I0740468

The Korean Kid

A Young Australian Pilot's Baptism Of Fire In The Jet Fighter Age

Rochelle Nicholls

16pt

Copyright Page from the Original Book

Copyright © Rochelle Nicholls

First published 2020

This book is copyright. Apart from any fair dealing for the purposes of private study, research, criticism or review as permitted under the Copyright Act, no part may be reproduced, stored in a retrieval system or transmitted in any form or by any means, electronic, mechanical, photocopying, recording or otherwise, without written permission.

The Australian Department of Defence has not participated in the research or production or exercised editorial control over the work's contents, and the views expressed and any conclusions reached herein do not necessarily represent those of the Commonwealth, which expressly disclaims any responsibility for the content or accuracy of the work.

All inquiries should be made to the publishers.

Big Sky Publishing Pty Ltd
PO Box 303, Newport, NSW 2106, Australia
Phone: 1300 364 611
Fax: (61 2) 9918 2396
Email: info@bigskypublishing.com.au
Web: www.bigskypublishing.com.au

Cover design and typesetting: Think Productions
Printed in China by Jilin GIGO International

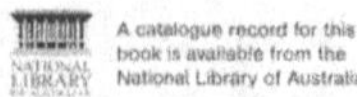
A catalogue record for this book is available from the National Library of Australia

TABLE OF CONTENTS

For Smithy
and nil those who sleep on the faraway hills of Korea.
Lest we forget.

UNIT CONVERSIONS

As far as is practical, the empirical units of measurement used in aviation in the 1950s and 1960s have been used in this book, particularly in reference to speed and altitude. Conversion factors for these measurements to metric units are provided below:

Speed:

1 mile per hour = 1.61 kilometres per hour

1 knot = 1.85 kilometres per hour

Mass:

1 pound = 0.45 kilograms

Length:

1 foot = 0.31 metres

1 yard = 0.91 metres

1 mile = 1609.34 metres

FOREWORD

To command a squadron, a commanding officer must lead and inspire the myriad of men and women who contribute to achieving the missions required of them in the name of the nation. But equally, a commanding officer will be inspired by all the members of a squadron as they give their all, be they aircrew, maintainers, logisticians or the various other support personnel.

For me, as the current commanding officer of 77 Squadron, my inspiration is not just limited to those who serve today, but also to all those who have been part of the "Double Sevens' since its formation during World War II.

This book about Jim Kichenside is definitely a story of inspiration for not only me but also for all the members of my squadron. When asked to provide this foreword, I couldn't readily recall the name Kichenside-we all know the names and the legends of past members of 77 Squadron like Cresswell, Spence, Drummond and Binskin. I am so grateful for having had the opportunity to learn about Jim Kichenside, and especially to Rochelle Nicholls for writing this book.

The story of Jim Kichenside is above all a story of resilience-starting from his days as a youth living in Sydney and questioning where his future would lie, through to becoming a key member of 77 Squadron flying Meteors as a sergeant pilot over Korea during that war. I was in awe when I read of Jim having flown 83 missions in just his first ten weeks in country-to be assigned his own aircraft, Meteor A77-316, by his CO, with the nose art "Korean Kid' painted on it is a testament to how highly respected he was amongst his pilot peers and the rest of the unit.

But Jim's story is much more than his experiences in the Korean War. Training as a fighter instructor on return from Korea and at the age of 22 he was amongst the highest graduates of his course. Following appointment as an officer and then promotion through the ranks to Squadron Leader, Jim then had the honour to command the RAAF Flight to the Antarctic throughout 1960-a tumultuous year for the Flight with the loss of a number of aircraft due to the savage conditions of the frozen continent.

The remainder of Jim's amazing Air Force flying career included time back flying Sabre fighter aircraft with both 77 and 79 Squadrons in South East Asia, culminating as a Wing Commander with his appointment as the commanding officer of 38 Squadron flying Caribou aircraft. In this role, Jim was called upon to lead and inspire his squadron through a difficult period, which he did admirably.

There is so much more to Jim Kichenside's story, including his life beyond the Air Force following his retirement at the age of 45, but I will leave that to the reader to explore for themselves through the pages of this marvellous book.

I am proud to be able to recommend this book on the life of Jim Kichenside-a man who lived up to the finest traditions of the Royal Australian Air Force. I look forward to Jim's story being a source of inspiration to the members of 77 squadron. Then. Now. Always.

Wing Commander Jason Easthope
Commanding Officer 77 Squadron
Royal Australian Air Force
July 2020

PROLOGUE

From up here, he can see the very curve of the earth. It is a hazy blue and white arc blurring distantly into the inverted dark bowl of space. A rumpled blanket of dusty mountains stretches below, veined with small rivers and the cat-scratches of roads. Outside, it is minus-50 degrees Fahrenheit and clouds hang like white islands suspended in a frozen blue sea.

They fly in a silence that is more ominous than the clamour of battle. He is alone in his cockpit, deep in enemy territory. It is a bloody nuisance to take a piss once he is suited up, so he never drinks on the day of a mission. Now his mouth and throat are dry and his tongue sticks to the roof of his mouth. The port wing and tail of the leader are bright in his peripheral vision, long white contrails flowing past him like pennants. The great engines whining at his elbows are the only sounds-that, and the rasp of his own breath inside the sweat-damp leather mask.

The radio squawks-'Target, boys!'

His stomach plummets as they all roll and veer and swoop, sixteen deadly silver eagles.

The barracks are a handful of squat buildings, a blip on the edge of a dirty town, but he knows they are thick with enemy: they are in the rooms like rats, in the trees like possums, and in the earth like wombats. Steel barrels of automatic weapons thrust through the slits of windows-they are preparing to fight the dragon's breath of air power with their antique guns. But the enemy also have heavy bullets. He imagines each one as a distinct entity, engraved in their odd crooked characters with a destination-*wing, tail, tank*-and with somebody's name: *it might be his name today.*

As he and the other silver fliers fall upon the target, tracer fire erupts like fireworks, those jagged bullets tearing past his face, which is protected only by the flimsy membrane of the canopy. He sees some as though in slow motion, black streaks in the flawless blue air. The radio explodes with voices. Jets are rolling away, pulling up, covering those still driving hard for the ground at close to the speed of sound. And that is his job-to hold the stick forward and hold his breath against the agony of the dive and never lift his eyes. His gaze locks onto an outbuilding which might be an ammo store. His thumb goes down. He barely glimpses the contrail of the rockets, or the upsurge of dust and smoke; he is already roaring away in a sweep of wings and jet exhaust as a steep hill rears up before him.

'That one's bust-one for you, Jimmy.'

Then the flash. He sees it beside him in the sky, like a new and blinding sun born of a violent mating between tracer fire and aircraft belly.

'That's a hit-he's taken a hit!'

A bright flamingo tail of pink and orange fire fills the whole sky. Some said later they had seen the white flower of a parachute.

The fifteen survivors stayed, orbiting through the flak as RAAF Meteor A77-316 went down, calling despairingly until the plane hit the ground and exploded.

1

CHAPTER I

THE BOY IN THE PORCH

He who would learn to fly one day must first learn to stand and walk and run and climb and dance; one cannot fly into flying.
—Friedrich Nietzsche

46 Roseby Street
Marrickville, Sydney
July 27, 1940

Drip.
Pause.
Drip, drip.

The boy scrunched up into a ball and hauled the blanket over his head. He could not sleep: the rain was too loud in the dark and the roof was leaking, sploshing onto a spot in the exact centre of his bed. The flimsy gauze enclosing the porch did nothing to muffle the noisy symphony of frogs and crickets in the yard. And now the blanket was hot and scratchy over his face. It smelled of Sundays-of the same yellow soap his mother scrubbed his hair with before church, where Nola and Jo whispered and wriggled and kicked their feet against the pews. The boy would soon be ten – too old to fidget through the sermons.

Ten. Not just soon – tomorrow! This was the other reason he could not fall asleep. He wished he had a wristwatch. What if midnight had passed and it was already his birthday? What if there was a bicycle waiting for him in the hall? A red one – a bright red one with a silver bell on the handle and a shiny brown leather seat. His whole body suddenly clenched with agonised longing. A bike ... Any bike would be good, even if it was made from scrap steel held together with old wire. But a *new bike ... a new red bike...*

The boy threw back the blanket and gulped a lungful of air, the night moist on his hot face. He would check the clock in the kitchen. And then take one little peek into the hall. He had swung his legs over the side of the cot and his bare feet were on the damp floorboards when another sound reached his ears above the dark drumming of rain.

The voices were muffled, as they always were. He knew his mother and father did not want to be overheard, but in this shoebox of a house, nothing was ever private. The boy sat very still, holding his breath in the dark. There was a sudden crescendo, then the sharp slam of a door and no more voices – only rain and crickets and frogs. He lay back down on his damp woollen blankets in the dark. Of course, there would be no red bike in the hall.

***

Roseby Street in Marrickville was working class. It was home to carpenters and postmen and greengrocers – even a preacher. A mighty mansion had once stood there, by the Cooks River in Sydney's inner west, complete with sandstone ramparts, marble busts, and exotic animals grazing its lawns. But in 1940, the great folly of *The Warren* was gone, subsumed by the tide of an ever-expanding city[1]. There were no millionaires left in Roseby Street: just rows of washing and backyard veggie beds and an SP bookie around the corner.

The boys of Roseby Street were mostly urchins in ill-fitting hand-me-downs: children of the Depression who were now children of World War II. They competed fiercely over bottletops and marbles, and begged (or pinched) sugared buns from Kirkland's Bakery up the road. Because almost nobody in Roseby Street had money for a car, the bumpy asphalt became a racing strip for their billycarts, chalked boldly across with the lines of cricket and hopscotch. And a mile or two's walk along the nearby river, brown and muddy and flat, was Mascot Aerodrome. In 1940, there were Tiger Moths daubed khaki and green swooping in and out, training young Australian pilots for the skies of war[2]. It was just the place for a boy who craved adventure: or escape.

Built from local sandstone and featuring more than 30 rooms and an impressive art collection, The Warren was built in Marrickville by Sydney business magnate Thomas Holt around 1865. The name derived from the rabbits Holt bred for hunting in the grounds. The mansion was demolished after World War I to create a housing estate for returned service personnel [Illustrated Sydney News, 17 March 1870 p.361; courtesy of the State Library of New South Wales, TNI 15].

James Kichenside dreamed of escape. When he was born on July 28, 1930, his hometown of Sydney was in freefall under the weight of a worldwide financial crisis. The fallout from World War I had stalled the British economy, meaning drastic cuts to imports of Australian wheat and wool: by 1930, the value of Australian grain and fibre exports had halved. The Australian government was forced to take large loans from London to maintain vital public infrastructure projects and services. On October 22, 1929, the Scullin Labor government took power after a year of labour unrest, pledging to protect Australian wages and working conditions, despite the nation's five-and-a-half million-pound deficit. But just seven days later, panicked sellers on the New York Stock Exchange traded nearly sixteen million shares in a single day – four times the normal volume – heralding the worst economic crisis since the Panic of 1893[3].

James Charles Kichenside was his parents' Depression baby. He was named James for his maternal grandfather, James Rutherford, and Charles for his own father. Rutherford, a toiling sharefarmer from the north coast of New South Wales, was so delighted at the tribute that he took a train to spend the Christmas of 1930 in Marrickville with his little namesake. But soon after his arrival at the Kichenside house at 27 Roseby Street, tragedy struck. Rutherford collapsed of a massive heart attack on Christmas

Eve, and died on the floor in the arms of his daughter, Dulcie[4].

Before the 1929 crash, the suburb of Marrickville, just 6 kilometres from Sydney's centre, had been a hub of light industry, its factories churning out blankets and bricks and bathtubs[5]. By 1932, however, the national unemployment rate had skyrocketed from around five per cent to almost twenty per cent[6]. In Marrickville, brick-making operations were shut down and the big General Motors automotive plant on Carrington Road closed as car sales crashed by ninety-five per cent[7]. Men sweated in hopeless queues in search of a day's work. Some foremen simply flung 'job tickets' into the air to be snatched up by the quickest and fittest. Vicious fights over these tickets left many injured, but those who did manage to snare one were often then thrust into back-breaking working conditions for little pay. The pervading sense of powerlessness and despair of the Great Depression drove Australian suicide rates to unprecedented levels.

The Kichensides were initially fortunate. Charles clung to his job as a telegraphist at the General Post Office in the city, so his family were not among the 60,000 men, women and children dependent on the paltry welfare payment known as the 'susso'. But in May 1931, at risk of defaulting on a spiralling foreign debt, the Federal Government and the six Australian states agreed to a twenty per cent reduction in expenditure and increased taxation. Wages were slashed and working hours increased from forty-four to forty-eight hours per week. The profession of telegraphy came under additional threat from the commercial advent of the telephone and teleprinter[8]. Postal workers had already taken a ten per cent wage cut under the Scullin government's *Financial Emergency Act (1931-1933)*[9] and in 1933, Charles Kichenside's position at the GPO was abolished[10].

Families evicted from their homes, their possessions around their feet, were a tragically common sight on the streets of Sydney during the Great Depression. In 1933, Charles Kichenside lost his job at the General Post Office and his family were forced to leave their home in Roseby Street,

Marrickville [photographer Sam Hood, Alamy, image ID: DY1002]

The Kichensides had to leave their cottage at 27 Roseby Street and move into a cheap apartment in nearby Day Street. That building also housed a butcher's shop which masqueraded as an illegal bookmaker (although when cornered by authorities, the butcher protested that he 'only did it to oblige his customers')[11]. Pretty, ladylike Dulcie Kichenside was mortified. However, the Kichensides' tenure here was short-lived. In 1934, Charles scrambled back into a job at the GPO, and they moved hastily away from Day Street into a house around the corner on Illawarra Road[12].

James Kichenside (left), aged 4, and his elder sister Valda, aged 9, in 1934, around the time their father lost his job during the Great Depression [Kichenside family collection].

***

Despite the many upheavals of the Depression, it was afterwards that the crunch came for the Kichenside family.

By 1936, with devaluation of the Australian pound and restoration of international trading links, the Australian economy was on a slow path to recovery. Charles Kichenside even had a little money put aside. He was growing weary, however, of the claustrophobia of industrial Marrickville. Watching his children – James, now six years old, Valda, eleven, and new baby Nola

– play on grubby asphalt while his wife Dulcie talked longingly of the green fields of her youth on the north coast, he wanted something brighter and cleaner for them. But his conscience warred with the thought of leaving Marrickville. His widowed mother, Ellen (Nellie) Kichenside, still lived around the corner at 46 Roseby Street and he visited her every day – he could not so easily abandon the old lady. But with his ear to the world at his telegraphist's station, Charles knew there was affordable land and pretty houses available on the northern outskirts of the city. It would mean a long commute every day, but by 1936, he had decided. He and Dulcie took the children out of the industrial fug and rented a house in Beecroft, seventeen miles away.

'*The house in Beecroft*' was to become a sorrowful mantra in the Kichenside household: a phrase reserved for bitter *sotto voce* arguments and stolen moments of longing and despair.

Despite Charles' conscience, the move to Beecroft was initially a welcome therapy for his years of sacrifice and endurance. His father, master stonemason William Kichenside, had been blinded in an industrial accident in 1899, when Charles was five years old; by the time he turned twelve, the family was nearly destitute and Charles left school to try to support his parents[13]. He rose from errand boy to telegraphist with the national postal service, and when William died in 1918, Charles continued diligently caring for his mother. He was twenty-nine years old before he left home to accept a promotion at Lismore, on the New South Wales north coast. It was here he married Dulcie Rutherford, the daughter of a local farmer, in 1924, bringing his new bride back to Marrickville to again be near his mother.

Charles had once dreamed of becoming a florist, and in 1936, Beecroft was a tranquil enclave of genteel houses with private tennis courts and the lush gardens he loved[14]. Charles and Dulcie's fourth child, Joan, was born not long after the move. Dulcie learned to play golf and tennis. The children played in an enormous grassy yard overlooking peaceful orchards and farmland. And their house on Boronia Avenue rang with laughter and ease and comfort.

However, after two years, Charles' guilt over his mother resurfaced. Although his children visited Nellie during their school vacations, the old lady was lonely. Dulcie contended it would be simplest to just bring Nellie to them in Beecroft. But Charles could not take the old lady out of her marital home. He proposed using some of their savings to renovate and extend his mother's Marrickville cottage to create space for them all to live together there.

Dulcie wept and stormed, but Charles, with one of his rare bursts of implacability, was adamant. A taxi truck came wheezing along Boronia Avenue and stopped outside number 29. All of their furniture and books and clothes and pillows and toys were piled into it. They went back. And something in Charles and Dulcie's marriage broke.

James Kichenside (rear) pictured with his younger sisters Joan (front left) and Nola (right) in 1938. The family had spent two years in Sydney's tranquil northern suburbs before returning in 1938 to live with James' grandmother in Marrickville [Kichenside family collection].

***

Nellie Kichenside's cottage at 46 Roseby Street, barely two bedrooms and a kitchen, groaned dreadfully with the admission of another six residents. The impact was perhaps greatest on eight-year-old James.

Charles brought men in to build on a new bedroom and extra living space, and the family's modest savings disappeared into a maw of joists, nails, paint and plaster. But shoe-horning seven people into the cottage in comfort remained a physical impossibility. Nellie, as matriarch and house owner, had the bedroom with the fireplace off the kitchen. Charles and Dulcie squeezed into the tiny front room. Nola, aged five, three-year-old Joan, and teenage Valda bunked in the new bedroom at the back of the house. However, there was nowhere for young James but the back porch.

Desperate to save the last of his money and sanity, Charles sent the costly tradesmen away and enlisted a neighbour, Frederick 'Rowly' Rowlands, to enclose the veranda for his son. The World War I veteran was an amateur carpenter and used old windows and plastic sheeting to create James' bedroom. But when it rained, the whole construct leaked, and any breeze made it shiver with draughts. The boy had no privacy and nowhere quiet to study. Anyone wanting to use the outhouse had to pass through this makeshift bedroom. And at night, his parents' voices, sometimes raised but mostly cold and acrimonious, invaded his dreams through the thin walls. As the shadow of World War II descended on Sydney and the de Havilland Moths looped over the aerodrome, James Kichenside lay awake and dreamed of flying away.

CHAPTER 2

FLIGHT DREAMS

It may be hard for an egg to turn into a bird: it would be a jolly sight harder for it to learn to fly while remaining an egg.

—C.S. Lewis

While his glimpses of airplanes through the fence at Mascot aerodrome fed James Kichenside's fantasies of a life beyond Roseby Street, the simple plywood and cloth flying machines also stoked another fire within his young soul: the craving for adventure.

Established as a private aerodrome in 1919 and acquired by the Commonwealth government in 1923, Mascot Aerodrome played host to some of the great pioneers of early Australian aviation. The site was within walking distance of James Kichenside's home in Marrickville in the 1930s [Alamy, image ID: PA670J]

As he and his mates crowded up to the barrier to watch the seemingly frail aircraft lifting so coolly into the air, James watched them spiral out of sight and wondered what far-flung destinations they might be roaring toward. Mascot was a place of infinite possibility, and one which had seen its share of great aviation moments. Ross and Keith Smith had landed their Vickers Vimy at the aerodrome in 1920 to celebrate winning the great air race from London to

Darwin[1]. Charles Kingsford Smith – after whom the airfield was re-christened in 1936 – had taken off from Mascot with Charles Ulm in 1927 to circumnavigate Australia in a Bristol Tourer, and returned in triumph ten days later[2]. Aviatrix Nancy Bird enrolled at Kingsford Smith's flying school at Mascot in 1932, aged just seventeen, and two years later became the youngest Australian woman to hold a pilot's licence[3].

Sir Charles Kingsford Smith (left), with Charles Ulm (right), Harry Lyon and James Warner, completed the first crossing of the Pacific Ocean by air in 1928. In 1936, the Mascot Aerodrome was renamed Sydney Kingsford Smith Airport in his honour [Charles T.P Ulm collection of historical aviation photographs, ca.1920-1934, image ID: FL1052943. Courtesy of the Mitchell Library, State Library of New South Wales].

In 1935, at 19 years of age, Nancy Bird became the youngest Australian woman to gain a commercial pilot's licence. She took her first flying lesson with Sir Charles Kingsford Smith at Mascot aerodrome in August 1933 [Alamy, image ID: DY0G41].

Pilot' s licence ... those were magical words. The local lads all had dreams of what they would do if they had one: fly to school every day suggested one wag. Fly all the way to the North Pole, enthused another. But for the Marrickville boys, the cost of flying lessons and earning that precious licence – more than two hundred pounds, more than most of their fathers earned in a whole year – meant the dream had little more substance than the wispy white clouds streaking the blue sky above their heads.

But the outbreak of war brought yet more aircraft to Mascot to feed their fascination, and for some, like James Kichenside, the dream simply refused to fade.

In the late 1930s, Australia had seemed on the cusp of a new era of stability and achievement following the trials of the Great Depression. Assisted immigration from Britain was reintroduced, a direct radiotelephone link established between Canberra and Washington DC, and the 1938 British Empire Games were held in Sydney with Australia leading the medal tally. Robert Gordon Menzies became Prime Minister in 1939 after the sudden death of Joseph Lyons. But Menzies was in power for just four months when, on September 3, 1939, Australia followed Britain in declaring war on Germany following its invasion of Poland. World War II had begun.

Suddenly there were soldiers in Sydney's streets – infantrymen in khaki, sailors in cocked hats, and airmen in smart navy blue. American accents mingled with the broad Australian, and shouts about Japan and Nazism echoed from newsboys on street corners. There were ration books and blackouts and air raid drills. The 1942 national austerity campaigned urged all Australians to tighten their belts: to consume less, make do, and, according to new Prime Minister John

Curtin, 'strip every luxurious impulse'[4]. James' mother Dulcie concocted pies and stews from cheap cuts of meat and blemished vegetables, squeezed a few chickens into the tiny back yard and grew beans on a trellis against the fence. She took a job in a local store as thousands of men enlisted and women joined the war effort on the home front. But Dulcie also determinedly kept up appearances, curling her dark hair and rouging her cheeks before any outing. She refused to give up her beloved golf and her pretty white sports skirts and shoes. Her son watched her grimly hanging on to her dreams and standards, and clung equally grimly to his own.

With his job in communications, Charles Kichenside had a protected role exempted from service. He still took the train every day to the massive sandstone edifice of the General Post Office, and James went with him on Saturdays, earning pennies by delivering telegrams. Sydney was taking the threat of Japanese attack extremely seriously, and the GPO was partially encased in timber cladding, with loudspeakers mounted on the façade and the clock tower dismantled to make the building less distinctive[5]. Charles was an air raid warden too: a very important job, even if he was not in khaki. James was proud of his father, who, when he was the same age as James was now, had been financially supporting his entire family. James could not help knowing how the disastrous renovations at Roseby Street had hurt his father, and why then he could not have the bike he wanted, or his sisters the ballet and piano lessons they hankered after: and why flying lessons were out of the question. It was a confusing sensation for the boy, with his admiration for his father tainted by the unrest at home, and his guilty attraction to the dark-blue airmen's uniforms while he trudged the streets delivering telegrams.

The General Post Office in Martin Place, Sydney, pictured in c.1901. The Victorian Italian Renaissance style building was constructed over 25 years from 1866 and is now listed on New South Wales and Commonwealth heritage registers. The GP

***

In 1942, Singapore and New Guinea fell to the advancing Japanese, and the war finally reached Australia. Broome and Darwin were assailed from the air, and in May 1942, Japanese midget submarines attacked Sydney Harbour. Twelve-year-old James began to change. He had always been a clever child – while at school in Beecroft, he had been promoted from second up to third class, and in his last two years of junior school at Marrickville West, he competed enthusiastically, despite conceding a year in age to most of his classmates. But when he completed his final primary year, in 1941, the headmaster sent a letter to the boy's parents advising to keep him back a year before starting high school: to let him mature a little more before the rigors of senior education.

James' hot pride was stung. He protested furiously at the prospect of repeating a year he had sailed through academically. His mother hesitated, but his father, seeing a growing jut in the boy's chin and a new steel in his eyes, conceded. So James went on to Kogarah High School unimpeded, graduating twenty-eighth of 160 in his Intermediate Certificate class and earning a place at Sydney Technical High School in Paddington for his final two years of education. He was even made a prefect at both schools, despite openly admitting a growing preference for sport over study.

Sydney Technical High School First XI cricket team, 1947. James Kichenside (front row, second from right) had captained the Second XI to a premiership in 1945 at age 15, and been promoted to the First XI as a talented pace bowler [Kichenside family collection].

With prefect badges on his blazers, James Kichenside's burgeoning leadership talents were clear on the sports field too. As atomic bombs fell on Hiroshima and Nagasaki in 1945, he captained the Sydney Technical High Second XI cricket team to the High Schools' premiership. In 1947, he was promoted to the First XI as a promising medium-fast bowler. Charles Kichenside, who had been a handy amateur cricketer himself, vowed never to chastise the boy again for practising his bowling against the front wall of the house. Perhaps cricket was the boy's ticket out of the greyness of suburban life.

But Charles also wanted to see James finish school well. He supported his son's subject choices of mathematics, English, physics, and chemistry – even French – hoping it would it would lead to a secure, well-paying job such as his own at the GPO. But the boy's health faltered as he neared the crucial final examinations. He was riven with discomfort from wisdom teeth which refused to emerge properly. And the crowded house and his draughty bedroom meant quiet and peace for serious study was virtually unobtainable. The result – he did not receive a matriculation certificate.

Back in 1938, as his parents warred over leaving the house in Beecroft, James had been excited at the prospect of moving back to Marrickville to live with his beloved grandmother. Now, when it was raining into his bedroom or he made Saturday afternoon walks to the airfield fence, he vowed again to escape, to make something of himself – to somehow spread his wings and fly.

CHAPTER 3

THE DREAM FULFILLED

No one should negotiate their dreams.
Dreams must be free to fly high.
—Jesse Jackson

Options seemed limited for a boy leaving school without a matriculation certificate in 1947. War-time prime minister John Curtin and his successor Ben Chifley's command economy had driven Australian unemployment to record lows, and with a queue of returned servicemen crowding into jobs before him, the boy seemed destined for difficult times[1]. But James Kichenside – who now liked to be known as Jim – was, like his father, resourceful, energetic and proud. He caddied at the local golf course, ran deliveries for the local butcher, and at night, carried trays of ice-cream at the Hoyts Marrickville cinema. When the big spenders came in to the theatre with their flash girlfriends, Jim always seemed to get their tips. He was clean-cut and deferential, but with a puckish twinkle in his eye that instinctively drew people to him.

Jim was also a great favourite with his uncle, Edwin 'Ted' Boyter, who had married Dulcie's sister Eileen and lived at Woodburn on the New South Wales north coast. Dulcie had been the ninth of her father James Rutherford's eleven children, and when she was just six years old, her mother had died while giving birth, leaving little Dulcie to be raised by her elder sisters. Dulcie and Eileen had always been close and, before World War II broke out, Dulcie would take her children to spend every summer on the Boyter farm. While the Kichensides had little spare cash, Ted Boyter had made big money in dairying: by the mid-1930s, he owned three farms and was conspicuous in sleepy Woodburn for the big shiny American car he drove. His only son, Jack, was a strapping lad who appeared destined to follow in his father's footsteps – a good student, Boy Scout, and President of the Woodburn Junior Farmers club. When World War II came, twenty-two year-old Jack became Lance-Sergeant Boyter, combat instructor with the 41st Australian Infantry Battalion AIF[2]. But when he returned to the farm in 1945, it was with the shock announcement that he would not be staying – he intended to join the police force in the dirty metropolis of Sydney.

Jack's decision devastated Ted Boyter. While his daughter Marie was a handy lass who worked hard on the farm, Ted was desperate to hand his agricultural enterprise on to a male relative.

He had taken a great fancy to young Jim during the summers the boy spent at the farm, and now wrote to Dulcie offering to put the boy through agricultural college with a view to joining Ted at the dairy. The lures were all there. The Boyter family were wealthy, established and respected. Jim would receive a first-class education and a guaranteed future. But Dulcie did not miss the stricken look that flashed through the boy's eyes when the proposal was put to him. He lowered his head, then looked up at her with a burning gaze, half proud, half pleading. 'Money isn't everything, Mother,' he said. 'I'd rather be broke and happy than do something that makes me miserable.'

Dulcie decided not to tell Charles that.

***

While confident he did not want to be a dairy farmer, and despite the school guidance counsellor noting the boy's 'strong drive to succeed' on his final report, Jim Kichenside left school in 1947 with little idea of what to do next.

He toyed with the idea of going to night school to redo his Matriculation, then answered an advertisement for a trainee accountant with the Saywell companies in the city. The Saywell family, originally from Nottinghamshire, England, had prospered in Australia from investments in mining, wine, tramways and real estate[3]. Jim got the job and took it with typical doggedness, going to night school four times a week and hanging on a train strap to the office every day.

One of his daily tasks at Saywells was preparing a brief on stock exchange trends from the financial columns in the newspapers. Tuesday, April 26, 1949, was an ordinary day, but on that day, this menial office chore was to change his life.

Jim permitted himself a peep at the back pages of the *Sydney Morning Herald* as he trawled through share prices and bond options. Among the accounts of South Sydney trouncing Manly Warringah in rugby league and Roman Step winning the Handicap at Randwick, was a small advertisement featuring a picture of a fresh-faced pilot[4].

'*Think you'd make a flier?*'

Jim sat very still. He could not move or take his eyes from the boy in the flying suit grinning up out of the paper. The stylised lad looked no older than himself. A real, actual, genuine boy pilot.

'*Fly with the RAAF! Aircrew Trainees Wanted!*'

Heart beating like a hammer, the boy glanced around the office to see if anyone was watching. He dared not tear the advertisement from the page, but he took a pencil, wiped his sweating palms on his trousers, and, very quietly, began to copy the advertisement onto a ledger pad. Then he folded the page over and over into a tiny square and shoved it deep into his trouser pocket.

He was a disciplined boy, and he did not look at the tightly folded note again until he had alighted from the train that evening at Tempe Station. Again, he cast a guilty glance around the crowds as he reached into his pocket and fingered the precious paper. He left the station for the short twilight walk home, crossed the cricket field without a glance, then broke into a run, satchel bouncing against his hip and his stiff collar threatening to choke him.

Tonight, he did not go home. He ran all the way up the hill to nearby Richardson's Lookout, where he flung himself, panting, upon his favourite bench. It was a clear evening and across the murky river, Mascot Aerodrome spread out before him, its runways like a great map of a new world. He finally pulled the paper from his pocket and smoothed it across his knee, re-read the words he had already committed to memory:

> *'Here is your opportunity to win your wings and take off on a new career—in the air! If you are between 18 and 23, and fit, apply now for selection as trainee Pilot or Navigator.'*

Royal Air Force pilot Douglas Bader lost both legs in a flying accident in 1931. He returned to fly with the RAF in 1939 and was credited with more than 22 aerial victories in World War II [Alamy, image ID: B4TD6B].

'Win your wings...' He tasted the words like wine. The old litany of the names of legendary pilots began to roll through his head like tickertape: Charles Kingsford Smith, Bert Hinkler, Charles Ulm. And the fighter aces his father had read aloud about from the papers during the war: Douglas Bader, who had flown in the Battle of Britain with two prosthetic legs; Clive Caldwell, who'd come out of the war with more kills than any other Australian airman...

'If selected you will be able to make flying your career under the most attractive

> *conditions—liberal scale of pay and allowances, free uniforms, accommodation, medical and dental care, and all the regular benefits of the RAAF.'*

Darkness was beginning to drift down. The sinking sun made the distant wings of the planes shine. He tasted the words again: *liberal* ... *free* ... *attractive* ... *benefits* ... The boy had never blamed his parents for the discomforts of the Roseby Street years, but he had never silenced the inner monologue that told him one day he would leave. He walked home in time for dinner, and in the regular confusion, nobody noticed his unusual silence.

Flying Curtiss P-40 Tomahawks and Kittyhawks in North Africa and the Pacific, RAAF air ace Clive Caldwell shot down more than 28 enemy aircraft during World War II [image ID: FL1712955, courtesy of the Mitchell Library, State Library of New South Wales].

The next day, he went to see 'Mister Tom' Saywell to hand in his notice. He told the old man he had a dream to be a fighter pilot. The old man looked at the eager young face across the shiny mahogany desktop, then extended a wiry hand and said, 'We'll be sorry to lose you, son, but you have my blessing.'

It was then that the boy concluded he ought to tell his parents what he'd done.

Their reactions were not what he expected. His mother, normally so passionate, consented almost at once, but his mild-mannered father leapt out of his armchair like he'd sat on a porcupine. 'What you've got to think about, son, is security!' he barked. 'Saywells – it's a job for life! You'll have money, a nice house, steak for supper every night if you want it!'

But the boy could not stop himself. 'And when I'm 65, IT I get a gold watch then die a year later?' he retorted. 'That's not what I want out of life, Dad. I have a dream – and I don't want to regret not following it.'

It was a blow, but not a fatal one. Charles shot back immediately, 'You're not 21 yet-I won't sign anything. You're making a big mistake, going for the glamour of the uniform.'

The boy's denial was immediate, although behind his back, he guiltily crossed his fingers. He had seen the way men (and women) stopped in the street to shake the hands of the boys in blue during the war, to admire them like they were winged demigods.

That night, the boy lay on his cot in the dark and waited for the voices to filter through the walls, sure there would be a new pitch in the rancour. But the door opened softly and Nola came padding onto the porch in her long nightgown. His bed springs creaked as she perched on the edge.

Are you here to holler at me?' he said gruffly. He knew she would have heard every word of the earlier row – the neighbours up the street probably had too.

'Silly.' She tweaked his big toe through the blankets, making him squirm. 'Anyway, sssh.' Her voice dropped to a whisper. 'I just came to say: whatever you do, don't get killed, alright?'

'Huh?'

'Just stay alive, okay? If you die, you'll break Mother's heart.' And she was gone.

***

There were 1200 applicants from all over Australia for the RAAF No.4 Training Course in 1949. The boy kept a poker face at home, but his insides were churning. The application forms had asked only for an Intermediate pass, but he was sure his lack of a Matric would count against him. He had been a prefect throughout high school, and a premiership-winning cricket captain – *would that help*? Then, what if his father would not sign his application? And the question that churned in him worst of all – he had never set foot near a real aircraft: *would that be the killer blow?*

It was not. Dulcie persuaded Charles to sign the papers, and on July 12, 1949, Jim was invited to the RAAF base at Bradfield Park in north Sydney for two days of IQ tests, physical aptitude trials, interviews and medicals[5]. The result came in the form of a yellow telegram, like the many he had delivered as a child.

'*Selected—depart in 10 days—notify acceptance immediately.*'

The boy would never know, but the assessors had scrawled in big letters across his papers, 'Good type – LOOK!'[6]

There was a muted dinner at home to celebrate. Jim kept catching Nola's eye across the crowded table; his father said almost nothing.

The train to Melbourne from Sydney's Central Station had dozens of other recruits on board, all travelling second class. The boy had never been so far from home before. They all slept where they sat, and shared bags of candy and packets of sandwiches and tall stories.

At Spencer Street station in the heart of Melbourne, there was no time to gape at the grand buildings and crowds. There were three-tonne trucks with canvas covers waiting outside the station, and the young men were all bundled into the backs for the journey to the flight training school at Point Cook. The boy nudged the lad beside him in the fusty darkness and murmured, 'What are they trying to do, hide us from the enemy or stop us from changing our minds?'

CHAPTER 4

FLEDGLINGS

Every take-off is optional. Every landing is mandatory.
—Pilot's adage

No.1 Flying Training School
RAAF Base Point Cook, Victoria
January 1950

'Switch on!'

It was a bull's roar, right behind his head. Heart hammering, he reached up and flicked the little toggle up; in its leather and sheepskin flying glove, his hand felt heavy as lead.

Out of the corner of his eye, he saw the instructor wave his own gloved hand nonchalantly at his assistant, who stepped in and neatly swung the prop. The engine sputtered and growled to life. The whole floor of the plane was vibrating with the sound; through the leather helmet, his ears were full of noise. The boy wondered how such a small, cheerful-looking machine could make so much racket.

Then the chocks were jerked away and they were moving. His heart leapt up into his throat – with the plane's nose tilted up, he could see nothing out the front but sky and distant treetops. *God, if he hit something before they even took off* He knew all the other lads were watching – some of them already had years of flying experience, and he felt the weight of that like a stone in his stomach.

'Look over the side, boy – you might see something to interest you!'

They puttered down the tarmac like a grounded budgie, now weaving slowly so as to catch sight of the runway in front. The windsock was taut and pointing straight at him. *Well, that was one thing he COULD remember—take off into the wind.*

'Throttle!'

Just in time, he reached up and jerked the goggles down over his eyes as the throttle opened and the engine's rumble became a roar. The plane accelerated down the strip, the prop a blur before him, two pairs of yellow wings bright in his peripheral vision. The plane bounced twice, the tail wheel lifted, and suddenly they were level.

'Forty knots! And – up!'

Just like that. One minute, they were rumbling along the macadamised strip – the next, the ground was falling away and cold air was rushing past his face.

'Level off!'

He saw the airspeed indicator reach 60 miles per hour, but he could not keep his eyes from the receding bush and buildings and flat brown paddocks below. And there was the sea – huge and endlessly blue. It was all being left behind – the ridiculous cares of earthbound life, the heavy burden of the everyday. Up here was where the action was!

'Left! Come about left!'

He jumped slightly, recalled to his duties. Left bank, left rudder and – miracle of miracles – the little yellow bird soared happily away to the left. *This was EASY – this was alright.*

***

Australia's air forces underwent a significant restructure at the end of World War II in 1945. Many personnel, including high-ranking officers, were demobilised and RAAF strength reduced from over 182,000 personnel to around 8000[1]. The permanent Air Force was re-formed in July 1947 with 16 operational squadrons, including fighters, heavy bomber and transport wings, a tactical reconnaissance squadron, and support units. But most RAAF personnel were only offered two-year contracts and by April 1949, many units were neither fully staffed nor properly equipped[2]. However, the 1949 federal election victory by the Menzies-led Liberal party saw spending on all three defence forces increase by nearly 50 per cent, with a significant component of funding devoted to recruitment and training[3].

The boys arriving at No.1 Flying Training School at Point Cook, Victoria, in August 1949 were the fourth intake of post-war air force recruits. The flying school was established in 1912, and when the RAAF was formed in 1921, Point Cook was already a well-developed facility on the shores of Port Phillip Bay, near Melbourne. The boy was one of the youngest of the 150 accepted into 4 Course, at barely 19 years old. Facing him was 18 months – twice the length of wartime courses – of fierce competition for places as navigators, signallers, and, most coveted of all, pilots.

Jim Kichenside in his first week of RAAF pilot training, No. 1 Flying Training School, Point Cook, August 1949 [Kichenside family collection].

For the first five months, the young men revolved through an unrelenting schedule of lectures on navigation, meteorology, engineering, communications and aerodynamics. The cobwebs of the classrooms were blown away with hours of physical training with a drill sergeant barking at their heels, and by pitiless weekly inspections of quarters, with recruit Col King ruefully recalling Warrant Officers even inspecting the tops of doors for dust[4].

But for all the bellowing and drill, the aircraft park at Point Cook was a boys' own dream of fighter aircraft. Beaufighters, Kittyhawks, Boomerangs and Spitfires were lined up right alongside the Tiger Moths they would be learning to fly in. The boy found himself sketching restless pictures of cloud formations and aileron set-ups on his notepads during classes. He thought guiltily of his father when they were pressed to reach a standard of 15 words per minute in Morse code. But even the relentless examinations could not stop his gaze drifting out the window to the blue seaside skies, and his ears straying to the runways as planes taxied and made their graceful circuits of the airfield.

And then 1950 arrived. Five months had gone, and, almost overnight, so had 75 of his classmates, ground down by the inexorable demands and standards of RAAF life. The boy, despite never gaining that final piece of paper from his high school years, had found the academic portion of flight training well within his capabilities. Sydney Technical High had a strong maths and engineering focus and he had always done well in physics and English: these subjects all stood him in excellent stead at flight school.

But he wasted no time celebrating making the first cut, for before him was the greatest challenge to date: flying for the very first time.

The 75 remaining recruits in 4 Course were introduced to the de Havilland DH.82 Tiger Moth and informed they had 10 hours to impress. The boy knew that many of his classmates – about one-third – had already flown recreationally; some had as much as 120 hours in the pilot's seat. But, as one RAAF instructor was quick to scoff, many would have been better off without it, coming as it often did from old-time instructors not much bothered about bad habits. 'If you've got enough money,' he sneered, 'even a monkey can learn how to fly.'

The de Havilland DH.82 Tiger Moth biplane was first manufactured in Britain in 1931. More than 1100 were built under licence in Australia and the DH.82 became a primary trainer aircraft for the RAAF between 1940 and 1957 [Australian War Memorial, accession no. AGO 135/2].

Despite their fragile appearance, dual-seat Tiger Moths had been used as a primary trainer by the RAAF throughout World War II. Powered by a 120 hp engine, with maximum speed of 175 kilometres per hour (94 knots), the controls were simple—sideways movement of the column operated the ailerons to control banking in turns, fore and aft motion moved the elevators on the tail to raise or lower the nose. The rudder was operated by foot controls and engine speed by a throttle.

To make the next cut, the recruits had to be flying solo within 10 hours. The boy never hesitated: his natural confidence made up for any shortfall in experience, and he had the firm touch on the controls the Tiger Moth loved. Within eight hours, he was in the sky alone, without an instructor in the back hollering, 'You fool, are you trying to kill me?' He was exhilarated, and realised only later, lying in his bunk in the dark, that he had sung most of the way around that first solo circuit.

***

The CAC Wirraway, whose name was adapted from an indigenous word for 'challenge', was employed in a light bomber/ground attack role by the RAAF in World War II. The Wirraway was then used as a training aircraft before being retired from service in 1959 [Australian War Memorial, accession no.000713].

At the conclusion of flight grading, only 31 members of the class remained. Now, every flight was assessed. The young pilots spent another 55 hours on Tiger Moths, driving the old aircraft into acrobatics, formation flying and landing on rough grass strips. With the Moth's range of around 500 kilometres, they were sent across country amongst variable winds which could blow the plane off-course, and learned to fly in cloud, with its giddying loss of orientation, on instruments alone.

The remaining 150 hours were spent in the Australian-built Wirraway fighter, a cranky radial engine monoplane that had seen service in New Guinea during World War II. It was said if you could fly a Wirraway well, you could fly anything. At 27 feet long, it was barely four feet longer than the Moth but had an extra 12 feet of wingspan, and was so noisy it was almost impossible to hear the instructor in the rear seat. But the main challenge of the old plane was a tendency to drop a wing, especially on landing. There were no simulators to learn to combat this – the young pilots quickly learned to criss-cross the aileron using opposite rudder and a bit of brake: too slow and the wing could contact the ground, sometimes with fatal consequences. In March 1951, trainee pilot Jimmy Cass and his instructor Flight Lieutenant Ronald Johnstone were killed when their Wirraway crashed into Port Phillip Bay after failing to gain height on take-off and one wingtip hitting the water, sending the aircraft cartwheeling into the bay[5].

Amid this barrage of training and gradings and flying hours, the weeks and months of 1950 were sliding away in a blur of aviation fuel and sweat. But on June 25, 1950, another kind of barrage began – one which would transform all of their lives.

Intermittent monsoonal showers were falling over the Korean peninsula in the early hours of Sunday June 25, 1950, when a massive fusillade of howitzer and mortar shells thundered over the 38th parallel, an arbitrary line separating the Communist hermit kingdom of North Korea from its southern counterpart. The shells were swiftly followed by Soviet T-34 tanks, then North Korean ground troops were pouring across a sleepily defended border into the south. By June 28, the South Korean capital was in flames and its citizens and army in retreat before the monstrous onslaught[6]. East Asia was once again at war.

***

London Hotel
Port Melbourne, Victoria
July 1, 1950

No.1 Flying Training School was a dry camp on weekdays, but on the weekends, the trainee airmen congregated in the back bar of the art deco London Hotel on Melbourne's historic waterfront. The youngsters drank lemon squash and enviously watched their older compatriots downing beers and the occasional cheeky whiskey.

July 1, 1950, was a grey Saturday Talk in the bar was desultory like the dank weather outside; a few boys were pushing coasters around the sticky little tables, toying with straws and watching the grey drizzle mournfully. Terrible flying weather.

The South Korean capital, Seoul, was overrun by North Korean troops within days of the invasion in June 1950. The capital would change hands four times during the course of the war, and much of its infrastructure was destroyed [Australian War Memorial, accession no. P02201.022].

Suddenly the hotel doors flew back and Vance Drummond came shouldering through the throng, clutching a newspaper, high colour in his lean, tanned face. It was as though the sun itself had burst into the dingy old bar. Drummond had trained with the New Zealand Air Force during World War II and with his superior age (he was 23) and experience, was flying right at the top of 4 Course[7]. When Drummond spoke, all the lads listened. Now he waved the paper breathlessly and, slotting himself into a place at the bar, smoothed it out in front of a dozen curious faces.

'Were on, boys.'

The headline covered half the front page of *The Age*. 'RAAF Fighter Unit to Help US in Korea,' someone read over Drummond's shoulder[8]. 'The RAAF's 77th fighter squadron, now in Japan, will assist American forces in the defence of Southern Korea.'

'But 77 are already over in Japan,' another said. 'Whafs this got to do with us?'

Drummond turned and eyed the speaker. 'Trust me,' he said, 'it's got everything to do with us.'

CHAPTER 5

THE LAND OF THE MORNING CALM

God too, has sinned, that's what I used to think. He looked down on this blazing hell, and he remained silent.

—Hwang Sok-yong, *The Guest*

Sunday, June 25, 1950, was almost the exact midpoint of the 20th century. It also loomed as the flashpoint for a new international war-the first war of the nuclear age.

The Korean peninsula, jutting off the east Asian mainland between China and Russia to the west and Japan to the east, rolls from frigid mountains to fertile plains and swampy coastland scattered with thousands of islands. Sandwiched between the regional superpowers, Koreas recent history is one of subjugation and territorial annexation. The Korean people are descended from central Asian nomads who were first conquered by China in 108BC. While internal rule was restored by the indigenous Koryo (918-1392 AD) and Chosin kingdoms (1392-1897 AD), the peninsula was annexed by Japan early in the twentieth century. Japanese troops were first sent to Korea in 1904 to counter the Soviet occupation of southern Manchuria during the Boxer Uprising of 1900. The resulting Russo-Japanese War realised two years of horrendous slaughter. The 1905 Treaty of Portsmouth saw Japan handed exclusive dominion on the Korean peninsula, including disbanding the Korean army and assuming control of the police and judiciary[1]. For the next 35 years, Japan maintained a merciless rule, using Korea as a springboard for expansionist plans into northern Asia. Thousands of Koreans were forced to work in factories and farms or conscripted into the Japanese army, and 200,000 Korean women became comfort women' to Japanese military personnel during the war in the Pacific[2].

Korean independence from Japan was first mooted at the 1943 Cairo Conference at which the United States, United Kingdom and China convened to determine the future of Japanese-occupied Asia. Independence would take the form of a trusteeship overseen by both the United States and the USSR, with the peninsula divided into north and south along the 38th parallel. At midnight on August 10, 1945, the day after the obliteration of Nagasaki with an atomic bomb which ended World War II, the border at the 38th parallel was instituted. Within just three weeks, Korea were once again occupied by foreign powers – Russia in the north and the US in the south – an arrangement intended to continue until the two halves of the divided land could be reunified.

But plans for unification stalled when the North, now an established communist regime with a well-armed military force, refused to take part in 1948 UN elections for a unity government, and former resistance fighter Kim Il-Sung came to power. The democratic South, with two-thirds of the population and most of the light industry and arable land, was led by the Princeton-educated anti-communist dictator Syngman Rhee. The two opposing ideologies meant border skirmishes were common, costing an estimated 10,000 lives before the 1950 war even began.

Taken into exile in Manchuria as a child, North Korean president Kim Il-Sung had been a guerrilla commander in the struggle against Japanese occupation before fleeing to the Soviet Union in 1942. There, he became a major in the Red Army before he was installed as chairman of the North Korean Communist party. Not only did he reject the 1948 UN elections, but Kim determined to retake the south of the peninsula by force. His cause was strengthened by the communist victory over the Kuomintang-led government in the Chinese Civil War of 1949. Kim enlisted the support of both Chinese Communist party chairman Mao Zedong and Russian president Joseph Stalin, who, believing the US would not act over a minor territory such as Korea, backed Kim's invasion plans and supplied both tanks and heavy artillery[3].

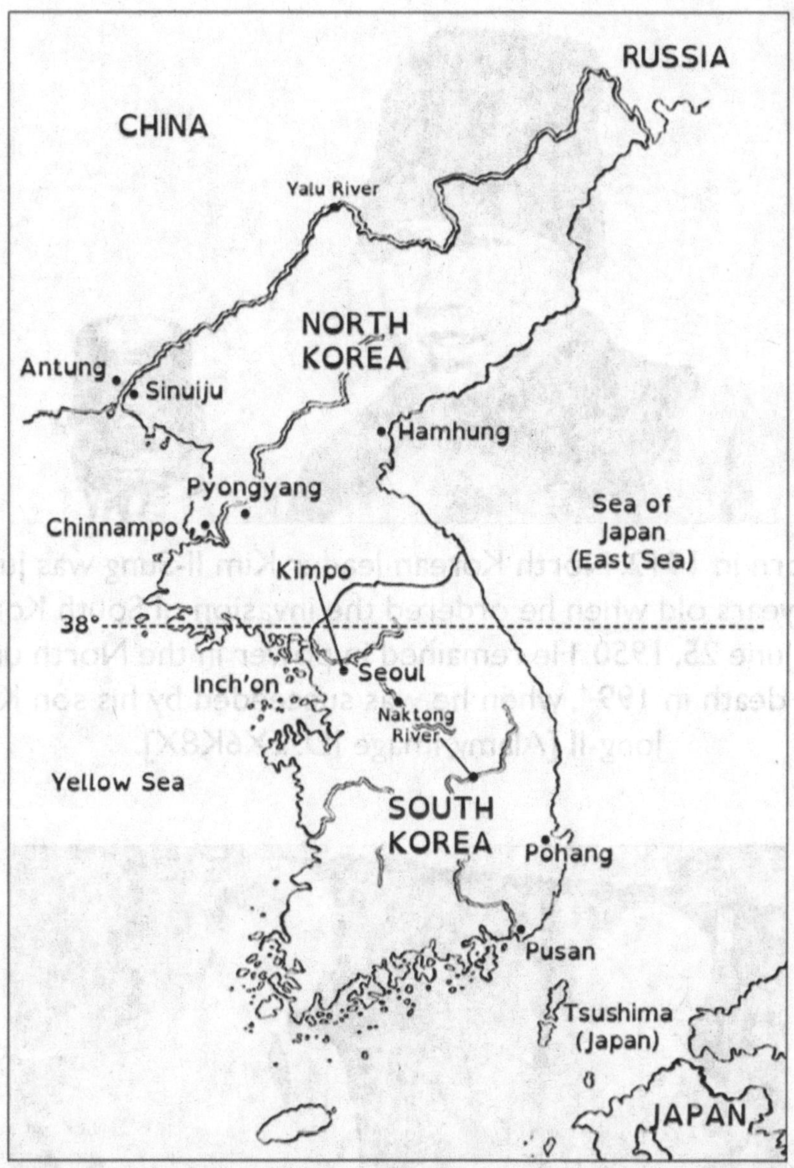

With a centuries-long history of invasion and occupation, in 1945, the Korean peninsula was liberated from Japanese rule and arbitrarily divided along latitude 38°N. The onset of the Cold War saw this temporary measure solidified with a well-armed Communist regime in the north and a US-backed administration in the south.

Born in 1912, North Korean leader Kim Il-Sung was just 38 years old when he ordered the invasion of South Korea on June 25, 1950. He remained in power in the North until his death in 1994, when he was succeeded by his son Kim Jong-Il [Alamy, image ID: EX6K8X].

South Korean president Syngman Rhee (left) greets the Australian Minister for Air William McMahon (right) during a visit to Seoul in November 1952. Rhee received a Ph.D.

from Princeton University in the United States in 1910, the same year Korea was annexed by Japan, and spent the next 30 years as a spokesman for Korean independence, mainly from a self-imposed exile in Hawaii. He died in 1965 at the age of 90 [Australian War Memorial, accession no. JK0538].

Warnings of an impending invasion of southern Korea had come as early as 1946, when the commander of the US occupation force, General John Reed Hodge, alerted Washington to a potential northern offensive. In March 1950, Major General Charles Willoughby, intelligence chief to the Supreme Commander Allied Powers in Tokyo, reported a massive build-up of northern troops moving south; the CIA predicted a North Korean attack by June[4].

But it was still an unprepared South which was overrun by northern troops on June 25, 1950. Seventy-five thousand North Korea soldiers stormed across the 38th parallel virtually unopposed, and within three days, the South Korean capital, Seoul, had fallen.

***

News of the invasion reached Australia at 0830 on June 26, 1950, via the Australian mission in Tokyo. Minister for External Affairs Percy Spender issued a statement declaring an imminent threat to the wider region: 'If southern Korea falls under the domination of Communist imperialism, the strategic picture of Asia ... will undergo a radical change and will increase the dangers to the whole of South and South-East Asia.'[5]

On the same day, the United Nations Security Council (UNSC) called on its members to assist in repelling the North Korean forces. However, in backing to the northern invasion, Stalin had misread US President Harry S. Truman, who was determined the UN would take decisive action to protect southern Korea. US forces were immediately deployed in South Korea with World War II supremo General Douglas MacArthur in charge. Russia at the time was boycotting the UN over its refusal to recognise the new Chinese communist government, so therefore was unable to veto the move, which was quickly followed by a further 20 UN member nations – including Australia – committing to protect the security of South Korea[6].

As part of this hastily convened UN response, on June 29, 1950, Prime Minister Robert Menzies committed Australian naval forces to the conflict. On the same day, the Australian cabinet approved a British request for an RAAF squadron of Lincoln bombers to be dispatched to the burgeoning civil conflict in Malaya. General MacArthur, who had personally made an audacious flight over the South Korean battlefields on June 29, immediately recognised the criticality of air power in curbing the advance of northern troops. US Air Force F-80 Shooting Star jets were already based in Japan, but could only carry sufficient fuel for 15 minutes flying time over Korea: longer-range fighters were needed, and quickly.

Australia's No.77 Squadron RAAF had been based at Iwakuni, in southern Japan, as part of the British Commonwealth Occupation Force (BCOF) since the end of World War II. Iwakuni was within 200 kilometres of Korea, well within range of 77 Squadron's P-51 Mustang fighters. The Head of BCOF, Lieutenant General George Stratemeyer, described 77 Squadron as the best fighter squadron in Japan, with 25 pilots and 26 planes ready to go. MacArthur approached Sir Horace Robertson, the Commander-in-Chief of Australian BCOF forces, to request 77 Squadron's participation in Korea as proof of its strategic commitment to both the United States and the UN. On June 30, 1950, 77 Squadron were given their orders to fly, and the RAAF was back on a war footing[7].

CHAPTER 6

SWIFT TO DESTROY

He who commands the height, commands the fight.
—Fighter pilot's adage

Sergeant's Mess, 77 Squadron RAAF
Iwakuni Air Base, Japan
Sunday June 25, 1950

Pale morning sunlight drifted in long hazy rays through the windows. It was very quiet. Outside, birds twittered sleepily from the trees standing sentinel over the old grey building. Inside was a scene of destruction.

The floors were strewn with paper streamers and beer cans. Platters of food lay abandoned on tables sticky with beer and overturned glasses. A paper palm tree drooped sadly in one corner. Inert bodies were propped against walls and in chairs, some snoring with heads tilted and mouths wide; others were stretched, smiling in their sleep, on the hard timber floors, still in their Hawaiian shirts.

A telephone rang, strident as a fire alarm in the silence. Nobody moved.

The phone shrilled on and on. Finally, a bleary-eyed young airman lifted his head from where it had been pillowed on his arms beside a half-eaten plate of sandwiches. He eyed the phone balefully, then swayed at last to his feet, almost stumbled over an inert body snoring beside the table, and staggered to answer it. He listened for a moment, his forehead resting against the coolness of the wall. 'Yeah?' he said finally. 'Sorry, mate – you can't pull that one on me.' And he put the receiver down with a groan.

At that moment, the door beside him opened and a tall, lean man in blue stepped through. The young pilot turned and, blearily recollecting his role as duty sergeant, pulled himself into a salute. 'Good morning, sir.' Trying not to slur.

Squadron Leader Graham Strout smothered a smile. His own Hawaiian shirt was now at the bottom of a kitbag and he was back in freshly pressed blue serge, but he could not grudge his boys their sore heads or late start. Some of them had been away from Australia for seven years and now were just hours away from returning home: they deserved a party.

'Did I hear the phone just now, Trebilco?'

'Yes, sir, but it was just one of them Yanks, trying for a stir, sir.'

A stir?'

'He tried to tell me there was fighting over in Korea – that we were wanted over there right away. I told him, well ... it was a pretty bad joke, sir.'

Strout's eyebrows flickered up, but he smiled. 'Don't worry, son-those planes are staying packed up, just as they are. Now, how about we get these boys on their feet?'

When the phone rang again, just moments later it seemed, Strout himself answered it. Then he held up a hand for silence. The men collecting glasses and sweeping floors and holding damp dishtowels to their foreheads all stopped, caught by Strout's set expression. When he replaced the receiver, Strout's eyes found those of Ray Trebilco first. 'I'm sorry, son,' he said quietly. 'It was true.'

***

The fateful phone call to 77 Squadron's base in Japan came just hours after North Korean troops crossed the 38th parallel on June 25, 1950.

No.77 Squadron was the last remaining Australian air presence in Japan following the Japanese surrender in World War II in 1945. The squadron was formed in 1942 when the bombing of Darwin brought home the paucity of RAAF resources in northern Australia, with only

14 old Wirraways stationed in the northern capital. Three new RAAF units were formed – Nos.75, 76, and 77 Squadrons.77 Squadron was born at Pearce in Western Australia, with its crest proclaiming 'Swift to Destroy' below the motif of a 'grumpy monkey'. Under the command of the 21-year-old Squadron Leader Dick Cresswell, 77 Squadron, flying US P-40E Kittyhawks, saw active service in both northern Australia and the Pacific, including Milne Bay, Rabaul, and Labuan, throughout the remainder of World War II[1].

In February 1946, the squadron, now equipped with P-51 Mustangs, joined BCOF forces in Japan as part of No.81 Fighter Wing RAAF alongside No.76 and 82 fighter squadrons, No.381 Base Squadron, and No.481 Maintenance Squadron. Their BCOF duties were largely confined to local surveillance, but 77 Squadron prided themselves on maintaining a high level of combat readiness. By 1949, Nos.76 and 82 Squadrons had left Japan but 77 Squadron stayed on until June 1950, when the Australian government decreed all remaining elements of BCOF be withdrawn. The squadron packed up and celebrated with a three-day shipwreck-themed party beginning on June 24, 1950. But at the eleventh hour, a new war gate crashed the party.

No.77 Squadron's piston-engine Mustangs were critical to MacArthur's plan to use air power to halt the North Korean advance. With a top speed over 700 kilometres per hour, the P-51 was armed with six .50 calibre machine guns, bombs, armour-piercing rockets, and napalm tanks. When fitted with drop-tanks, the Mustang also had a range of more than 2500 kilometres, unlike the gas-guzzling USAF F-80 Shooting Star jets – ideal to strike at North Korean airfields and supply lines[2].

No.77 Squadron RAAF had been stationed in Japan as part of the British Commonwealth Occupation Force since the end of World War II. The long-range capabilities of their P-51 Mustangs made them crucial to General MacArthur's plan to use air power to slow the North Korean advance [Australian War Memorial, accession no. JK1027].

***

Back at Point Cook, the boys of No.4 training course were galvanised by the onset of air action in Korea. They were left in no doubt they too, would be in the air over the peninsula as soon as they were qualified. Instructors ramped up preparations on and off the airfield, with lectures on the geopolitics of the situation running alongside a new intensity in the flying program. And the boys scrambled for every newspaper they could lay hands on, devouring the headlines as North Korean troops continued to hammer a path through the South.

Trainee pilot Jim Kichenside in flying gear, Point Cook, 1950. The outbreak of the Korean War in June 1950 added extra impetus to the RAAF pilot training program [Kichenside family collection].

***

While South Korea had almost three times the population of the North, at 21 million, after the failed 1948 elections, the United States had deliberately kept the South lightly armed to reduce the likelihood of conflict on the peninsula. Now, with only 100,000 troops and 16 aircraft, southern forces were quickly crushed by the North's 200,000 well-trained fighters, backed by 1000 artillery pieces, 150 T-34 Soviet tanks and 154 aircraft, including Ilyushin 11-10 ground-attack planes and Yakovlev Yak-9 fighters. The first five days of the war saw the South Korean capital Seoul captured and the South suffer more than 44,000 casualties. South Korean and US ground troops were driven back to defensive positions around the port of Pusan in the southeast[3]. It was only the UN's superior air power which slowed the northern advance in those first bloody weeks.

By July 2, 1950, 77 Squadron's Mustangs were in the skies, with Strout at their head. Within days, UN aircraft had destroyed all of the North Korean Yaks and most of the Ilyushin fighters, flying up to 300 sorties a day, mainly on dead reckoning. But just five days into the campaign, 77 Squadron suffered their first casualty when Strout was shot down while on a strike against the North Korean railway at Samchok[4]. It was a stark reminder of the dangers they were facing against a well-armed and fast-moving enemy: as squadron CO Lou Spence told the assembled squadron: A lot of you others won't be here either at the end. (You've) got to realise – it's a real war.'[5]

Despite the heavy casualties inflicted from the air, Kim Il-Sung drove his forces onward with the demand that they achieve victory by August 15, 1950. And by early August, his DPRK armies had occupied virtually all of South Korea except for 130 square kilometres around Pusan. No.77 Squadron had established a rudimentary airfield at nearby Taegu and missions became increasingly hazardous as the battle for control of the southeast raged into September[6]. Flying up to five times a day, No.77 Squadron was awarded the Duke of Gloucester Cup in August 1950 as the most efficient squadron in the RAAF, and Lou Spence earned the US Legion of Merit[7]. Spence often flew multiple missions each day on top of his punishing command role, but on September 9, 1950, just one week before he was due to be posted out to London, an exhausted Spence failed to pull out of a strafing run at

Angang-ni; his Mustang exploded on impact in the centre of the town, and Spence was never seen again[8]. The loss of their leader had a devastating impact on morale at No.77 Squadron. Dick Cresswell, the first ever commanding officer of 77 Squadron in 1942 and now a Wing Commander, was dispatched immediately to Korea to assume command, and the World War II hero led his pilots from the front, flying 11 sorties in his first week in Korea[9].

The Yakovlev Yak-9 single-engine fighter (foreground) had been heavily used by Soviet forces in World War II, and surplus aircraft were supplied to communist states including North Korea after the war to develop their air power. In the background is a North American P- 51A Mustang fighter [Alamy, image ID: DCGYKH].

Despite the horrendous toll, the campaign at Pusan saved the UN in Korea. By September 12, General Walker declared the UN toehold firming, and the emphasis on air power was vindicated. Just days later, on September 15, MacArthur mounted a massive counterattack against North Korea at the dangerous tidal port of Inchon, near Seoul. The risky amphibious landing of 70,000 US troops behind enemy lines liberated the South Korean capital and cut food and ammunition supplies to enemy divisions further south; the momentum of the war suddenly swung dramatically back to the UN[10].

Success at Inchon drove MacArthur to push ground troops north across the 38th parallel for the first time, barrelling through North Korea toward the Chinese border on the Yalu River. Australian troops from the 3rd Battalion, Royal Australian Regiment (3RAR), saw fierce hand-to-hand fighting north of Pyongyang at Sinanju on October 22. The battalion, known as 'Old Faithful', had been committed to Korea in late July, and took their first casualties on October 25 when eight Australians were killed at the Battle of Broken Bridge as they advanced north on the Taeryong River. Four days later, a further nine Australian soldiers died at Chongju, including the commanding officer of 3RAR, Lieutenant Colonel Charles Green.

In November, the US 24th Division had reached within 29 kilometres of the Manchu border and 77 Squadron were flying in support of ground troops advancing along the Taeryong. The move infuriated China, which responded by pouring 300,000 troops across the Yalu in order to 'drive the warmonger MacArthur into the sea, as announced on Radio Peking. As UN forces hammered toward Pyongyang in late October, 77 Squadron were relocated to a bombed-out airfield at Pohang on the east coast of South Korea as part of the new 35th Fighter Group. Winter descended. The rapidly deteriorating conditions earned the place the nickname 'Frozen Chosin'. The men froze in skimpy tents pitched alongside the concrete runways where they were buffeted by-20°C winds, and ill-equipped ground staff had to urinate on their own hands to unstick them from frozen aircraft parts.

On October 19, 1950, UN forces captured the North Korean capital. MacArthur trumpeted that the war would be over by Christmas, and the first 50-mission veterans of 77 Squadron were sent home, with the end of the war seemingly in sight[11]. But MacArthur was still determined to reach the Manchurian border, a further 250 kilometres to the north, and sent the US 8th Army and 10th Corps forward, with US, Australian, and South African Mustang squadrons in support. 77 Squadron had again been relocated, now to Yonpo airfield at Hamhung in North Korea, and the men continued to suffer in the depths of a winter so severe it saw wings iced over, aircraft brakes seized, and even the emergency water supply under the ejection seats frozen solid – an unhappy prospect for any pilot having to then sit upon it. The battle of Chosin Reservoir in November 1950 was fought in temperatures as low as-47°Q after the war, some US servicemen displayed bumper stickers proclaiming the words of President Harry S. Truman: 'Once upon a time, hell froze over. We were there.'[12]

But as northern forces were driven back, Chinese leader Mao Zedong followed them with a massive Second Offensive, pouring thousands of fresh troops across the frozen Yalu River to prolong the war through the hell of winter. By November, UN ground forces were in retreat south of the 38th parallel, Pyongyang was lost, and the fighting was within a few kilometres of Hamhung. No.77 Squadron were evacuated to Pusan, and by January 5, 1951, Chinese forces had recaptured Seoul.

***

China's entry into the war introduced a new and deadly element to the air campaign: the

Soviet Mikoyan-Gurevich MiG-15 fighter jet, or more simply referred to by its combatants as the MiG. With a super-light airframe, swept-wing design, and engine copied from the Rolls-Royce Nene centrifugal compressor jet engine, the MiG was a superb climber, handled like a sports car at high altitudes, and could reach level speeds close to 1000 kilometres per hour. Hunting in packs which could exceed 150 aircraft, the MiG was a fearsome new adversary for the World War II-era United Nations fighter aircraft.

On November 8, 1950, the first jet air battle in history was fought above Sinuiju in North Korea. A US 5th Air Force Shooting Star jet shot down one MiG in providing cover for 77 Squadron as they strafed enemy troops to protect 3RAR and UN ground troops. The MiGs then vanished as quickly as they had appeared, sweeping insolently back across the border to their base at Antung in Manchuria. UN aircraft were barred from crossing the Yalu into Chinese territory, and US President Truman refused to grant MacArthur his dearest wish of bombing across the border, fearing the inevitable casualties would weaken the UN forces against any future Soviet involvement. So with a super-fast, highly manoeuvrable new enemy at the gates, it was now up to UN fighters to both continue their ground attack and interdiction roles and to intercept the waves of MiGs before they could advance too far south.

The Mikoyan-Gurevich MiG-15 jet was one of the first swept-wing fighters capable of operating in the transonic range (close to the speed of sound). It had thinner control surfaces than first-generation jets, a more powerful engine and better high-altitude flight characteristics, with a ceiling of 50,900 ft and climbing rate of 9,200 ft per minute [Alamy, image ID: 2B0AGPN].

The USAF was swift to respond to the MiG threat with a swept-wing fighter of its own in the form of the American F-86A Sabre jet. Boasting a similar swept-wing design to the MiG-15, the F-86 could outfly and out-handle the MiG below 30,000 feet, and the US pilots were far better trained and more experienced than their Chinese counterparts, despite the presence of the wily Soviet tutors who were also rumoured to be flying combat missions[13]. But while the introduction of the Sabre helped to slow the Communist advance by the end of January 1951, the carnage on the ground continued, with thousands of combatants and civilians injured or killed.

CHAPTER 7

WINGS

Go to the edge of the cliffandjump off.
Build your wings on the way down.
—Ray Bradbury

No.1 Flying Training School
RAAF Base Point Cook, Victoria
February 1951

As graduation neared in early 1951, the boy began having trouble sleeping.

This was not remarkable in itself, given the fiercely competitive and tightly wound state of many trainees faced with both daily assessments and increasingly bad news from Korea. But when the boy began to go off his food, having always been a robust eater, he was dispatched to the base infirmary. The boy kept his mouth tightly closed during the examination, which soon ruled out nervous disorders and problems with the liver, heart, lungs or stomach. It was when the doctor made to peer into his throat that the first involuntary gasp of discomfort came.

The old dental trouble which had cost the boy his Matriculation Certificate had re-emerged

– or rather, not emerged. An X-ray revealed his wisdom teeth were intractably hooked into his jaw and growing sideways, radiating pain whenever he attempted to talk, chew or sleep. There was no choice but to operate, which meant 12 days in the infirmary, where the boy sipped ice-cream and glumly watched the Wirraways performing hypnotic circuits of the base. But even after the operation, pain persisted in the side of his face. A further X-ray revealed that the dogfight the dental surgeon had had with his teeth had fractured his jaw. The result: he would not be able to wear a flying mask for another six weeks while the fracture healed.

Jim Kichenside's initial reaction was one of fury. *Six weeks grounded—six weeks of advanced flying lost!* The boy vowed that if that surgeon ever returned to his room, he'd rearrange *his* teeth and jaw. And then the worst realisation dawned – if he missed all that training, he would not graduate. His colleagues from 4 Course would leave without him-they would be among the dogfights in Korean skies and he'd end up in the GPO transcribing telegrams alongside his father.

So the old man had won.

The boy spent several days in physical and spiritual agony before Squadron Leader Paul Metzler came to see him. Metzler was more than just commander of the flight school: he took a real interest in his trainees and saw them as the exciting future of the RAAF[1]. Now he came to present the boy with the solution he craved: he would be retained at flight school and given a chance to graduate, but to complete the advanced flying requirements, he would have to drop back to join 5 Course, delaying his graduation for six months.

Six months! The war might be over before then! But it was better than a kick in the pants and a one-way ticket back to Sydney. He had no choice but to take the deal as offered. Two weeks later, the boys from 4 Course were presented with their wings. The boy, on the other hand, packed his kit to shift in with the lads from 5 Course. He shook hands with his old mates, with Vance Drummond and Bruce Thomson and the others, who all clapped him on the back and said see you soon'. They were going to war; he was staying in the classroom.

***

February 1951 saw the onset of the communist Fourth Phase campaign in Korea. After being initially repelled by the UN's Operation Thunderbolt counteroffensive early in 1951, North Korean and Chinese forces retaliated on February 11 in the twisting valleys around Hoengsong, inflicting a devastating defeat on the UN which cost the lives of up to 12,000 South Koreans and 1900 American troops. Both sides collided over the battle for Seoul on March 16, 1951, where a revitalised US Eighth Army retook the city, albeit destroying much of it with aerial and artillery bombardments. It was the fourth and final time Seoul was to change hands, although on April 22, Chinese forces launched another major offensive on the capital. The 27th British Commonwealth Brigade, including 3RAR, were dispatched to the valley of the Kapyong River, northeast of Seoul, where, over two days of fierce fighting on April 22-23, the Chinese advance was stalled, at the cost of 32 Australian lives. The battalion were later awarded a US Presidential citation for their courage at Kapyong[2].

In the skies, the toll among No.77 Squadron's pilots was mounting, with the deaths of Donald Ellis three days before Christmas in 1950 and Geoffrey Stephens shot down near Seoul two weeks later. Gordon Harvey survived being shot down on January 19, 1951, but became the first Australian airman captured by North Korean forces. He was held in horrific conditions for more than two years. Aircraft failures cost the lives of Ken Royal on February 6 and Harry Strange on March 19, with Strange falling to his death after his parachute failed to open when he was forced to bail out over the blockaded port of Wonsan. The battle of Chipyong-ni, on 13-15 February, became known as the Gettysburg of the Korean War' for both the ferocity of the Chinese infantry attacks and the desperate efforts of outnumbered UN forces to repel them in the air and on the ground. 77 Squadron pilots KC Matthews and Sinclair Squiers were both killed in action[3].

Despite the toll on its defence forces, Australian public interest in Korea was lukewarm. Two world wars in the first half of the twentieth century and the attendant cycles of grief and austerity meant many Australians were exhausted by the toll of war. Australia was never directly threatened by the Korean conflict, and in some sectors, Korea actually proved a boon, such as through the demand for wool for uniforms during the severe Korean winters.

As the battle for control of the peninsula see-sawed, MacArthur was still desperate to strike at the Chinese across the Manchurian border. However, President Truman continued to refuse to sanction such a move, prompting MacArthur to loudly complain about the President's lack of support. Truman reacted furiously: on April 11, 1951, MacArthur was sacked, and General Matthew Ridgway installed in his place[4].

In that same week, the RAAF would reshape its own air campaign in Korea and change the face of its operations forever.

***

One group very much aware of the mounting air casualty toll in Korea were the 31 hopefuls left in No.5 Flight Training Course at Point Cook. The war had electrified the group – nobody wanted to be left behind when the final cut for fighter pilot places was made in July. They filled their heads to bursting with tactics, jet aerodynamics and astronavigation, and lived every day in the air, dive-bombing, barrel-rolling, night flying and pushing the old Wirraways to their limits: always with Korea looming on the horizon.

Standards were high and competition intense. In 5 Course, the boy was reunited with Colin King, a young de Havilland aircraft engineering apprentice he had met in Sydney during selection interviews back in 1949. While both were accepted into 4 Course, King had to stay behind until he could secure a release from his apprenticeship; when he did eventually arrive at Point Cook, now to join 5 Course, the boy was the first to shake his hand. But while their friendship was warm, King was a formidable rival:

on top of his trade knowledge and academic prowess, King had been flying since age 15, earning shillings as a casual farm labourer to fund his passion, and now he was leaving nothing in the hangar to finish the course as number one. They were joined by Max Outhwaite, a lad from the NSW Central Coast whose diminutive stature belied his natural skill in the air, and the distinctive towering figure of South Australian Ken Smith, with his red hair and prominent nose. The quartet were both friends and friendly rivals, all determined to emerge from 5 Course as nothing less than incumbent fighter pilots[5].

Portrait of Sergeant Colin Kang painted in 1952 by Sir Ivor Hele, CBE, Australia's longest serving war artist. King, who graduated from No.5 Course with the Most Proficient Pilot award, was also later awarded the Distinguished Flying Medal for his service in Korea [Australian War Memorial, accession no. ART40333].

Ken Smith (left) and Lionel Cowper (right) outside the airmen's accommodation at Kimpo air base in Korea, March 1952 [Australian War Memorial, accession no. P08301.004].

***

Trainees at Point Cook were graded on physical fitness in addition to their classroom and airborne performance. Participation in competitive sports was seen as a critical element of preparation for the stress of future combat, and trainees played rugby or soccer in the winter and cricket in the summer. With six months headstart on his 5 Course colleagues in the classroom, the Point Cook instructors were well aware of Jim Kichenside's propensity to become bored. He had been captain of the 4 Course cricket team, and now the chief flying instructor, an avid cricketer himself, saw that the boy was granted the same role in 5 Course. To further ensure the boy was kept busy, the instructor added the responsibilities of repairing wickets, coaching and organising matches.

While the boy was a good golfer, dabbled with soccer, and twice represented Victorian Combined Services in rugby union, the instinctive hand-eye coordination that made Jim Kichenside a natural fighter pilot helped him excel at cricket. Point Cook's base chaplain, the legendary wartime padre Thomas 'Dave' Beyer, was a cricket aficionado and made an approach to the iconic Melbourne Cricket Club about the boy and his dangerous fast-medium bowling[6]. The MCC, home to Australian Test players including Warwick Armstrong, Bill Ponsford, and the boy's own idol, Fred 'The Demon Bowler' SpofForth, showed immediate interest, and at any other time, the boy might have flung off the traces and dived at a chance to play in the famous red and blue[7]. But the dream to be a fighter pilot outweighed even his love of the whites and the willow. While flattered, he declined the approach in favour of his burgeoning military career.

***

In early 1951, with the enemy Fourth Phase campaign as background, 77 Squadron came under pressure from the controlling US Air Force to double their rate of operations. By April, they were flying over 20 sorties a day targeting bridges and airfields around the Yalu River – a deadly interdiction campaign against an enemy rebuilding infrastructure as fast as it was destroyed, backed by a jet air force which could deploy more than 100 MiGs in a single sweep[8].

By the end of March 1951, 77 had been flying against the Chinese MiG fighters for five months and the casualty toll was grim: 16 aircraft lost and 13 pilots captured, missing or killed. Within weeks of the MiG entering the war in November 1950, the RAAF, like the USAF, were scrambling for a more competitive aircraft to replace the old P-51 Mustangs. The American-built Sabre was first choice, but the USAF had earmarked them all for their own use. The RAAF already had a small contingent of first-generation single-engine de Havilland Vampire jets, but they were too light and underpowered to compete with the MiG. It was BCOF head George Stratemeyer who made the recommendation conveyed by Australian Minister for Air William McMahon to Cabinet on December 4, 1950: to re-equip 77 Squadron with the twin engine British Gloster Meteor jet[9].

The twin-engine Gloster Meteor was the first jet to fly with the Royal Air Force and was the only Allied jet to fly in combat during World War II. Ninety-three Meteor F.8s and six T.7 trainers were purchased by the RAAF for use in Korea in response to the entry of the MiG-15 into the conflict [Peter Williams, image ID: 014R].into the conflict [Peter Williams, image ID: 014R].

Built by the Gloster Aircraft Company, the first Meteors flew in late 1939 as the Royal Air Force sought a jet fighter for use in the

European theatre[10]. In 1951, the Australian government ordered 35 straight-wing Meteor F.8s and four Meteor T.7 trainers at an estimated cost of £2.5 million. The first 17 aircraft arrived in Japan on February 24; another 82 were to follow[11]. With both sides now moving away from piston-engine fighter aircraft, Korea had become the first war of the jet age.

On April 6, 1951, 77 Squadron were withdrawn from all active combat duties to commence jet conversion training at Iwakuni under pilots from the RAF. Many RAAF pilots found the jets simple to fly, despite the unnerving quiet of the engines compared to the roar of the Mustang's big Merlin. While it was more fuel hungry than the Mustang, and had almost 1000 kilometres less range, the Meteor could operate up to 44,000 feet with a top speed 250 kilometres per hour greater. Squadron CO Dick Cresswell saw a role for the Meteor as an air interceptor, particularly at altitudes around 15-20,000 feet, and General Partridge, commander of the 5th Air Force, agreed, although with reservations: after personally test-flying the aircraft, he noted that compared to the Sabre, it lacked serious agility and acceleration at higher altitudes[12].

But as the war approached its first anniversary in mid-1951, the air war was entering a fearsome new phase. The UN had doubled down on truce talks at the ancient Korean capital of Kaesong with increased air aggression, aiming to force the North into a ceasefire. But China and North Korea responded with larger formations of MiGs than ever, also sending a further 700,000 ground troops into the conflict. In 77 Squadron's absence, just 89 USAF Sabres had remained to combat more than 1,100 Chinese jet aircraft. The squadron were now summoned back to Korea to resume active operations, but before the new Meteors could be sanctioned by BCOF for combat, they had to be retrofitted with radio compasses: it was July 29, 1951, before Australians flew their first operational missions as jet pilots out of their new base at Kimpo, north-west of Seoul[13].

***

Graduate pilot Jim Kichenside with wings' displayed on his uniform, August 1951 [Kichenside family collection].

At Point Cook, exams and flying tests also finished at the end of July 1951. The young men of 5 Course had earned a formidable reputation for self-confidence and skill, with one instructor wryly referring to them as a 'bunch of reprobates'[14]. But on August 2, 1951, 21 trainee pilots graduated on the Point Cook parade ground, led by course dux Ken Smith; Col King was a close second and awarded as Most Proficient Pilot. Minister for Air William McMahon was on hand to present the group, including Jim Kichenside, with their wings[15].

From more than 1500 applicants, just 10 graduates would go on to operational fighter training. Smith, King, Max Outhwaite and the boy were all in that ten.

***

Marrickville, Sydney
August 4, 1951

He smoothed the blue lapels of the smart belted jacket, checked the shine on his shoes and bent to flick away a speck of dust before he stepped off the train. The white wings on his chest gleamed in the late Sydney sunlight.

He walked. As the boy turned into the familiarity of Roseby Street, a hail reached him from number 48. His neighbour, Rowly, who had constructed his makeshift bedroom on the back porch, was smoking on his front step. Now, he came down the front steps with his familiar limping gait and clasped the boy's hand across the fence. 'So, you're in blue, mate,' he said. 'Well, then – we'd best take you up the road for a beer.'

Jim grinned. 'I'm sure you know just the place,' he replied.

But as they turned to go, another voice followed them, this time from number 46. 'Where are you blokes off to?'

It was the boy's father, standing on the front porch in his shirt sleeves. The boy hesitated. His mother had been at Point Cook for the graduation ceremony but his father had not, citing commitments to his own mother; the boy had felt the sting keenly.

'Were just going for a beer, Dad,' he said. 'Won't be long.'

Their eyes met and held. His father eyed the blue serge and white wings for an instant that seemed a lifetime. 'Wait for me,' Charles Kichenside said.

'But, Dad,' the boy protested, wondering why he couldn't keep his own mouth shut, you don't drink beer.'

His father did not reply as he came down the steps, shrugging into his coat. They walked the length of the block in silence; as though he sensed what was coming, Rowly had drifted back. 'I don't drink beer,' Charles said finally, 'because we all needed shoes and food on the table instead.'

The boy kept his eyes ahead as they walked, but said quietly, 'Like the bicycle?'

'Yes.' Equally quiet. 'Just like the bike.'

They walked on in silence into the gathering dusk. Then the boy said, 'I'll get the first round, Dad.'

PART
TWO
71

CHAPTER 8

REAL FLY BOYS

There are old pilots and bold pilots, but there are no old, bold pilots.
—Pilot's adage

Forster, NSW
December 1951

The boy thought Heaven must look like this.

The earth was a faraway panorama of ocean as dark and blue as a sapphire, the green land fringed with perfect white dunes. All around him were great heaped white clouds as big as hills. And he could fly amongst them all: fast – so very fast. The part that lifted his heart most, however, was that up here it was so quiet. There was no deafening roar of a great pumping piston engine, no huge vibration of propeller – just the low whine of the Nene jet turbine behind him. It made a high-pitched steaming sound, like the hairdryers his mother sat beneath to set her hair each week. That thought made him smile as he rolled the Vampire easily to starboard and opened the throttle and *flew.*

It came not as a bang or a jolt but as an abrupt heavy slowing of the aircraft, as though he had flown deep into a patch of molasses. The jet heaved once and hissed, then the whine of the turbine faded. He rattled the stick – *nothing.* The Vampire's tail immediately began to sink, like that of a wounded bird.

For an instant, the beautiful jewelled panorama around him turned to shades of grey. There was a buzzing in his ears, as though the cockpit were suddenly infested with wasps. The altimeter was dialling downward, and it was that fact which jerked him back to the bright coloured world. His eyes refocussed on the gauges: 25,000 feet, 24,000, 23,000...

He shifted in his seat and felt the crackle of papers beneath his flying suit. The pilot notes. He struggled briefly with the harness in the tight little cockpit and hauled the folded wad of notes out from his inside pocket. *Flameout* ... flipping pages ... *Engine re-light sequence* ... more pages...

18,000 feet...

Finally, the damned right page. Re-lighting in the air. Note: practice relighting is NOT to be encouraged. Despite himself, he very nearly laughed.

Close high-pressure cock ... If above 15,000 feet, no-relight should be attempted.

A glance at the altimeter: 16,000 feet, 15,500 feet...

Once below 15,000 feet, re-lighting may be carried out. Throttle: closed. Windmilling: 1000 rpm. Press and hold re-light button, turn on HP cock, count five, release button[1].

Press and hold – count five – release.

Nothing happened.

12,000 feet...

***

The early days of jet fighter training in the RAAF meant – quite literally – flying by the seat of one's pants. In 1951, there were no dual-seat jet training aircraft in Australia for pilots making the transition from piston-engine fighters to jets. Aspiring jet pilots learned the theory of jet engine function and aerodynamics in the classroom, then in the air, they were immediately on their own. Furthermore, there were no modern G-suits available to help withstand the high forces of turning and banking – pilots had to simply tighten their abdominal muscles and try to ward off an impending blackout.

The deteriorating situation in Korea had only amplified pressure on the RAAF to hastily train and deploy a new generation of jet pilots. The advent of the Meteor and pressure on 77 Squadron to return swiftly to their air interceptor role – and the loss of 13 pilots – culminated in a hasty and barely coordinated operational training program in 1951 for graduate pilots preparing for overseas combat.

To speed up their transition and maximise time in the air, five of the 5 Course 'Reprobates' were sent to the Operational Training Unit at Williamtown RAAF base near Newcastle, NSW, and five to No.23 Squadron at Archerfield in Brisbane. This latter included the boy, Col King, Ken Smith, and Max Outhwaite. Here, their fighter debut came in the P-51 Mustang which, although withdrawn from combat operations in Korea, remained the keystone of RAAF fighter training. The Reprobates would spend 70 hours in the legendary old fighter. With no dual-seater available, they were forced to prepare by executing flapless landings from the rear seat in a Wirraway to mimic the blind approach of the Mustang, whose massive Merlin engine obscured almost all forward vision during the approach. And then at last – for King and the boy had both waited more than two years for this day – a first solo flight in the indomitable old warhorse[2].

***

August 29, 1951, marked a bitter first confrontation between RAAF Meteors and enemy MiGs in Korea.

A flight of eight Meteors and 26 US Sabres were *en route* for Chongju, north-west of Pyongyang, when they were hit by a swarm of MiGs bearing down out of the sun at one thousand kilometres per hour[3]. Ron Guthrie's Meteor was hit and he was forced to eject at 33,000 feet; Guthrie had over 30 minutes floating earthward in a parachute to contemplate his landing in enemy territory, where he was captured by North Korean troops. He was held for more than two years in horrific conditions, including being locked in a small wooden packing case, tethered and publicly tormented on North Korean streets, and ordered to dig his own grave at gunpoint[4].

As confrontations with the MiG continued, the inferiority of the Meteor in high-altitude combat became steadily more apparent. Its maximum speed of 950 kilometres per hour was more than 10 per cent slower than the MiG. Its straight-wing design was also a limiting factor: aircraft with swept-back wings reach higher speeds before shock-waves build over the wing (compressibility), leading to potential loss of control. The MiG was also lighter, more compact, and could climb faster. And while the Meteor had excellent firepower with its four 20 millimetre cannons, it was not fitted for carrying bombs or approved for rocketry – both critical for a successful role in ground attack[5]. It seemed the Meteor was in a fight with one hand tied behind its back.

***

From Archerfield, the Reprobates moved to No.3 Squadron at RAAF Fairbairn in Canberra for advanced Mustang flying, including line-astern chasing, quarter attacks, and engine failure drills. With reports of Ron Guthrie's capture ringing in their ears, the young pilots also took part in a ground-based Escape and Evasion exercise where they were bundled out of the base in a covered truck and shunted out individually at points up to 50 kilometres away; 'home' was the peak of a local mountain, with police and army cadets in the role of North Korean troops stalking them through the bush. It was a stark reminder of the vulnerability of grounded pilots.

Advanced training at Fairbairn also meant night-flying in all weathers. King had a near miss when the flaps on his Mustang failed one night in a stiff cross-breeze[6]. The OIC of night flying at Fairbairn was Flight Lieutenant Ian 'Bill' Purssey, a 28-year-old Queenslander who had flown Kittyhawks and Mustangs in North Africa and Italy during World War II. On returning home, Purssey had remained in the Citizen Air Force in Brisbane, then joined up again full-time in 1951 as calls grew for experienced men to lead the young tyros of the reshaped RAAF[7]. Like his young charges, Purssey himself was now destined for aerial combat over Korea – where he and the boy would meet again on the darkest of days.

***

In Korea, the Meteor was in trouble. Its role as an interceptor was under question as it struggled to combat the superior speed and agility of the enemy MiGs. No.77 Squadron CO Dick Cresswell had completed his tour in late August 1951 and been replaced by Wing Commander Gordon Steege, a decorated World War II fighter pilot whose arrival in Korea was greeted by almost daily incursions by swarms of MiGs. In his monthly report for August 1951, Steege wrote despairingly, 'Unless the MiGs are operated unintelligently, Meteors are not going to account for many.'[8]

And with casualties and the aircraft damage toll mounting, after only a fortnight in Korea, Steege acted: on September 6, 1951, 77 Squadron were withdrawn from air combat operations in the volatile region in the northwest of North

Korea known as MiG Alley. Their new role: bomber escort and airfield defence around Kimpo.

Being taken out of the front line was a huge blow to the young Australian pilots' pride. And the decision came as communist forces threw everything at regaining air superiority: in October 1951, over 3000 MiGs were massed on the Chinese border. And with 77 already out of the front line, the superiority of the communist jets forced UN operations into a further backdown when, after losing 55 aircrew in one week, the USAF had little choice but to halt daylight bombing operations[9].

***

In November 1951, the five Reprobates were again transferred, this time to No.76 Squadron, the Fighter Operational Training Unit at RAAF Base Williamtown, to complete their Mustang phase. The focus shifted to gunnery and attack training, including live firing at both ground and aerial targets towed behind lead aircraft or naval vessels. With the high-altitude attack capabilities of the MiG now well known, the young pilots pushed the Mustangs to their limits, despite the moratorium on No.77 Squadron's frontline combat operations in Korea. They were risky days, for in taking the Mustang above 35,000 feet, the old aircraft had to be nursed in the low-density atmosphere which could induce a deadly stall during hard turns. But Korea was in the gunsights of these young men, and they were determined to be more than ready.

***

Despite 77 Squadron's withdrawal from the heat of air-to-air combat in MiG Alley, and despite being awarded a Presidential Citation by South Korea leader Syngman Rhee for their meritorious service, the casualties among Australian pilots in Korea continued. Three RAAF airmen were lost in a single day on December 1, 1951, when a flight of 14 Meteors were set upon by more than 50 MiGs near Pyongyang. Ducking and diving, Bruce Gogerly managed to bring one MiG down – the first confirmed MiG kill for 77 Squadron in North Korean skies. But Don Armit's bullet-riddled Meteor crashed and exploded, and the boy's former bunkmates in No.4 Course, Bruce Thomson and Vance Drummond, were both shot down and captured. The following day, 77 Squadron was informed their air-to-air combat role in Korea had been officially terminated[10].

***

The final phase of fighter training for the Reprobates came in late December 1951, when the five transferred to No.75 Vampire Squadron at Williamtown for a first – and brief – taste of jet operations. With no Meteors in Australia, the group spent 30 hours in the first-generation de Havilland Vampire FB.31 fighter, a single-seat jet with one Rolls Royce Nene turbo engine, a rounded plywood fuselage, and distinctive twin tail booms.

The Vampire jet was relatively new to the RAAF, with the first 50 only delivered in 1949[11]. Instruction on the new jet was still evolving in 1951, with no dual-seat training aircraft until 1953, few experienced instructors, and limited theory on both the jet engine and the plane's aerodynamic characteristics. The Vampire was a far different proposition to the reassuring substance and proven record of the Mustang. Fire was a real risk with the Vampire's plywood construction, and the ultra-light controls meant greater anticipation and thrust adjustment were required during formation flying. The Vampire also had an unholy thirst, particularly during low-altitude exercises such as air-to-ground rocketry and dive-bombing. There was no ejection seat, and the cramped cockpit was extremely tight for a pilot wearing a parachute; to bail out, the entire aircraft had to be rolled upside down to allow the pilot to fall out. The boy faced this prospect on his very first Vampire flight.

A jet engine compresses air then adds fuel and ignites it to generate forward thrust. Fuel starvation, compressor stall, or ingestion of foreign matter can lead to flameout: a sudden and often irreversible engine halt. On the boy's first solo flight, he climbed to 30,000 feet as directed and turned north of RAAF Base Williamtown towards Forster to start a series of basic turns and aerobatics. Then the engine simply quit. The re-light sequence failed. He was far from the base and his only options were to bail out (risking the aircraft crashing in a civilian area) or make a forced landing. Quick calculations indicated he might be able to glide back to Williamtown or at least bail out somewhere close by, perhaps over the sea. For 25 agonising minutes, the boy and the disabled jet floated back toward the base where the entire squadron had gathered on the tarmac, hearts in mouths, while a senior officer desperately radioed to the young pilot. But the boy coasted quietly in over their heads, made a deep landing, and braked a few yards short of the end of the runway. Col King recalled, It was a superb effort for a pilot with only 300 hours experience, and a tribute to good pilot selection and efficient training.'[12]

A pair of de Havilland Vampire fighters (left, centre) flank a MiG-15 jet during a flypast at the 2017 Southport airshow. The first Vampires were acquired by the RAAF in 1949, but these first-generation jets were too light and underpowered to be considered for active combat in Korea against the MiG, recognition of which drove the Australian decision to equip No.77 Squadron with the Meteor F.8 [Alamy, image ID: K88FWE].

The boy was flying again the next day. It was just like falling off a horse – he had to get straight back in the saddle. But the Vampire was not finished with him yet. The early Vampires had the 'elephant ear' air intakes positioned on top of the fuselage to prevent ingestion of debris into the engine turbines. But in high speed flight, this altered the aerodynamics of the jet so as to cause a critical nose-down pitch and loss of elevator control at the onset of compressibility.

A plunge of up to 15,000 feet could occur in seconds, with the pilot potentially blacking out under the severe G-forces of the plummeting aircraft. Soon after the Forster incident, the boy encountered one such rogue aircraft. During a training flight, the jet suddenly dived, completely out of control, plunging to below 4000 feet before the boy regained the upper hand. Six pilots were lost during these early days of jet training on Vampires; while some fatalities related to structural faults, others were aerodynamic: with no ejection seat, pilots were trapped in an unstoppable, and often fatal, high-speed vertical dive.

***

By the end of 1951, one in four pilots from 77 Squadron were missing in action or had been killed over Korea.

Despite the gaping hole it left in the UN's interceptor capabilities, in late 1951, 77 Squadron remained confined to low-altitude airfield defence duties. The main threat they faced was from 'Bedcheck Charlies'—nuisance bi-planes dropping fragmentation bombs over the airfield in order to damage parked aircraft. Meanwhile, massed formations of MiGs were making thousands of sorties as far south as Seoul, sometimes flying right over the heads of the members of 77

Squadron at Kimpo. Morale plummeted as another Korean winter plunged the dejected airmen into weeks of subzero temperatures, snow piling up around their tents as they were forced to watch the war from the sidelines.

The arrival of new CO, Wing Commander Ron Susans, on December 26, 1951, brought an immediate and decisive agitation for return to combat. Despite its lack of bomb racks and untried rocketry capabilities, Susans saw a new potential for the Meteor as a ground-attack aircraft, with its rugged airframe and preference to work at lower altitudes. General Frank Everest, new head of the 5th Air Force, was also unhappy with 77 Squadron's limited contribution and gave the all-clear to re-enter the war in a ground-attack role. Against flak traps, anti-aircraft installations, and well-armed ground troops with rifles pointed at the sky, Susans knew ground-attack would be even more hazardous than air-to-air combat. But with his men losing heart by the day Susans also understood the criticality of restoring a full operational commitment. He led the first Meteor ground-attack mission himself on January 8, 1952[13].

However, General Everest's concession had one grave condition – he wanted 1000 sorties a month from the revamped squadron: a massive task with only 20 aircraft serviceable to fly at any time and less than 30 pilots to fly them[14].

No.77 Squadron needed more pilots – right now.

***

By February 1952, the Reprobates were students no more. The lectures, the drilling, the inspections and gradings were over, and the boy, Smith, King, and Outhwaite were sergeant pilots: fully fledged members of the RAAF pilot fraternity. The boy now had 399 hours in his logbook, albeit with only 30 hours on jets. Their kitbags were packed to join the first war of the jet age in the windswept icy skies over Korea. They would spend a few days getting to know the Meteor in Japan then it was straight to the front.

'We knew some of us would die,' Col King said. 'But of course: "it won't be me!"'

CHAPTER 9

THE PILOT AND THE PRINCESS

Oho, wouldst like it? Then so shall it be. Doff thy rags, and don these splendors, lad! It is a brief happiness, but will be not less keen for that.
—Mark Twain, *The Prince and the Pauper*

Enmore Theatre
Newtown, Sydney
Christmas 1950

'Oh, dear! Beryl, do you have any spare batteries? Mine do run down so fast!' The pretty blonde girl shook her pencil torch despairingly, which only made the thin beam of light gutter then flicker out. 'That's the third time this month – the boss will slay me if I ask her for any more!'

Her friend squeezed her arm. 'Here, take mine,' she said, slipping the torch into her hand. 'I'll stay out here and take tickets if you show people to their seats.'

The blonde girl kissed her friend impulsively on the cheek and scampered up the stairs to her station at the theatre door. 'You're the best! I'll buy you something nice for Christmas!'

The girl named Beryl shook her head and took her own position at the base of the theatre stairs, smiling at each patron as they handed her their tickets. It was a pretty smile. Her teeth were small and perfectly white, like pearls. Hers was a delicate bone structure and the eyes beneath the curling chestnut hair were intensely blue. But there was something very kind in the smile she gave them all – the sticky-fingered children clutching sweets, the shy lovers arm in arm, the big spenders in their garish suits.

And then she saw him. A solitary figure immaculate in blue, standing in the doorway.

***

At the end of 1950, before his wisdom teeth curtailed his dreams of graduation from flight school with 4 Course, the boy had felt himself standing on the threshold of manhood: a real career, with income and security and the chance of promotion. These were all the things he had learned were important from his father: his father who had worked for the postal service since he was virtually a child and seemed destined to remain there, secure and comfortable, for life.

So during the Christmas break at the end of 1950, when the air cadets were granted a few precious days of leave, the boy had returned to Sydney to see his mother, father and sisters – and to renew an old acquaintance.

He had been a little nervous about it. Beryl Sjoberg was a year older than he was. As children, they had played together and had demure little picnics on the banks of the Cooks River. She was the prettiest girl in Marrickville, with her glossy auburn curls and the blue eyes so unlike the greys and browns of the other girls. But he had hardly seen her for seven years, since he'd gone off to Sydney Technical High at age 12 and she had taken domestic science at Enmore Tech. She'd then found a job in a city store selling hosiery and handbags, and he would sometimes pass that way while walking from Central Station to his school in Paddington. But at 15, he could hardly step into *that* type of store, so he had to content himself with a wave through the window.

Now, when he felt his prospects in life were assured, the compulsion to reunite with Beryl Sjoberg was irresistible.

Beryl Kichenside pictured at Shoal Bay, Port Stephens, NSW. The rear of the photograph is inscribed, 'To my darling Jim, all my love forever' [Kichenside family collection].

It did not start well. He walked to the Sjoberg house at 77 Livingstone Road in Petersham – a two mile walk from Marrickville which gave him plenty of opportunity to rehearse what he'd say. He was dressed in his air force blues and, despite the beautifully pressed serge and highly polished shoes, suddenly felt conspicuous, like walking about dressed for a costume party. But he had no choice – he still did not have enough money to buy civilian clothes beyond his best suit and cricket whites. Suddenly that lack of money reared up inside him like a snake. What right had he to ask out the best girl in the neighbourhood when he was still a man of only one suit? Would Beryl's parents even remember who he was? And what if she was at home in the parlour with some other bloke when he arrived?

When Beryl's mother answered his knock, he blurted out, 'Well, I've established myself – I've come back to marry your daughter.'

Florence Sjoberg told him her only child was not at home[1]. Beryl was in nearby Enmore, working as an usherette at the theatre. So he walked again, and there she was, flashlight and all, and he said, 'Hello, Beryl' – while silently cursing himself for having still not come up with any more impressive opening gambit.

But she smiled – *that smile!*-and said, ‘Hello, Jim.’

***

Beryl Sjoberg and Jim Kichenside quite literally came from opposite sides of the tracks. They were born within 100 yards of one another, Beryl in 1929 at her parents’ rented home at 411 Illawarra Road, south of Marrickville station, and Jim just north of the station in 1930 at a private cottage hospice. They were both children of the Depression, and both of their fathers worked for the Postmaster-General. But while the Kichenside family always had food on the table, the Sjoberg family were not so fortunate.

Beryl’s father, World War I serviceman William Olaf ‘Ossie’ Sjoberg, lost his job during the Depression. It was another rung on the hard-luck ladder of Ossie Sjoberg’s life. His own father, Louis, had gotten into business trouble in the late 1890s and run off to New Zealand, leaving behind two children and a pregnant wife, Mary, who raised the babies with the help of her sister. But tragedy struck in 1912 when both Mary and her sister drowned in a boating accident on Sydney Harbour, leaving now 17-yearold Ossie and his sister Lilian orphaned in industrial inner-city Sydney[2].

It was a far cry from the royal Scandinavian heritage of his Sjoberg ancestry, descending from two lines of ancient Scandinavian kings. Beryl Sjoberg's great-great-grandmother, Johanna Larsdotter (1793-1873) was a direct descendant of Gustaf I Vasa (King of Sweden 1523-1560, during the reign of Henry VIII in England) and his successor Erik XIV (1560-1568). Gustaf's own father Erik was beheaded by the Danish king Kirstian II at the Stockholm Bloodbath of 1520 with 90 other nobles. Gustaf inspired a peasant revolution to force the Danish out and retake the throne. However, despite her royal lineage, a fateful extramarital relationship was to condemn Johanna Larsdotter to penury. She was born in Hössna, a village on the Swedish west coast, and went with her brother to the city of Goteborg to find work, in the early nineteenth century, taking a position in the home of Frans Gideon Funch, a powerful local official; he was married at the time with 11 children of his own.

In 1823, Johanna fell pregnant. Her son Johan Frans was brought up in Punch's house, but Johanna refused to reveal the identity of his father. She later left Punch's house to marry Stockholm carpenter Gustaf Sjoberg, and 10-year-old Frans took his name. Frans Sjoberg went on to become a well-known musician and composer, but it was not until he was 40 years old that Johanna confirmed Funch as his father after keeping her secret for four decades.

Frans and his wife Carolina Borgstrom had nine children, of whom the fourth, Frans Ludvig 'Louis' Sjoberg (1854-1923), was a talented artist who studied at the Royal Academy in Stockholm from the age of 13[3]. However, his studies were interrupted by continual dalliance and in 1880, he migrated to Australia to escape escalating social scandals. He worked as a painter-decorator on some of the colony's most prominent buildings, including Her Majesty's Theatre in Sydney, and married Mary Elizabeth Hodges in 1894. His son Ossie Sjoberg, Beryl's father, was born the following year, before his father fled to New Zealand.

Jim Kichenside, on the other hand, came from much sterner stock. His Kichenside descendants originated in the area around Fetcham in Surrey, England, as far back as 1744. His grandfather William (1853-1918) was a third-generation brick-maker, a skill he brought to Australia when he was 24 years old. But unlike the royal lineage of the Sjobergs, Jim Kichenside's heritage was tied to the First Fleet and Australia's convict past. The feudal agrarian societies of 17th century England were shattered by the social upheaval of the Industrial Revolution, Napoleonic Wars, and a population explosion that drove the poor and desperate to cities where they became vulnerable to a criminal underclass focussed on both survival and obtaining a share of the opulence of the wealthy minority. Draconian laws enacted to protect private property meant a fourfold increase in the number of offenses attracting penal transportation.

For seventeen-year-old Ann Martin, it started with a silk handkerchief. Her theft conviction of this delicate accessory in 1787 earned her seven years transportation from Surrey to Sydney, where she formed a relationship with convicted highwayman William Miller. Miller was pardoned in 1802 and given a land grant in the area of present-day Circular Quay. At age eight, their daughter Sarah Martin was indentured as a household servant to William Cox, a wealthy pastoralist, magistrate, and a close friend of Governor Macquarie. She fell pregnant to Cox's son James when she was 17. Young Cox was betrothed to someone else and induced another convict assigned to his father, convicted thief Christian Sternbeck, to marry Sarah and raise the child; Sternbeck was offered a pardon and a land grant if he agreed.

Sarah bore Sternbeck three children, and the youngest, Elizabeth, was married in 1836 at 14 years old to Samuel Upton. The two had 15 children. Their third child, Mary Ann, born less than 2 years after the marriage, was 22 when she married 18-year-old Scottish immigrant Daniel Rutherford and bore him 8 children. The Rutherford family left their home in the NSW Shoalhaven for the north coast due to severe flooding around Nowra. Their third child, James (1863-1930) became a farmer at Woodburn. He married 14-year-old Kate Husking and her ninth child, Dulcie, was the boy's mother.

However, despite her royal Swedish lineage, Beryl Sjoberg also had convict heritage. Her grandmother, Mary Hodges, was the granddaughter of convict William Hodges, who was convicted in 1799 of stealing a box of clothes and transported, aged 17. But he was pardoned in 1812, married a wealthy widow and became a prosperous Sydney publican[4].

So Beryl and Jim's relationship formed the confluence of two ancient lineages – the ancient trades and the ancient kings – united by the convicts whose descendants would later populate modern Australia.

***

In the first week of July 1951, as their stint at Point Cook drew to a close, the boy received leave to travel to The Entrance on the NSW Central Coast to act as groomsman at Max Outhwaite's wedding[5]. The bride, with her misty veil and bouquet of sweet-scented orchids, was just about the prettiest thing he'd seen. It set him to serious thinking. And on the long return journey, he made a very important stopover at a rented bungalow in Petersham with a ring in his blazer pocket.

It was a time for acceptance, and a time for truths. Beryl confessed to Jim that a childhood accident had left her unable to bear children. He said that was okay. But as the time for departure for Korea became increasingly hectic, so too did the relationship. In December, Jim received a letter at Williamtown bearing the news – Beryl was pregnant. After the initial shock, there was delight. Beryl had never aspired to a fancy career or wealthy lifestyle – she wanted a cosy home and a family of her own. She and Jim had planned to marry after he returned from Korea: now the wedding was brought forward to January 25, 1952, five weeks before his departure. There was now a 44 per cent casualty rate among RAAF pilots in Korea, and if Jim was killed, Beryl would at least receive a war widow's pension. Ken Smith came down from Williamtown to Summer Hill in Sydney to stand as best man. The young couple snatched a few days' honeymoon at Williamtown, but when the boy flew out for Korea in February 1952, he had been married just six weeks.

Hie wedding of Beryl Sjoberg and Jim Kichenside, January 25, 1952, just six weeks before Jim was deployed to Korea. L-R: best man Ken Smith, Jim's sister Nola Kichenside, Jim Kichenside, Beryl Sjoberg, Beryl's father Ossie Sjoberg [Kichenside family collection].

CHAPTER 10

EIGHT HOURS

Be glad you're even alive. Be furious you're going to die.

—Joseph Heller, *Catch-22*

Pilots' quarters
Iwakuni Air Base, Japan
March 9, 1952

Max pushed the main door open and looked down the corridor. He hesitated for an instant, checked the door number, then dumped his kitbag inside the first bedroom. He and the boy looked down the corridor again; all the doors were open, but the silence was profound.

'Seems a little empty around here,' Max said, a frown creasing his forehead.

The boy moved past him and peered into the next room, then the next. All were neatly made up, but with no personal possessions within. 'Strange,' he breathed. 'Where are they? Are we in the right place?'

'Looking for your mates?' A tall sergeant had come in behind them.

Both Max and the boy snapped to a salute. Then the boy said, 'Yes, sir. Smith and King, sir.'

'Gone, last week,' the sergeant said.

Startled looks.

'You mean, they've finished their conversion? They're already over there?'

'Look,' said the sergeant, you blokes will be lucky if you get 10 hours on wings here before you go too. They've lost that many pilots they're screaming for more. So, take my advice – keep your mouths shut, camp down on the strip, and fly every minute you've got the chance.'

***

Early 1952 and Wing Commander Susans had met General Everest's stipulation for a 25 per cent increase in sortie rate by 77 Squadron over Korea. The interdiction rate rose to over 1000 missions per month in their battle against enemy convoys, trains, and infrastructure[1]. But while the struggle for performance at high altitude was no longer their chief issue, flying low over hostile territory exposed a new and significant vulnerability in the Meteor.

Attached under the belly of the aircraft was a ventral tank which added an extra 175 gallons of fuel to extend the range of the aircraft. While the tank could be dropped using a handle on the instrument panel, the added weight affected the aircraft handling, particularly in pulling out of a dive. The position of the tank on the aircraft underbelly also made it vulnerable to enemy fire, and Susans was well aware of the risk, declaring in an official report in March 1952, It is a perpetual menace for, when empty of fuel and full of gas, (the ventral tank) presents just the type of target the enemy wants.'[2] Two pilots were lost to ventral tank hits on a single day on January 27, 1952, during a mission to Haeju: Mark Browne-Gaylord's plane was hit in the belly and he was given immediate clearance to return to Kimpo, but the aircraft vanished on the return journey. Bruce Gillan was hit while attacking a locomotive and, with flames issuing from the ventral tank, he ejected, but despite an extensive search, no trace of him was ever found.

On February 6, 1952, JT 'Butch' Hannan was leading an attack on targets in the Sibyong-Ni area when his Meteor was also hit in the ventral tank. The aircraft was burning when he ejected, parachuting into the hands of enemy forces. Richard 'Dick' Robinson, another graduate of 5 Course, was killed when his Meteor exploded after the ventral tank was hit while strafing targets in Haeju on February 16. He was the first casualty of the 5 Course Reprobates. And the day before the boy and Max Outhwaite arrived in Japan, on March 8, 1952, another 5

Course colleague, Ian Cranston, was killed when he was shot down near Kaesong; the plane's ventral tank was hit and exploded before Cranston could eject. He had been in Korea just eight weeks[3]. Ian Cranston was only 23 years old when he died; he had won the Most Outstanding Sportsman award in 5 Course and played rugby for Australia against the New Zealand All Blacks in 1951. Cranston, like the boy, was also a graduate of Sydney Technical High School[4].

The casualty rate meant the three-month Meteor conversion which 77 Squadron pilots had undertaken in 1951 was no longer an option. Young pilots were needed as fodder for the cannons of war. Meteor conversion training still took place out of the Iwakuni Air Base in southern Japan. When the boy and Max Outhwaite arrived in March 1952, it was winter – the kind of winter the boy from temperate Sydney had never imagined. It had been cold sometimes at Point Cook in southern Victoria, with its chilly winds off Port Phillip Bay. But at Iwakuni, beyond the long grey runway, frozen hills lay streaked with snow and wreathed with ominous grey cloud. The ocean they had flown over on the descent had not been like an Australian ocean, blue and playful: it was steel-grey and dotted with rocky black islands like malignant warts.

Neither the boy nor Max had ever been outside Australia before, nor flown in such luxury as the Qantas DC-4 Skymaster service to Japan via Darwin and Hong Kong. There were comfortable seats, meals on trays, and freedom to smoke and sleep. Despite all their bravado, they were as excited as schoolboys at flying over turquoise seas and coral reefs and palm trees. But Hong Kong, while impossibly exotic with its harbour of junks, did not provide a friendly welcome-they were held over for a frustrating three days because of a typhoon. By the time they taxiied into Japan, they had been more than 33 hours in the air and 96 hours in transit.

Modern-day Iwakuni is an industrial city of over 135,000 population, but in 1952, it was a small town on the Nishiki river delta at the southern end of Honshu island, just 30 kilometres from the devastated city of Hiroshima. Its streets were populated by dancehalls, rickshaws, and cormorant fishermen. The famous Kintai Bridge, constructed in 1673 but destroyed in 1950 by typhoon Kijiya, stood half ruined across the river. The scene might have been pretty, with the little town nestling in a patchwork of paddy fields inhabited by sacred white snakes, but the stench from fields fertilised with human excrement was overwhelming.

The base had a single concrete runway, a slipway for flying boats, and accommodation for 4000 personnel. It had been a training site for Japanese Kamikaze pilots in World War II, and still bore the scars of Allied bombing[5]'. But the new arrivals had eyes for little beyond the sleek silver Meteor jets parked outside the hangars. There were three – a T.7 dual-seat trainer and two F.8 single-seat jets. They were beautiful, with their twin cigar-shaped Rolls Royce Derwent engines, 20mm cannons withsemi-armour-piercing ammunition that could disable a tank, and up to 8 rockets slung beneath each wing.

There was little time for admiring the slick new machine: it was straight into training. Conversion placed a big emphasis on twin-engine handling and engine-failure procedures. Few had flown a twin-engine aircraft before – the second engine provided more power, but also meant they had to learn to fly it on one in an emergency. With the engines well out on the wings, the aircraft yawed badly toward any disabled engine, requiring counter-rudder to balance it. However, the Meteor lacked a powered rudder, so strong legs were needed to push down on one pedal to sufficiently displace the rudder.

RAAF pilots outside the Sergeants' Mess at Iwakuni, Japan, March 1952. Jim Kichenside is third from left; Max Outhwaite second from left [Kichenside family collection].

The pressure for replacement pilots in Korea meant many of the RAAF pilots arriving at Iwakuni in 1952 had less than ten hours of conversion training on the Meteor [Peter Williams, image ID: 18 ICR].

Such was the desperaton for pilots in Korea that most sergeant pilots now received less than 10 hours conversion training. Col King and Ken Smith had just 6.5 hours; Jim Kichenside and Max Outhwaite had 8. There was no time for honky-tonk bars or sunbathing. They had to learn to fly a twin-engine jet aircraft from scratch – including handling, navigation, gunnery, communication, formation flying, and escape procedures – and be ready to fly it for interdiction and ground-attack in what amounted to less than one working day. The boy had five flights in the trainer and seven solo trips. The only operational training was three thirty-minute sorties firing rockets at a nearby island.

Before their departure, the young pilots were issued with survival gear, including the 'Mae West' yellow vest, a handful of US dollars, and a .38 revolver[6]. The boy looked at it, askance – sometimes at night, as he lay in his bunk in this strange place, he swore he could feel the vibration of the big Chinese guns across the sea; this little pistol felt like a peashooter in comparison. The boy knew there were Yankee pilots who would swap the snub-nosed little gun for a big-ass Colt 45, provided a pair of fur-lined flying boots or an Aussie slouch hat were thrown into the bargain. But funny as that seemed, the thought of Ron Guthrie and Butch Hannan, of his mates Vance Drummond and Bruce Thomson, made him tuck the peashooter a little firmer into the holster and make sure it was always well oiled and armed.

And then, after just eight hours of air-time, it was time to go. There would be no more training – no more preparation. The war was here.

Jim Kichenside with a Gloster Meteor F.8 in 1952. Jim received just 8 hours of conversion training on the aircraft at Iwakuni before he was deployed to the front line in Korea in March 1952 [Kichenside family collection].

***

Pilots' quarters
Iwakuni Air Base, Japan
March 18, 1952

When they received their orders, it took only moments to pack. Max went to the mess for a final beer, but the boy lingered over his few possessions, smoothing non-existent creases from blue serge and crisp shirts.

There was a soft shuffle from the doorway behind him, and he turned.

She was small and slender, with a perfectly oval face framed in two curtains of perfectly black, perfectly shiny hair.

The living quarters at Iwakuni had been comfortable, with neat rooms, spotlessly laundered linens, steam heating and 'room-girls': pretty local girls who polished and washed, ironed and mended and tidied. The boy found them difficult to get used to – both their subservience and how happy and gentle they were in their lowly role. Disciplined, obedient and doll-like, they were nothing like the girls at home.

He scrambled for his scanty Japanese. 'Minnie-san,' he said, '*konnichi wa*'

Minnie bowed and indicated the kitbag and the neat piles of clothing on the bed: clothing she had personally washed and pressed. 'You go, Jim-boy-san? You go now Korea?'

He nodded. 'Tomorrow. I've packed all my things, thanks.' This was too complicated a sentence for her, but she followed his gaze to the empty closet and nodded. Then her eyes returned to his face.

'You come.'

He hesitated, unsure whether he had understood, but she stepped back from the doorway and beckoned. Still, he hesitated. These girls were of the highest moral character and the pilots had all been warned severely to treat them with respect or risk having them replaced with a room-boy: a far less interesting prospect. Likewise, the girls could lose their jobs for fraternising with the pilots. But Minnie, impatient now, returned to the room and took his elbow. 'Come.'

Australian personnel were under strict instructions to treat the 'room girls', who tended the men's quarters at Iwakuni, with respect or risk having them replaced with 'room boys' [Australian War Memorial, accession no. P02032.001].

A cold winter sunset roared in great scarlet contrails over the snow-streaked hills. They walked in silence out of the base and into the town, he frustrated at his lack of language, she seemingly satisfied at moving like a small shadow at his side. He could hear the ocean, black and guttural, in the dark. The thin silhouettes of trees stretched in frozen supplication toward the cold, distant stars. They crossed a bridge and she stopped outside a small building with an upwardly curving roof. '*Shirasaki Hachimangu,*' she said, and at his blank look, pointed down at his shoes. He saw rows of shoes in pigeon-holes by the temple doors, so obediently bent down and removed his own before she led him inside.

The temple was lit only by rows of candles. She tugged at the neck of her dress, and pulled over her head a thin necklace made of cotton twine. She handed it to a small man who stood behind the main altar. He made a complicated sign over it, then bowed. The twine had clearly been blessed. Now Minnie handed it to the boy, and he put it in his pocket with his own awkward bow.

Leaving this strange haven the next day, with just a short flight across the sea between himself and the war, he slipped the cotton twine over his head and tucked it beneath his shirt.

CHAPTER 11

THE FRONT LINE

Real courage is when you know you re licked before you begin, but you begin anyway and see it through no matter what.

—Harper Lee, *To Kill A Mockingbird*

Kimpo Air Base K-14
South Korea
March 19, 1952

The noise was so terrific it swept over him in a great wave. As he and Max stepped gratefully out of the muddy, rattling truck onto the tarmac, their ears were assailed with the scream of jets on runways, taking off in pairs one after another, wingtips separated by as little as 20 feet. There was, too, the familiar roar of the great Merlin engines of P-51 Mustangs, the growl of massive B-29 Superfortress bombers, with their escorts like a herd of worker bees around a queen. One F-80 Shooting Star jet was trailing a badly damaged stabiliser as it taxied drunkenly toward the American lines. There were trucks and jeeps hustling like ants, men in flying suits and greasy overalls and blue serge overcoats, Asian faces and white faces and African-American faces, all with something to do and somewhere to be. The boy's heart was hammering: he had come a long way to be in this place, so far the seasons themselves were reversed. This was the front line.

In 1952, Kimpo Air Base K-14 had one of the highest aircraft traffic rates in the world, sometimes with a touchdown every 15 seconds and aircraft at times landing from both ends of the runway (with strict instructions to keep right). Kimpo was just 50 kilometres from the 38th parallel and within striking distance of the Yalu, where the hot action was. The noise and pace were unrelenting – there were nonstop patrols and searchlights and sirens and the tramp of hundreds of boots in the vast tent city adjoining the runways.

A C-47 transport had flown the boy and Max out of Iwakuni and within an hour they were in Seoul. It was a bone-shaking 25 kilometre truck ride to the impoverished town of Kimpo through the bombed-out streets of the capital. Seoul was a city in ruins: the snow was grey with ash and debris, devastated buildings and bare trees stood like skeletons on empty frozen streets, and ragged people begged in the icy wind. It had been a place of murder when Kim Il-Sung's troops first won the city in 1950 and slaughtered Syngman Rhee's followers as they tried to flee. When Kim's troops withdrew, Rhee returned and his men slaughtered those who had welcomed the communists. And so it went on, back and forth, destruction and retribution.

Within an hour of his arrival at No.77 Squadron's base at Kimpo in Korea on March 19, 1952, Jim Kichenside was in the air flying on patrol [Kichenside family collection].

Like the hasty Meteor conversion program at Iwakuni, there was no time for niceties in Korea. The boy had been at Kimpo only an hour – barely time to report to Wing headquarters and show a copy of his orders – when both he and Max were thrust into the line-up for patrols[1]. The boy flew as wingman – a kind of bodyguard and lookout-to World War II veteran Phil Hamilton-Foster and had his first glimpse of

Korea from the seat of a fighter. Smooth fields of snow, rivers like veins, the rumpled stone of hostile mountains – he saw the desolate winter landscape with a flyers eye: deadly narrow valleys, the absence of flat places for emergency landings. Suddenly the peashooter' in the holster at his shoulder was more of a reassuring weight.

The harsh topography of Korea, as viewed from the air. Pilots quickly recognised that emergency landing places were few, and the narrow valleys and steep terrain made ground-attack missions a deadly challenge [Arthur Gulliver, State Library of Victoria, image ID: H2002.199/4015].

***

When he returned and signed his aircraft back in, the boy was assigned to a tent in one of the vast anonymous rows beside the tarmac.

He realised he was walking alone, lugging his kitbag, as the other pilots filtered away to their own cubbies. Even through his fur-lined flying boots, his feet were freezing in the foul-smelling muddy slush of melting snow.

But here were familiar faces at last. Ken Smith, the top of his ginger head almost brushing the tent roof: Smithy, who he had not seen since his own wedding back in January. How faraway and fantastical that day now seemed, as though it had happened to someone else. The dark earnest face of Col King, the naked electric bulb casting shadows beneath his high cheekbones. And Lionel Cowper, thin and clever, the oldest of the group at 24. The Reprobates were back together, with Max in another tent just down the row.

The tent, only 4 metres by 4, was as dark as a den but surprisingly warm in the glow of a large oil heater. 'That's your spot, mate.' Smithy indicated a stretcher near the door, spread with grey blankets. The wooden floor creaked under his boots as the boy laid his kitbag beside the cot and hung up his flying jacket on a peg hammered into the plywood wall. He knew without asking that this had been Ian Cranston's bunk. The boy realised the dark charcoal scratches on the wall above the cot represented missions, all lined up like soldiers – and what an abrupt halt they came to.

'Feel like a beer?' That was Cowper, watching him from his own corner where he was stretched on his cot, writing a letter.

'Feel like two,' said the boy.

***

In March 1952, Seoul changed hands for the fourth time as General Ridgeway again drove the North Korea and Chinese forces out after a ten-week offensive. The value of the southern capital by this stage was symbolic – there was no light or power, and food and water were scarce. UN air forces also launched a new interdiction operation, Operation Saturate, focussed on inflicting heavy damage to infrastructure in the North. March was a hectic month for 77 Squadron, with 1007 sorties in their new ground-attack role[2]. For the boy, March 26, 1952, brought his first real test.

In his first seven days at the front, he had chiefly flown patrol and familiarisation missions, absorbing the formations and tactics of the squadron, always flying in a pair. On March 25, intelligence came in that there were huts outside the northern port of Chinnampo concealing a concentration of enemy troops. The area, as a key transport hub on the west coast of North

Korea, was very heavily defended. Moreover, Chinese troops were known for their cunning, moving at night, disguising trucks as haystacks and equipping their troops with white winter uniforms. Terrified civilians fled before them, leaving empty houses as ideal hiding places for anti-aircraft guns or ground troops with rifles that could strike a jet at up to 3000 feet[3]. Today, Double-Seven would surprise them at sunrise.

Dawn on March 26 was piercingly cold. They rumbled down to the tarmac in the dark back of a truck, gear hanging loose. Nobody talked. The strip was a slippery silver arrow beneath the searchlights, surmounted by glistening white barricades of snow. He felt ice prickling on the exposed skin of his face. Two by two, they took off in the dark, Frost on the outside of the canopy, condensation trickling on the inside.

Chinnampo stood on a marshy delta where the Taedong River emptied into the Yellow Sea. First light Fell on dirty brown hills and the meandering grey river. 'We have target, heading 2-5-0.' Tinny voices through the radio. The mission began to break apart, wheeling left and right. He gripped the stick and followed left.

He circled as four went for the huts – hard and flat and deadly as eagles. Even from up here, he saw rockets bursting up a great hail of debris and dust, then one struck a building: the whole structure heaved then partly collapsed.

'They're out, they're out – go, go, go.'

White-clad figures were fleeing across the snow-covered landscape, dozens of them; it seemed like hundreds, going for guns and going for cover.

'Follow me in, kid.'

And the scuttling white ants became larger and suddenly they were people – human beings scrambling for the scrub and a chance at survival, their own weapons now flung harmlessly across their backs as they fled.

He had loaded the cannons himself the day before, pulled the barrels through and oiled the guns – the 20 millimetre shells were as long as his hands. In training, he had seen them obliterate solid timber targets, leaving nothing but a mist of matchwood in the air, punching holes in armour-plated trucks like giant fists.

Number One's wake was streaking for the ground and the boy jammed the stick forward, swooping after him. Bodies were falling as cannon fire cut a swathe through the fleeing troops. The snow was turning red. *He couldn't shoot running men in the back.* But these were enemy – when they got into cover, they'd turn like cornered tigers. Flak was already flying, the silver streaks of tracer fire bursting up like a hail of stars. He rolled and dipped instinctively: then there was a thud and the jet shook itself fiercely, like a smacked cat. Another thud and a crack as a bullet hit the canopy. Suddenly the fight seemed a whole lot fairer.

If I'm going to get out of here, the best thing I can do is shoot.

The heavy *yak-yak-yak* of cannon.

Lethal effect.

That sight will never leave you—ever.

***

The water-stained walls of the tent were lit only by the blue glow of a single hurricane lantern. They sat in the semi-dark, swaddled in blankets but still so cold the chill seeped into their very bones. The vast tent city, with its searchlights and icy moon, was a stage around them, all silver and black and shadow. The silver Meteors were quiet on the tarmac, like well-mannered horses at rest in their nightly stable.

Australian personnel at Kimpo K-14 airfield were accommodated in rows of makeshift tents alongside the runways. The tents were dark and stuffy in summer and stood in a slushy quagmire of snow and mud during the Korean winter [Kichenside family collection].

Cowper had a bottle of Scotch: it was the best, and only, form of therapy, he reckoned. He handed the bottle around before taking a long pull at it himself. With his pointed chin and large eyes, he looked like a schoolboy in the shadows.

'The first question you have to ask yourself is – am I prepared to kill?' he said.

'It's a hard one,' Smithy said quietly, extending a hand for the bottle.

'You're not talking about small bullets.' King nursed the bottle in his turn for a moment, then shook his head and took a gulp.

'But when you see the devastation, towns being flattened, people living under sheets of iron in bomb craters ... You've got to do something.' Smithy's voice was quiet but firm.

'So, you're coming in and you see tracer fire coming at you, and every now and again something hits you – you've just got to say to yourself, well, if it's got my name on it, bad luck,' said Cowper.

And the boy heard his own voice. 'It's not a thing you'd want to do – it's a thing you have to do. It's your job.'

But when he closed his eyes that night, the image of red-stained snow and the unmoving dead seemed burned into his retinas. The entire sweep had lasted less than three minutes. But he wondered how many years would pass before it would grey out in his mind.

***

Haeju, North Korea
March 30, 1952

Lionel Cowper's Meteor was shot down the next day, north-west of Haeju, in North Korea.

Cowper was Number Four in a six-plane sortie against enemy warehouses. Col King was in the same flight. He saw a fireball tumbling across the countryside and heard mission leader Phil Hamilton-Foster calling in vain for a check-in from Blue Four[4].

There was, once more, an empty bunk in the Reprobates' tent.

CHAPTER 12

THE KOREAN KID

Behind the mountains are more mountains.
—Korean adage

While the Reprobates of 5 Course were inexperienced in combat, they were probably better trained than many of their counterparts, with their 18 months – or in the boy's case, two years – at flight school. But throughout all the lectures and classes, all the gradings and theorising and carefully controlled drills, their mortality had never been in question. They had never had to weigh the life of another against their own or fill the crosshairs with a living target and squeeze fire. Or be left to mourn. They had been boys, even in Iwakuni with their new wings pinned proudly on their chests and their elevated status as Meteor pilots.

Now, the boy and his tent-mates were confronted daily by the empty corner where the kitbag labelled 'Cowper' had stood. Now, there were no more snowball fights. They were out every day alongside the ground crews, buffeted by freezing winds and driving blizzards, sweeping and scraping their wings free of snow and ice.

While water pipes froze, beer froze, nose and ears and eyes froze, their eyes remained fixed on their targets: barracks and buildings, ammo dumps, gun posts, factories, trucks and trains, blasting and strafing through smoke and flying debris and flak. But inevitably there were people in the crosshairs, and animals too. There were enemy soldiers in convoys and on patrols, hidden among civilians and shanties where women and children and chickens and donkeys and cats lived. And despite their fierce desire to fly and fight, few of these young gladiators wanted to shoot at living things. Col King, after his first shots in anger, found there was no more anger – *anguish,* he said, would be a better word[1].

The survival rate of ground-attack pilots in Korea was significantly worse than that of aerial combat or bomber pilots. Strafing dives at 300 metres per second left little margin for error. Rocket attacks required a very low angle of approach, often amid a hail of anti-aircraft fire, and the pilots had to hold on and deliver the rocket then pull out at the right instant or risk overshooting into a mountain or being brought down by telegraph wires or flying flak. The capabilities – physical and emotional – of the young Reprobates and their counterparts were put severely to the test again on April 13, 1952, just two weeks after Lionel Cowper's death.

April 13 was Easter Sunday, and the squadron attended a service on the tarmac at dawn. The weather had been bad, but it cleared that day, and following religious observances, operations resumed with 69 sorties for the day, including an attack on stores installations in the Haeju area. On that mission was Sergeant Maxwell 'Bluey' Colebrook, a 25-year-old West Australian on his second tour of Korea after accumulating 101 missions in his first[2]. There were known heavy-gun positions around Haeju, and Colebrook's plane was hit by ground fire. His Number One, Peter Middleton, heard Bluey call, I'm hit', then saw the ventral tank aflame. Colebrook radioed he was heading for home, but when Middleton returned to Kimpo, there was no sign of either the tall, red-headed Colebrook or his aircraft[3].

The squadron scrambled, clambering furiously into gun belts and flying boots. Ground crews strapped pilots in. Fuel, pneumatics, rudder, elevator, canopy – check, check, check. Starter buttons for Number One and Two engines. Spearing back into hostile airspace. Circling and calling.

While it was common for pilots to fly two missions a day, on that terrible day, the boy and many of his colleagues each flew four. They returned repeatedly to the area Colebrook had been hit, being pinged and dented by tracer fire themselves as they orbited, rotating again and again through refuelling and re-arming until last light, fighting the physical demands of G-forces to search for their lost mate. But no sign of Bluey Colebrook was ever found; he remains missing, presumed killed in action.

Twenty-five-year-old Western Australian Maxwell Colebrook spent 339 days in service with No.77 Squadron in Korea. He was on his second tour in April 1952 when he disappeared after his aircraft was hit by ground fire; his body has never been recovered [Australian War Memorial, accession no. JK0077].

Ron Susans, who had to give the order to cease the search, was very conscious of the impact. With no counselling or other support available, all he could do was encourage his boys to build a cricket pitch near the runway and try to think of something else.

The respite was brief.

***

Kimpo Air Base K-14
South Korea
April 22, 1952

The boy was now a veteran of 46 missions, but he had been unable to suppress a chill when the teletype clattered through the orders from headquarters a week after Blue Colebrook went missing. *Another rocket attack on Chinnampo.* Deputy squadron CO Bill Bennett led the morning briefing, using the big relief model of North Korea. The boy found it hard to pay attention, for the word still rattled around in his head like flak: *Chinnampo. Red stains in the snow.*

'She's right to go, Jim.' Leading Aircraftman Kev Felton, in his dark blue overalls, pushed an oily rag into his back pocket and stepped back from the aircraft.

'Good, mate. Thanks.' The boy climbed up into the cockpit; Felton leaned over to help him strap in, pulling another rag, this time a clean one, from his top pocket and polishing the canopy.

Jim Kichenside being strapped in to Meteor A77-139. In his first six weeks at the front, he flew almost 50 missions [Kichenside family collection].

The boy reached for the radio. 'Red One from Red Four.' A spurt of static. Engines were whining to life around him. 'Shit. Red One from Red Four.' More static. He turned urgently to Felton. 'The radio's on the blink; have we got a spare fuelled up?' He knew big Bill Purssey was already strapped in as a reserve at the back of the line; despite the ugly memory Chinnampo stirred in him, there was no way he was being left behind.

Felton was already tugging at the buckles of the harness. 'Yeah, mate – take 163.'

Kichenside vaulted out of the cockpit and dashed down the tarmac, counting off the tail numbers, Felton on his heels as he went up the side of A77-163 like a spider.

'Red One from Red Four.' This time, Bennett's voice echoed clearly back to him, and the boy gave Felton a thumbs-up.

'Get it rolling, kid.'

It was not permissible to start both engines simultaneously; the boy reached for the starboard start button, but when he pressed and released it, nothing happened[4]. 'Christ, no – don't do this...' All around him, jets were starting to taxi. A fierce stab at the button, holding it down until his knuckles turned white. Absolutely nothing. He turned an anguished face up to Felton. But he was already being waved out of the line-up; he could do nothing but watch as Purssey taxied past him in 189. The boy was still sitting there, stationary, as the last boiling wash of take-off turbulence spread a silver ripple of heat over the strip.

Felton already had the side panel off. 'Bastard of a thing,' the boy heard him muttering. 'I bet it's not the first time it's done this...'

With a sigh, the boy shrugged out of his harness and shimmied down the side of the jet. He couldn't bear the thought of returning to stew in his dark tent. He sat on a stack of tyres and listened to Felton tapping and murmuring inside the fuselage. Despite his present discomfiture, he liked Felton a lot. The young mechanic had only been in Kimpo a few days, but he had already won plenty of friends for his clean work and willingness. The lack of hangars at Kimpo meant the ground crews spent their time outdoors, where frostbite was endemic. Felton's pain tolerance would become legend in 77 Squadron: his bare hands would be split and bleeding and he'd be still working.

The boy now sat watching him moodily, the spring sun prickling on the back of his neck. He liked Bill Purssey too, and it would be stupid to resent him just because he'd drawn a functioning aircraft. He'd met Purssey in those far-distant days back at Fairbairn, looping around moonlit Canberra in the old Mustangs. With his rumpled hair and firm chin, Purssey was a career military man, one of three brothers in the services and his father a veteran of both world wars. Today, Purssey was on his 131st and final mission – he'd be back on the Brisbane beaches by next week.

Flight Lieutenant Ian Goodwin "Bill" Purssey, pictured while flying with No.3 Mustang Squadron RAAF in northern Italy, 1945. The World War II veteran also served 142 days with No.77 Squadron in Korea [Australian War Memorial, accession no. MEA2240].

The distant whine of jets lifted heads along the line. They usually came back in fours, flying tight formation. If they came back without tanks or with gun ports blackened, there had been a fight – or a casualty. Felton was at his shoulder. They both silently counted them in. Then Felton said very quietly, 'Where's 189?'

It was like being kicked in the chest by a horse.

Susans' official account indicated A77-189 was hit by intense automatic fire over Chinnampo and the aircraft caught fire. Purssey was told by Bennett to jettison his ventral tank and head west over the sea, where rescue choppers could reach him away from enemy ground fire. But before he could drop the tank, the wing of the aircraft burnt through and, at 600 feet, Purssey had no time to open a parachute. The flaming aircraft crashed into the water south of Chinnampo; Purssey was listed as missing, presumed killed[5]. The news reached his mother on the eve of Anzac Day, 1952. She was presented with his posthumous DFC by Her Majesty Queen Elizabeth at a special investiture at Parliament House in Brisbane in 1954, during the Royal Tour[6].

No.77 Squadron had now lost 28 pilots.

It seemed the difference between living and dying in the skies above Korea was often down to sheer luck – a radio out, an engine on the blink, a substitution in the line-up. Any or all could mean the difference between coming home and not.

***

In his first six weeks at the front, Jim Kichenside had flown almost 50 missions and lived through the deaths of three colleagues. Susans couldn't help noticing the young man. Even among the hard-nosed World War II vets and the cocksure graduate pilots of 77 Squadron, the boy had a certain confidence and polish. But he was also a kid: the youngest of all Susans's 'lads', much as he hated to be reminded of it. As rain dragged into a fifth day after Purssey's death, Susans became increasingly concerned about the lack of flying and distraction, and summoned the boy to the large tent which comprised his office.

The next day, the boy was in the sky – now cloudless and blue again – but he flew alone, heading south away from the front. He was at the controls of battle-damaged A77-446, *en route* for Iwakuni, where major aircraft servicing and damage repairs were carried out. There was a roster system among the pilots for taking damaged planes to Japan and ferrying replacements back – a welcome, if brief, respite from the front. The boy wondered if his turn today was a tactic by Susans to take his mind off Purssey, despite the fact his face ached from trying to not show a thing.

The replacement for 446 was another repaired Meteor: A77-316[7]. The regular test pilot at Iwakuni was on sick leave, so on April 29, the boy gave 316 four test flights, then another the next day before he signed it off as airworthy and turned its nose to Kimpo. When he returned, he was off on a rocket strike before he could even eat lunch. He had to leave 316 by the revetments for refuelling and jump straight into another plane. When he returned, 316 was nowhere to be seen.

The next day, he was summoned before Susans again, this time to the maintenance hut by the tarmac. He wondered for one awful moment what he had done wrong – if there was some problem with 316 he had overlooked. He'd had five flights in her and already had a proprietorial feeling toward her. *Or, worse,* his thoughts galloped on, *what if Susans thought the trip to Iwakuni had not been enough and he was somehow cracking up and everyone knew it?*

'Bullshit.' He said the word out loud. By the time he reached the tarmac, his head was up and his shoulders were defiantly back. He ignored the clench in his gut when he saw Susans standing by 316, surrounded by ground staff and several other pilots, including Smithy. The boy forced himself to keep walking straight, his face set.

But as he reached them, Susans smiled, and the others stepped back to allow him to shake the boy by the hand. 'Congratulations, kid,' he said.

Two unidentified ground crew from No.77 Squadron pose with the newly-anointed Gloster Meteor A77-316, 'The Korean Kid'. The aircraft was assigned to Jim Kichenside after he survived his first six weeks at the front [Australian War Memorial, accession no. P03741.002].

The boy eyed him. 'I – don't understand, sir.'

Susans nodded at the plane, its silver coat glinting in the sunlight, and something of his usual officious manner returned. It is standard practice, Sergeant, that after a period of consolidation, a pilot may fly the same aircraft whenever available or practical. With 50 missions to your name, we don't believe you are about to leave us any time soon. So, this is your ship.'

Mine.

He was aware of applause, his hand being shaken. Then they all moved back again because Susans was still speaking. 'As the youngest pilot in the squadron, it seems some felt it appropriate you be given the largest and most, ahem, *detailed* accoutrement to delineate your aircraft.'

Last night, the RAAF ground crew had got together with their American counterparts – experts in this field – and painted a skinny gunslinger on the nose of 316, with dual holsters and a mighty sombrero, a cowboy with a cigarette on his lip blowing a smoke-ring at the enemy. And above it was emblazoned the legend *The Korean Kid*. Colourful names were common among UN aircraft. Other Meteors had been christened *Littlest Angel, Top O' the Mornin, Die-R-Ear* (it'll pass anything), *Constipated* (can't be passed) and *Querida Mia.* Susans had named his own *Mart & Geoff* after his two sons[8]. But the CO was not keen on the big accompanying artworks so favoured by the Americans, and less so the large and lavish decoration they gave to 316: moves were apparently made to make the extravagant artwork the last of its type in 77 Squadron[9].

Now, the boy stepped forward. There were no hard edges on Meteor 316 – she was rounded and curved and sensuous and sleek. He ran a bare palm over the snub nose. He'd made a habit of changing the subject whenever the excruciating fact he was the youngest in the squadron was raised – now, he revelled in it. And a great swell of realisation rose up in him: in just six weeks, he had gone from novice to fully operational, even leading sections into action. Now he was also the proud custodian of 'his own' fighter aircraft. He was the Korean Kid.

Jim Kichenside with Meteor A77-316, 'The Korean Kid'. The logo, conceived by ground crews from the US Air Force, paid homage to Kichenside's status as the youngest pilot in No.77 Squadron [Kichenside family collection].

CHAPTER 13

CANNON FODDER

It doesn't make a damned bit of difference who wins the war to someone who I/8 dead.
—Joseph Heller, *Catch-22*

In May 1952, General Mark Clark took the reins as UN commander-in-chief from Matthew Ridgway and imposed a new air strategy, Air Pressure, which aimed to achieve the greatest damage for the lowest cost and highest political impact. The focus shifted to high-value targets such as North Korean hydroelectric power stations, untouched so far as they were considered necessary to restoration of a functional society in the north should peace be achieved.

No.77 Squadron's Meteors were now flying once more alongside American Sabres as far north as the Chongchon river, protecting fighter-bombers from the ever-present MiGs on top of their ground-attack role. The need for replacement pilots was so great the ten-hour Meteor conversion at Iwakuni was now *de rigueur.* But it took another death for the uneasy rumbling over the hasty transition of new pilots to the front to penetrate the public consciousness in Australia.

Pilot Officer Donald Robertson of Ivanhoe, Victoria, was one of the most outstanding post-World War II graduates from Point Cook. He was dux of No.1 Course and, while he was serious-minded and a little self-conscious, he was much admired by his colleagues; Col King proclaimed, 'No finer young officer ever served.'[1] Robertson flew his first mission in Korea on April 6, 1952, aged 22. Just 40 days later, on May 15, Robertson was killed near Masam-Ni. He had driven four rockets home in a dive before his aircraft was struck by enemy ground fire and crashed. His Meteor had been hit on a similar mission just one week before – now, it seemed, Robertson's luck had run out[2].

Pilot Officer Donald Robertson studies a map of Korea prior to flying a patrol mission in 1952. Robertson was killed when his aircraft was shot down on May 15; his grieving father sparked a campaign in Australia for public recognition of the conditions under which Australian pilots were serving in Korea [Australian War Memorial, accession no. JK0272].

Don Robertson was the 29th pilot from 77 Squadron to be captured or killed in Korea. But this death was different. At home, the war had had little impact on most Australians, with no direct threat to domestic security and a pervading desire to forget after the horrors of World War II. Just 60 people had farewelled the latest Australian reinforcements heading to Korea from Sydney compared to a crowd of over 10,000 in New Zealand[3]. But Don Robertson's father was not going to allow the death of his son to go unremarked.

Leonard Robertson's fierce devotion to peace stemmed from his own experience as a World War I veteran. As a young stockman from South Australia, he had served with the 5th Anzac Light Horse in Palestine and Gaza for three years which left him with, in his own words, shattered nerves'[4]. To compound his suffering, he was widowed suddenly in 1941 with three children to raise, including his clever, scholarly son Donald[5]. When Don was shot down in 1952, Len Robertson made the first of many public calls to 'stop the criminal stupidity in Korea. Through local and national media, he begged for Australia 'to rouse itself from its selfishness and apathy.'[6] He even appealed to the Australian Peace Council, founded in 1949 to encourage harmonious coexistence, for support.

Sadly, Peace Councils were often pro-Soviet and linked with the spread of communism, and as the Cold War heightened, Len Robertson's neighbours began to avoid him in the street for his perceived links with the feared ideology[7]. This was despite the fact the APC had appealed to Australians to write 10,000 letters to the UN Security Council calling for peace in Korea[8]. Len Robertson was entirely innocent of the political leanings of the group; he was focussed only on raising public awareness of the horrors of the war in Korea and the difficulties Australia's young pilots were experiencing[9].

Don Robertson's death coincided with the deepening of a complex political tug of war over the RAAF which had begun before the Korean War itself. The period following World War II was one of flux in Australia's diplomatic and military relationships. Following the end of hostilities in World War II in 1945, Australia committed 11,500 personnel to BCOF in Japan, including three fighter squadrons. This was reduced to a single squadron – No.77 Squadron – at the end of 1949 in favour of supporting British military commitments in Malaya against an unfolding Communist insurgency there. It was a politically complex arrangement, with Australia providing transports, bombers, and maintenance personnel into Malaya but reluctant to commit further lest Australia's involvement be construed by other Southeast Asian nations as favouring a hostile solution.

On June 15, 1950, Chief of the Imperial General Staff, Field Marshal Sir William Slim, had visited Melbourne for talks on provision of further Australian forces to the Empire: this time, to the Middle East, where there were fears any Soviet invasion would impact upon world oil supplies[10]. The North Atlantic Treaty Organization (NATO), founded in 1949 as a western alliance aimed at countering Soviet aggression in Europe, was calling for a massive build-up of forces in the region to deter Soviet ambitions. Britain particularly pressed its Commonwealth partners to provide offensive air power, presenting a new dilemma for Australian defence planners and their already overstretched air resources.

Just two weeks later, while heads were still being scratched, war erupted in Korea. The rapidity of the Australian response there meant its embryonic post-World War II air forces were strained almost to breaking point. But despite the desperate situation in Korea, with pilot losses and a shortage of replacements forcing personnel to undertake longer and more arduous tours with less and less preparation, the Menzies government remained focussed on the Communist threat to Australia through Indochina. A security review in September 1950 by the Joint Planning Committee concluded that no additional commitment in Korea should be undertaken if an effective contribution to Malaya is to be made.'[11]

In war-weakened Britain, Prime Minister Winston Churchill remained equally fixated on the threat of communist invasion in the Middle East. Finding Australia reluctant to commit to any action there, in August 1951, Churchill offered a new incentive. Australia could purchase brand new de Havilland FB.9 Vampire jet aircraft from Britain – enough for two fighter squadrons – on the proviso it agreed to station them in the Middle East the following year[12]. When the Australian Joint Intelligence Committee reported the Chinese threat in South-East Asia was, for now, reduced, and British Defence Minister Emanuel Shinwell added reassurances that Britain would maintain Malaya as a defence priority—a kind of buffer to Australia from a potential communist invasion from the north – the Menzies government acquiesced in March 1952[13].

In response to a potential Soviet invasion of the Middle East after World War II, British prime minister Winston Churchill (right) called on Australia to contribute to greater deterrent air power in the region. While Australian air forces were already stretched by commitments in Malaya and Korea, Australian prime minister Robert Menzies (left) agreed to dispatch No.75 and 76 Squadrons to Malta in July 1952 [Australian War Memorial, accession no.006414].

The government agreed to dispatch No 78 Fighter Wing (comprising No 75 and 76 Squadrons from RAAF William town) to Malta in July 1952[14]. Menzies' nostalgia for a dissolving imperial order was still influential on the Australian government's foreign policy decisions, but the decision was flagged as one '[giving] to many officers and men training and experience in an area which presents distinctive problems to air forces.'[15] The decision, however, left little operational air power in Australia and the overstretched forces in Korea with less prospect of relief than ever[16].

The decision set the stage for a complicated juggling of relations between Australia and both its traditional ally Britain and the increasingly important new one in the US. The US, following the signing of the ANZUS treaty in September 1951, was now pressing Australia for a greater commitment in Korea[17]. But in April 1952, Britain raised doubt on the future of air operations in Korea, arguing there was an urgent need to reinforce the Middle East, despite the potential disapproval of the US over the withdrawal of Commonwealth forces[18].

***

Early in 1952, Dick Cresswell, former CO of No.77 Squadron, now in charge of Fighter

Operations at RAAF Headquarters in Australia, had taken the matter of resourcing pilots in Korea to Chief of the Air Staff Air Chief Marshal Sir Donald Hardman, who agreed to give Korea greater emphasis. The Fighter Operational Conversion Unit (OCU) at Williamtown was established to speed up the supply of new pilots. But around the same time, the Australian government announced the commitment of No.78 Wing to Malta, and little else was done to help No.77 Squadron in the near term.

In April 1952, Air-Marshal Hardman visited Korea and returned to Australia proclaiming things are going extremely well.'[19] And on June 18, three weeks after Don Robertson's death, Minister for Air William McMahon addressed the Australian parliament and denied the claim fighter pilots in 77 Squadron were overworked, adding there was a substantial reserve of trained jet pilots at Williamtown'[20].

However, *Courier-Mail* correspondent Charles Madden countered that the shift from aerial combat to ground attack meant Australian pilots were making more sorties than ever, with some flying over 200 missions in a tour compared to the 100 which American pilots were capped at, and that the cumulative stresses were affecting even the strongest and fittest[21]. Upon his return from Korea in June, Wing Commander

Ron Susans confirmed 77 Squadron pilots were flying more missions than any other UN fighter squadron in Korea[22]. This prompted the Air Force Association to call for an investigation[23].

On June 18, 1952, the same day as McMahon's pronouncement in parliament, Air Force officials confirmed that some RAAF pilots had flown twice as many missions as Americans in the same fighter wing[24]. Just nine days later, RAAF pilots' operational tours of Korea were cut from nine months to six[25]. To assuage the pilot shortage, the RAF agreed to loan pilots to 77 Squadron, with six arriving in July 1952 alongside 77 Squadron's new Australian CO, Wing Commander Jack 'Congo' Kinninmont[26].

But the demands of the war and fiscal restraints of 1952-53 meant RAAF training was also being cut back just when it needed to be bolstered[27]. The 18-month flying course was cut to 12 months and broken up across three locations – initial training at Archerfield, Queensland, basic training at Uranquinty in New South Wales, and applied training at Point Cook in Victoria[28]. Furthermore, Menzies' follow-up visit to London in July 1952 met with an altered view on the Middle East by Churchill's government, with strategic priority returning to South-East Asia. However, the two RAAF squadrons had already departed for the Middle

East, and would remain there until December 1954[29].

***

Len Robertson's solo campaign had opened a door for heightened public awareness of the plight of Australian airmen in Korea, even if it had not been the direct catalyst for change at bureaucratic or operational levels. But such was his grief over the loss of his son, and the toll of his long letter-writing effort after his own World War I service, that he died in 1960, aged just 68[30].

***

Under the original terms of his deployment, Jim Kichenside was supposed to remain in Korea for nine months or 100 missions, whichever came first. By the end of May 1952, he had flown 83 missions in just ten weeks. King and Smith had already reached their 100-mission milestones. The boy was told he must stay on until a replacement arrived (although he wouldn't have gone home anyway). The high casualty rate had made Australian pilot deployments in Korea virtually open-ended.

Political fallout from Don Robertson's death, the Department of Air inquiry, and parliamentary debate reached Kimpo in June 1952. The boy and Max Outhwaite were abruptly pulled aside and sent to Japan on extended leave: 12 days, double the usual mid-term allowance.

There were none of the lurid escapades with which many returned from leave in Japan bearing tales – of dance halls and strippers and mind-altering substances. A short flight by Douglas C-47 (the military version of the venerable Douglas DC-3 passenger aircraft) over the Inland Sea, then a train from Tokyo brought Max and the boy to the quiet resort hotel of Kawana, with Mt Fuji as the backdrop. At Kawana, there were no tents or mud or army rations: instead, there were hot baths and linen sheets and green lawns and white bread. Col King and Smithy were already there. It was early summer, and the quartet played 18 holes of golf a day, caddied by teenage Japanese girls; a round cost ten cents, almost as much as the price of a room, but they said to hell with the expense. They had forgotten how to enjoy themselves – how to count strokes instead of missions. They ate big dinners every night, ordering everything off the menu, and slept late every morning.

With hot springs, bars, and superb golf courses nearby, the hotel at Kawana, Japan, provided welcome relief for Australian pilots on leave from the front. Jim Kichenside (second from right) is pictured during extended leave at Kawana in June 1952 [Kichenside family collection].

But while they were away, the carnage on the peninsula continued. On June 9, just weeks after shooting down a MiG near Pyongyang, John Surman was killed on a strafing run at Hwanju: he was 77 Squadron's 30th loss[31]. The boy and Max returned to operations at Kimpo on June 21 on what was nominally called a second tour. King and Smithy, too, had signed up for a second go without hesitation, even knowing that these extended tours had proved a death sentence for so many of their comrades.

How bitter and dreary life in Korea now seemed after the brilliant sunlight and clear skies of Japan. They were surrounded again by grey tarmac and blowing dust and hot grit, with little to do outside flying hours but swat flies and play endless rounds of gin rummy.

CHAPTER 14

SOMETHING WORSE IN THE WINGS

We call that person who has lost his father, an orphan; and a widower that man who has lost his wife. But that man who has known the immense unhappiness of losing a friend: by what name do we call him?

—Joseph Roux

Officers Mess, Kimpo Air Base K-14
South Korea
June 22, 1952

American beer had an odd bitter taste he had never got used to. Nonetheless, he nursed a glass in the crowded, dark fug of the mess, with its shroud of cigarette smoke hanging at the ceiling and the deafening roar of voices to drown his thoughts. He was glad of the noise, the strange mixed bedlam of American and Australian accents. Being earthbound gave him too much time to think; he wanted to be flying, where there was no time to dwell.

He tugged morosely at Minnie's twine necklace. It was beginning to fray in places; the sweat and heat of the Korean monsoon weren't doing it any good. Perhaps he ought to take it off a while, carry it in a pocket instead.

'G'day there, bud.' A damp, heavy hand on his shoulder. He knew this voice, this flash of white teeth in a lean brown face. The accent marked him out as Californian. The boy looked him up and down, trim and clean in his blue dress uniform, captain's bars pinned and polished. 'Dressed to impress?'

Yankee Jack threw back his head and laughed, then nodded at the door. 'There's a Skymaster on the way from Tokyo, and it's got my name on it.' He signalled to the barman. 'Whiskey – make it a double. Yeah, tallied my hundred two days ago.'

Going home. 'What're you going to do then?'

Jack shrugged. 'Who knows? But one thing's for sure – I won't be flying.' His eyes darkened for a moment, then he dug in his pocket and laid a bright object on the bar where it glinted, even in the dimness and smoke. 'I carried this on every mission, right through the Pacific and now here: I'd say it got me through.' He slid it toward the boy. 'Take it.'

The boy picked it up and turned it over in his fingers. It was an old American silver dollar, surprisingly warm and heavy, stamped 1886. He looked up at Jack, who was sipping his whiskey and watching him over the rim of the glass. With the privileges of officer status conferred on Australian sergeant pilots, Australian and American airmen regularly fraternised at Kimpo and many friendships were formed on both tarmacs and barstools. The US pilots could not believe the youth of the Australians, and at 28, Jack seemed vastly old and experienced to the 21-year-old boy. Nonetheless, they had hit it off immediately and often had a beer and a talk in the evenings.

'Listen, kid,' Yankee Jack said. 'You've got to play it smart.' Jack drained his glass and picked up the kitbag at his feet. 'But you've also got to stay lucky.'

The boy watched him go, the silver dollar still heavy in his palm. He realised he didn't even know Jack's surname.

The next day, on a four-man armed reconnaissance mission to Singak, near Inchon, the boy and his colleagues attacked a truck convoy while it was refuelling. Stationary vehicles were treated with great caution: the Chinese were masters of the art of decoys, setting up tempting-looking targets to draw aircraft into an area where they became targets themselves for concealed artillery. The Australian theory was to pick off the first and last vehicles in a convoy so none of them could escape. Now, trucks were in flames and the overheated countryside around them was catching fire. Even as the small arms fire erupted, the Meteors went around a second time and, as he bore down to just 200 feet, strafing through the billowing oily smoke, the boy saw a driver jump out of one of the trucks. He was on fire – a running flailing human torch, his clothing burned off and his very flesh aflame. The boy knew that image would be seared upon his brain forever.

But it is your job: you have to concentrate on the precision of your delivery. It is a kind of self preservation—to believe in the cause. You have been trained what to do and you do it. You concentrate on getting that weapon delivered to its target—nothing more.

Then there was a flash and a dreadful sound of disintegrating metal, and his wounded jet heeled over like a capsizing yacht. But even in that shortest of conversions in Iwakuni, in those eight hours of frantic cramming, he had learned one valuable lesson in flying a twin-engine plane: never turn the plane toward the side with the dead engine. He pumped the rudder and found he could still steer, rolling the jet away from its wounded limb as he called in.

'Keep the speed up to it, kid. Radio in and Land Right.'

And as he limped the jet back, bathed in sweat in the searing cockpit and dry-mouthed with delayed reaction, he tried to banish the *what-ifs:* if the ventral tank had been hit, or the wing blown off. What would a spinning tumbling descent to earth look and feel like? Would it be quick, or would it hurt to burn? But it hadn't happened. He slipped a hand into the pocket of his flying suit and his fingers closed hard around the silver dollar. *Thanks, Jack,* he thought. And he felt suddenly invincible.

***

Summer in Korea was not like summer in Sydney. Summer in Korea was monsoon, heavy stormy days, interminable and inescapable heat, flying insects crawling into ears and eyes day and night. Runways melting, smog and dust blown all the way from the Gobi Desert. Inches of torrential rain in spearing downpours, deadly low cloud.

July continued the build-up to massive raids on the North Korean capital planned for August. On the warm humid evening of July 7, the boy and three others were dispatched on armed reconnaissance to Chorwon, west of Pyongyang. He had been in Korea just four months, and this was his 100th mission. It was a Monday – if he had an American passport, he'd be home by Friday in time for a round at the pub with Rowly. But he was not going home.

He was flying A77-368, *Rosemary*. Technically, it was Bob Strawbridge's bird, even named after his girlfriend, but the boy knew Blue Colebrook had also been attached to 368 after doing damage to a MiG with it in November 1951[1]. Colebrook's name was a dull weight in the boy's chest. How long ago it all seemed, the anxious hopeless circling and strafing and radioing, and the long silent night that followed.

It was after 9pm when the flight returned with two trucks and two huts to their credit. Still bothered by the ghost of the man who had loved the plane, the boy wanted to linger on the tarmac and ensure the ground crew fed and watered 368 as it deserved. But the other pilots-Ramsay, Lushey, and Green – took him by the elbows and hustled him towards the mess, and as the tarmac lights and ghosts faded behind them, he allowed himself to go. The 100-mission milestone meant a party, and what better cure for melancholy than smoke and shouting and beer and noise? He knew, despite being the guest of honour, he'd still be picking up the tab for four cases of beer – half for the Airmen's bar and the remainder to the Officer's Mess. Smithy was the first to thrust a glass into his hand and clap him on the back, and soon, he was able to forget.

***

But tomorrow was another day, with enemy convoys on the move and flights from 77 Squadron taking off at five-minute intervals in pursuit. On July 8, the boy was in a group of three with Eric Ramsay and Allan Avery. Behind him, Smithy was taxiing, leading a flight that included Col King, Max Outhwaite, and rookie Hugh Howard, just six weeks into his tour. The boy glanced back once as he took off, oddly wishing he was with them.

His own flight was last to return, just behind a quartet led by Alan Philp. The seven pilots walked together along the tarmac, heading for the Flight Hut to sign back in and report three trucks destroyed. He saw Col King and Max just outside, and Howie Howard; then he started counting heads.

King could not speak. Max was smoking so hard he was coughing up as much as he was sucking in. Young Howard just stood with his head against the revetment. The boy peered around once more, even poked his head into the Flight Hut to check again. The great noisy vibrating airfield seemed to fall silent.

It was well after midnight, in the tent where nobody slept, when Col King, who the CO had earlier guided away to the bar and pushed a beer into each hand, began to talk. His voice was hoarse in the darkness, as though something inside him had broken and could never be mended. Smithy had led them out, aiming to rocket any enemy transport crossing their path. Young Howie was his wingman; King and Max flew top cover at 5000 feet, eyes peeled for MiGs. They had not long left the hot haze of Kimpo when they spotted a convoy in the hills to the north-west. 'Trucks!' Smithy was as keen as a hound off the leash. And with Howie close behind, he dived at them like an eagle with talons outstretched.

Tracer fire came to meet him.

From high above, King saw a great orange sheet of flame tumbling a mile across the hills. And Howard's anguished cry threatened to break the radio apart: 'Smithy's gone in!'[2]

Those words hung in the black air For hours. King, who had been through the entire war, From Point Cook to this day, with the big red-haired man, who had planned to travel back home to Australia with his best mate when it was all over. And the boy – the boy who had walked down the aisle to marry his sweetheart with big Smithy at his shoulder. The boy with

Minnie's lucky twine about his neck and Captain Jack's silver dollar in his flight suit pocket. Perhaps if he'd shared one of these talismans with Smithy ... Perhaps, if there hadn't been a party last night, with those four cases of beer.... Perhaps ... *If only* ... *Perhaps*...

Kenneth Dudley Smith was 77 Squadron's 31st casualty in Korea. He was 24 years old[3].

CHAPTER 15

THE LAST FLIGHT OF 316

Orr was crazy and could be grounded. All he had to do was ask; and as soon as he did, he would no longer be crazy and would have to fly more missions. Orr would be crazy to fly more missions and sane if he didn't, but if he was sane he had to fly them. If he flew them he was crazy and didn't have to; but if he didn't want to he was sane and had to.

—Joseph Heller, *Catch-22*

Both the boy and young Howie were in the air again the day following Smithy's death.

There was no choice – the burden on 5th Air Force fighter-bombers and 77 Squadron to maintain pressure around Pyongyang was unrelenting. Just two days later, on July 11, 1952, virtually every UN aircraft took part in the massive raids on the North Korean capital, with Meteors patrolling the Chongchon River to prevent MiG incursions. Over 1,200 sorties were flown that day, but with 77 Squadron on patrol, not one UN aircraft fell victim to a MiG. Much of Pyongyang was levelled[1].

August 1952 marked one year of Meteor operations in Korea, with over 8000 missions flown. But the pilot crisis continued. The RAF loaned a further six pilots in an attempt to bolster numbers; the group included two fliers from South Africa. One of these was World War II veteran Martinus Oelof Bergh. Bergh was an enormous man, an outstanding all-round sportsman with an accompanying daredevil nature: he had reportedly once gotten into a car following a night in the mess and raced it while blindfolded, getting directions only from his passengers by Morse Code tapped out on the dash[2].

August 27, 1952 was a significant day for the young Reprobates – it was to be Col King's last in a Meteor. He had been awarded a Distinguished Flying Medal two weeks earlier and he was, at last, going home. He saddled up one last time as part of a 16-man mission to rocket an important communist barracks at Chaeryong. The boy was also in the flight, and was delighted to be assigned his own aircraft, A77-316, which thusfar he had flown on less than 20 per cent of his missions. But on arrival at the Flight Hut, splashing down through the puddles strewing the runway after yesterday's downpour, he found

Oelof Bergh already strapped into 316. But he shrugged off the mix-up, and, anxious not to be left behind, dived for the reserve aircraft, A77-258.

He followed King to the target area, where they dived at the barracks through a fierce curtain of automatic fire. The area erupted into a haze of dust and smoke as the rockets struck home and plane after plane bore down upon the target. And then the cry came across the radio, 'Oelof is hit!' A77-316 was plummeting out of the sky, flames streaming from the fuselage. Then the starboard wing exploded. King saw Bergh eject, tumbling and falling until his parachute opened and he floated away, an ever-decreasing white speck, toward a nearby village.

The boy had not seen the parachute. But he had seen 316, breaking apart and in flames, tumbling end over end as it fell out of the sky. Then it hit the side of a hill and exploded. It was gone – his Kid. It was gone. *And if not for some stupid mixup, it might have been him with it.*

While the RAAF halted operations to search for the downed man, the enemy did not – if anything, the flak and tracer fire escalated, pinging off low-flying jets as pilots strained their eyes for a glimpse of a parachute. King circled, certain he had seen a running figure, but after three passes could see no more and was forced to turn back to Kimpo, his fuel so low his jet had to be towed off the runway. The next morning, when he should have been going home, King led a flight of four, including the boy, to search for Bergh. But the mission had to be aborted due to low cloud; Oelof Bergh was now officially listed as missing[3].

Kev Felton, who used to polish A77-316 until it shone, said to the boy, 'Well, we've lost the plane – but at least nobody ever got killed in it.' And he was right, for Oelof Bergh had not been killed. But as the 33rd pilot lost to the squadron, Bergh spent a harrowing year as a prisoner of war. Nobody in 77 Squadron would know until the armistice in 1953, when its seven captured pilots were repatriated, the true horror of what they endured. Australia was a signatory to the 1948 Geneva Convention which regulated treatment of prisoners, but North Korea and China were not. In all, 24 Australian soldiers and seven airmen were captured between 1950 and 1953. All survived the months and years of mistreatment except Private Horace Madden 3RAR, who perished in 1951 and was posthumously awarded the George Cross for his courage in captivity[4].

Five of the seven pilots from No.77 Squadron who were taken prisoner during the Korean War, shown here at Panmunjom after their release in September 1953: (back row): Ron Guthrie, Oelof Bergh, John 'Butch' Hannan; (front row): Vance Drummond, Bruce Thomson. Also pictured (white uniform) is Executive Officer No.77 Squadron, Squadron Leader Neville McNamara [Australian War Memorial, accession no. JK0855].

Prisoners were routinely stripped in the freezing winters or forced into sweat boxes for weeks at a time in summer. Untreated wounds festered with maggots. They were kept awake for days under interrogation, and had bamboo shards hammered under their fingernails. Some, like the boy's old 4 Course mates Vance Drummond and Bruce Thomson, attempted to escape – Drummond on three occasions from the notorious camp at Pinchon-Ni – but all were recaptured and tortured afresh. Others resorted to desperate means to both pass the time and infuriate their captors – US Lieutenant John Thornton rode an imaginary motorbike around and around his prison camp, a practice so irritating it prompted his North Korea captors to 'confiscate' his invisible machine[5].

All the Australian pilots were caught shortly after landing except Oelof Bergh, who evaded the enemy for a remarkable seven days before finally collapsing from lack of food and sleep. He was ferociously interrogated over his supposed knowledge of what the communist forces claimed was a UN germ warfare campaign, with American agents allegedly poisoning wells and spreading smallpox. Bergh spent much of his incarceration immersed up to his neck in a pit of freezing water[6].

***

As was the way of this rollercoaster war, there was no time for the boy to mourn his lost aircraft or dwell upon the fate of its occupant. The day following the search for Bergh, August 29, 1952, saw another All UN Air Effort' strike on Pyongyang. Airfields, power stations, government buildings, and factories were bombed and strafed. No.77 Squadron again flew patrols along the Chongchon River to protect the 420 fighter-bombers in the air that day. Against such a show of strength, there was barely a MiG to be seen[7]. But for the boy, the horrors and destruction of this war were now becoming the norm: he recorded the day's events in his logbook simply as 'fighter sweep, Pyongyang'.

But the war was not finished with him yet. On September 1, 1952, a typhoon blew up off the west coast of Japan. Allan Avery, who had flown alongside the boy on the day of Smithy's death, was taking his turn for a short rest at Iwakuni, as was Randy Green, who had shared the boy's 100th mission. With Engineering Officer Eric Johnston alongside, Avery was returning to Korear in a dual-seat Meteor, with Green as escort, when the aircraft were hit by the storm. Green managed to haul his Meteor back to Iwakuni, but the bodies of Avery and Johnston later found on the west coast of Japan. Their deaths brought the casualty count at 77 Squadron to 35[8].

The boy was fortunate not to add to that number on September 4 during a rocket strike mission; in all the smoke and dust, his aircraft A77-415 was hit in the tail section. For the second time, he had to ask for an emergency 'Land Right' landing – which was just as well, as the elevator and rudder controls were afterward found to be hanging by the proverbial thread.

On September 10, 1952, it finally ended. Jim Kichenside's 148 [t] and final mission was a mass strafing of enemy supply shelters alongside Max Outhwaite, Randy Green, Hugh Howard and 12 others. And as the weak autumn sun crept over Kimpo next morning, Congo Kinninmont came in while they were in the showers and told the boy and Max, 'You blokes are finished.'

***

Two weeks later, on September 24, 1952, the boy and Max arrived home in Sydney. They had trained together, flown in combat together, and now came home together on a Qantas charter with an overnight stop in Manila. Waiting for the boy was his young wife, and in her arms two-week-old baby Gary, born on September 5[9].

Soon after he arrived home, the boy was reunited briefly with Col King, and able to introduce his wife and child to his friend. King was mightily impressed that the youngest man in their squadron had spent months flying amid the deadly flak, trying to keep himself and his mates alive, while all the time bearing the additional emotional responsibility of a young spouse and baby at home.

The pilot, the princess and the baby: when Jim Kichenside returned home from Korea in late September 1952, he was greeted by wife Beryl and his newborn son Gary [Kichenside family collection].

But the boy, while the clear Sydney sky and its complete absence of tracer fire and enemy jets warmed him, could not rid himself of a grey haze that muffled life like a blanket. He tried going to his local in Marrickville for a beer with old mates who talked about their office jobs and Western Suburbs winning the football premiership. He listened as though through a thick pane of glass – he could see their lips moving but could not understand the words, as though the sound of rockets and bombs and falling masonry and exploding trucks reared up to obscure them. He looked at their ruddy, well-fed faces and saw gaunt columns of refugees: both their hungry, haunted faces, and the way they smiled and said thank you, even in the midst of their own terror and despair. And after a time, he stopped going to the pub.

Awake and asleep, he returned endlessly to Korea. He thought about what he privately named as wicked and selfish things – how he had enjoyed the adrenaline and the camaraderie, his guilty wish for two more missions to make it a square 150. Then he thought of the near misses, the *chak-chak* of cannon fire, and the litany of names would begin: Cranston, Cowper, Colebrook, Drummond, Thomson, Purssey, Bergh – and Smithy.

Was it skill, fate, destiny, or just luck that he was here and they were dead or so terribly damaged? And he would reach into his pocket for the silver dollar that always lay there, cold and heavy, and close his fingers hard around it.

It was Beryl's mother, Florence Sjoberg, who gave it a name. 'You went away a boy,' she said, 'and you came home a man.'

CHAPTER 16

WHAT ARE THOSE MEDALS FOR?

War is a stern teacher.
—Bruce Cumings, *North Korea—Another Country*

At 10am on July 27, 1953, Lt. Gen. William Harrison of the UN Command and Lt. Gen. Nam Il of the Korean People's Army met at the village of Panmunjom, just north of the 38th parallel. They met in silence, and for 10 minutes only; there was no representative from South Korea in attendance. The result was a signed armistice – a supposed end' to the war, with victory for neither side. Years of excruciating peace negotiations, comprising 575 meetings before the armistice was signed, had been continually hampered by the symbolic importance of the Cold War and neither side wanting to appear too eager for compromise. The result was almost 5 million casualties-more than half of which were civilians[1].

For 77 Squadron, the lead-up to the 1953 ceasefire meant another miserable winter and an even hotter summer under Korean skies. The tempo of operations remained high and the sad litany of losses continued as all around them, the war on the ground disintegrated into a stalemate. No.77 Squadron flew its final mission on 20 July, 1953—one week before the Armistice.

Korea was not the longest or costliest war of the twentieth century, but it was among the toughest. One veteran described it as commanded by experts, fought with outstanding bravery ... in some of the worst country in the world.'[2] Of the 17,808 Australians to serve in Korea, 340 were lost, including 41 RAAF and RAF pilots from No.77 Squadron.

Korea was a new breed of air war. During World War I, air warfare mainly comprised of reconnaissance and battlefield photography with some first-generation bombers. World War II saw aircraft used in direct support of ground and naval operations, but the air war over Korea witnessed the debut of air-to-air combat between jet aircraft. The switch to the Meteor made the RAAF one of the world's few air forces with aerial combat experience in the jet age. The commitment also provided a core of combat-experienced officers who would lead the Air Force for much of the ensuing decades.

The RAAF's contribution in Korea was also important to establishment of strong Australian security ties with the United States. The esteem in which No.77 Squadron was held in Washington was a significant factor in the ratification of the ANZUS Treaty in 1951. But while UN air power in Korea complicated Communist resupply and troop mobilisation efforts, interdiction operations also resulted in large numbers of aircraft and personnel lost, and underlined the critical need to tie aircraft operations to their capabilities[3].

Some pilots in No.77 Squadron felt they were let down by the Meteor. Ray Trebilco called it an inferior high altitude fighter.'[4] But as a ground attack aircraft, Col King and Jim Kichenside both opined the Meteor was safer than the Mustang, with dual engines and without the vulnerability of the Mustang's glycol cooling system. However, the Meteor's ventral fuel tank contributed to many casualties, as did the planning and conduct of operational training. The Meteor was never used again in combat by Australian forces. No.77 Squadron remained in Korea for a year after the armistice and by 1956, had converted to the Australian-built variant of the Sabre, the CA-27. Any surviving Meteors were either scrapped, used as target drones, or became museum pieces. In 2020, only one airworthy Meteor F.8 remained in Australia, at the Temora Aviation Museum, as a poignant reminder of Australia's 'forgotten war'.

***

No-one knew I was home from Korea. 'What are those medals for?' - they just didn't have a clue, really.

-Sgt (later Air Vice Marshal) Bill Collings, 77 Squadron RAAF

Australian veterans returning from the Korean conflict often arrived home to find their experiences had flown under the radar of public consciousness. For the nation at large, the Korean War had been little more an unwelcome addendum to the harrowing experience of the preceding world war. The extreme environmental conditions, savagery, and chaos of the Korean conflict went largely unrecognised as the country focussed on rebuilding and renewing after the economic and social destruction of World War II. For the young pilots of 77 Squadron, arriving quietly back in twos and threes, the homecoming was particularly muted.

The boy returned with a United States Air Medal awarded for valour, proficiency, and devotion to duty ... despite intense enemy ground fire and adverse weather conditions'. His service was also mentioned in Dispatches on March 17, 1953, with Her Majesty's high appreciation'[5]. But it was the year 2000 – 50 years after the outbreak of the conflict – before the Australian National Korean War Memorial was unveiled in

Canberra, with a field of 340 stainless steel poles representing the Australians who had perished in the conflict. In 2011, Labor Prime Minister Julia Gillard became the first Australian leader to commemorate Anzac Day in Korea, laying a wreath at the national war memorial in Seoul and meeting Australian veterans at Kapyong to commemorate the 60th anniversary of that bloody struggle[6]. But the war remains overshadowed by the historical bookends of World War II and Vietnam, and the censored and erratic coverage of the conflict left many Australians unconscious of the horrors its veterans endured or the relevance of the war for the ongoing strategic situation in east Asia.

Presentation of Mention in Dispatches to Jim Kichenside (left) at East Sale Air Force Base, 1953 [Kichenside family collection].

The Korean War was the first real test of the Western doctrine of containment, aimed at stemming the global spread of communism, and the first true demonstration of unity and cooperation by the new member states of the UN. But the 1970s television satire *M*A*S*H,* so beloved for its bittersweet portrayal of US army medics in Korea, also became emblematic of the fiasco and tragedy of the Korean War: a war in which British army private Bill Speakman won a Victoria Cross for holding off the enemy by throwing beer bottles; a war which saw the first heavy use of intravenous amphetamine by allied troops; where crates of Tootsie Rolls were supplied in place of mortar rounds and Pablo Picasso painted the 1951 expressionist critique *Massacre in Korea* to articulate his horror at the deaths of thousands of civilians.

Ironically, *M*A *S*H* stars Alan Alda and Jamie Farr both served with the US Army in Korea after the armistice. The serving UN ranks also included movie stars James Garner and Michael Caine, baseball Hall of Famer Ted Williams, and astronauts Neil Armstrong, Buzz Aldrin and John Glenn. The conflict has been immortalised in Hollywood through movies including *The Manchurian Candidate* with Frank Sinatra and Gregory Peck's *Pork Chop Hill.* Yet despite featuring thus in popular culture, the bloody conflict, heartache, and stalemate of the war in Korea remains a dark corner of Western memory. But can the world afford to forget a war that has never formally ended? What began as a struggle between opposing social and political ideologies remains a flashpoint in the international arm-wrestle between capitalism and communism, with ongoing implications for global security. And for Jim Kichenside and his RAAF compatriots, Korea remains both the springboard into the jet age and a battlefield where mates and innocence were lost forever.

PART
THREE

CHAPTER 17

ICE COLD TOP GUN

Antarctica has this mythic weight. It resides in the collective unconscious of so many people, and it makes this huge impact, just like outer space. It's like going to the moon.

—Jon Krakauer

It is the coldest and loneliest place on earth.

Ringed by turbulent seas, Antarctica, the world's fifth largest continent, lies in a permanent eerie silence only broken by the howl of katabatic winds roaring out of its interior. It is an arid, frozen desert where, in some regions, significant precipitation has not fallen for over two million years and temperatures can plunge below-90°C. Nowhere on earth is more hostile to life.

Antarctica is a world dominated by ice. Its 14 million square kilometres of ice comprise an area larger than Europe and twice the size of Australia, containing over three-quarters of the world's fresh water: a sheet of ice so gigantic it interacts with global oceanic and atmospheric circulation to affect climate on a worldwide scale. The continent was once the keystone of ancient

Gondwanaland, and now its prehistoric ice can be over 5 kilometres thick, submerging mountain ranges as high as the Alps so only their peaks protrude. Rivers of ice spill down from the central polar plateau to the sea as creeping megaglaciers, breaking off as icebergs so large they can drift in the world's oceans for up to ten years.

In 1960, it was to this pitiless, pristine wilderness that the boy-pilot came. Despite the danger of300kilometre per hour blizzards, ofwhiteouts and cloud and airborne mirages that could send a pilot smashing into an unseen peak, he came to fly and to join a proud tradition of RAAF pilots serving in the latitudes beyond 60 degrees south.

Antarctica, with its ever-changing landscape of ice, snow, and stone, is the coldest and windiest continent on earth, and continues to pose unique environmental challenges for scientists, explorers and aviators alike [Kichenside family collection].

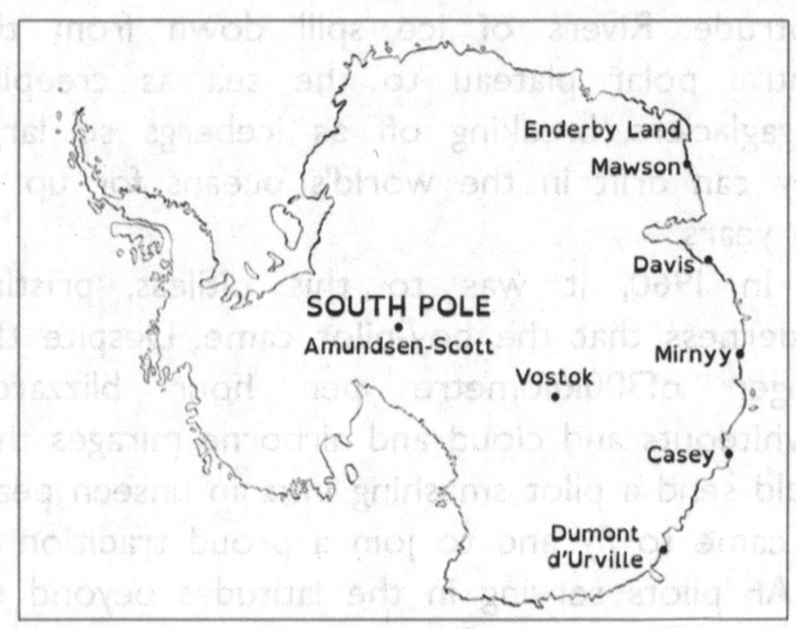

The location of Australian bases—Mawson, Davis, and Casey—in eastern Antarctica. The surrounding Australian Antarctic Territory comprises almost 42 per cent of the Antarctic continent.

***

The continent of Antarctica has long held a mythical fascination that has attracted explorers and pioneers since the time of the ancient Greeks, who believed a mysterious continent, *Terra Australis Incognita,* existed at the base of the earth to counterbalance the northern hemisphere. But it was not until 1773 that British navigator James Cook first ventured south of the Antarctic Circle in search of this legendary realm. While he reached latitude 71°10' south, pack ice kept his ships more than 250 kilometres from the Antarctic mainland, and it was the Russian expedition led by Gottlieb von Bellingshausen and Mikhail Lazarev who were first to sight the body of the continent when they discovered the Princess Martha Coast in 1820. Just a year later, American sealing captain John Davis claimed to have made the first landing on the east coast of mainland Antarctica. A new age of exploration and scientific discovery had begun in the Southern Ocean, with international interests from Britain, the United States, Russia and Australia all racing to secure claims on the frozen continent.

While John Davis reported reaching the continent in 1821, it was a further 74 years before the first undisputed footfall in 1895, when Norwegian whaler Henryk Bull reached Cape Adare in the ship *Antarctic*. Carsten Borchgrevink, a Norwegian scientist who had been teaching in Australia, had joined Bulls crew in Melbourne, and subsequently led a British expedition in 1898-1900 which was first to winter on the continent. His party included the first Australian to step onto mainland Antarctica, Tasmanian physicist Louis Bernacchi. Like Borchgrevink, Bernacchi s fascination with the Antarctic saw him return with British naval officer Robert Falcon Scotts 1901-04 expedition, which undertook the first major land exploration in the Antarctic while their ship, *Discovery,* was icebound in McMurdo Sound[1].

As part of this expedition, Scott, accompanied by ambitious young Irishman Ernest Shackleton and physician Edward Wilson, made the first attempt to reach the legendary 90 degrees south – the South Pole—in late 1902. They were forced to turn back before reaching their goal, suffering from frostbite, snow blindness, and scurvy, but Scott returned for a second attempt in 1910-11, this time equipped with three motor tractors, 19 Siberian ponies and 60 men. It became a desperate race when Norwegian explorer Roald Amundsen, who had originally planned to be first to reach the North Pole but was beaten to it by American Robert Peary in 1909, turned his attention to the south. Travelling fast with sledges and dogs, Amundsen reached the South Pole on December 14, 1911: 33 days before Scott. Finding the Norwegian flag planted at the Pole was a dreadful blow to the Brits. Exhausted and dispirited, Scott and his four companions perished on the return journey, just 17 kilometres from a supply depot that might have saved them.

Ernest Shackleton, who had fallen out with Scott before leading his own unsuccessful quest for the Pole in 1907-09, was nonetheless knighted for setting a new record for farthest south latitude on that trip, sledging to within 180 kilometres of the Pole. He made his party turn back when supplies ran critically low, and his strategic thinking undoubtedly saved their lives; Shackleton told his wife later, A live donkey is better than a dead lion'. The subsequent conquest of the Pole by Amundsen set Shackleton on a new goal: to cross the entire continent on foot, via the Pole, on what he extolled as the greatest polar journey ever attempted'.

Shackleton's 1914-17 British Imperial Transantarctic Expedition was indeed later heralded as one of the great feats of endurance in Antarctic exploration history, but the party were riven with setbacks, losing their ship, *Endurance*, crushed in pack ice off the Antarctic coast, forcing them into lifeboats and a journey of almost 1500 kilometres to South Georgia, off the east coast of South America, in April 1916. It was here Shackleton learned his depot-laying party had been stranded back on the other side of the continent since May 1915 after their own ship had drifted away. Shackleton returned to rescue the survivors in January 1917. The dream of a trans-Antarctic crossing was not realised until 1958 when British archaeologist Vivian Fuchs, with famed mountaineer Sir Edmund Hillary in his party, accomplished the feat[2].

Ernest Shackleton, Captain Robert Falcon Scott, and Dr. Edward Wilson during the British Discovery expedition of 1902, which included the first attempt to reach the South Pole [Alamy, image ID: W9K13T].

Young Australian geologist Douglas Mawson had been part of the 1907 Shackleton expedition, during which he and his University of Sydney mentor T. Edgeworth David made the first ascent of the Antarctic's highest active volcano, Mount Erebus, and was part of a trio to reach the South Magnetic Pole in January 1909. Mawson had his own tale of polar survival, He had returned to lead the 1911-14 Australasian Antarctic Expedition, and set out with two companions to explore George V Land coast in November 1912. The deaths of his companions saw him stranded alone, 160 kilometres from the rendezvous point with his ship. He trekked back through blizzards and crevasses with almost no food – only to witness the *Aurora* departing without him. But a search party had stayed behind and the group survived for almost a year on the ice before being rescued in 1914. Sir Edmund Hillary described Mawson's solo journey as probably the greatest story of lone survival in Polar exploration. Mawson also led the 1929-31 British-Australian-New Zealand Antarctic Research Expeditions (BANZARE), which garnered such extensive geographical, zoological and scientific data it took over 30 years to publish it all[3].

Sir Douglas Mawson (1882-1958), geologist and Antarctic explorer. In 1907, with Ernest Shackleton, Mawson travelled to within 161 kilometres of the South Pole. His 1911-14 expedition charted over 3200 kilometres of Antarctic coastline, and Mawson's joint British-Australian-New Zealand expedition of 1929-31 produced 13 volumes of reports on climate, weather, and the polar environment [Alamy, image ID: 2ADGXHJ].

***

Almost from the moment man set foot in the Antarctic, he realised the potential for aviation in traversing and surveying its vast frozen wilderness. Robert Falcon Scott, aboard a hydrogen balloon equipped with what he felt was a very inadequate basket', became the first man to fly above the Antarctic during the 1901-04 *Discovery* expedition. Douglas Mawson was equally innovative, combining his plan to use a single-engine Vickers REP Monoplane for reconnaissance during his 1911-14 expedition with promotion for the Antarctic cause. He flew the machine in a public demonstration in Adelaide prior to his departure, and even a crash landing failed to deter him: the machine was employed, *sans* wings, for overland transport in the Antarctic. When the engine finally seized, Mawson was forced to abandon his precious air tractor'; it was rediscovered, preserved in ice at Cape Denison, by Australian expeditioners in 2010[4]. Mawson spent almost 20 years planning his next venture into Antarctic aviation. His 1929-31 BANZARE expedition used a de Havilland DH.60G Gypsy Moth float plane for aerial surveying of what would become the Australian Antarctic Territory (AAT) (an area of 5,896,500km^2, comprising 42 per cent of the Antarctic continent)[5].

Mawson's use of the Moth came little over a year after the first successful powered aircraft flight in Antarctica, when Australian aviator Hubert Wilkins mapped uncharted Graham Land from a Lockheed Vega I monoplane in 1928. United States Navy admiral Richard Byrd made the first flight over the South Pole a year later in the Ford trimotor aircraft *Floyd Bennett,* and his expeditions of 1933, 1939 and 1946 all used aircraft for survey and photography[6].

The RAAF have been linked with Antarctic aviation since the time of Mawson's BANZARE expeditions. Defence pilots Stuart Campbell and Eric Douglas had charge of Mawson's Gypsy Moth, and used it to both guide his ship *Discovery* through the ice and make reconnaissance flights. In 1935, wealthy American adventurer and World War I pilot Lincoln Ellsworth attempted to traverse the Antarctic by air, having made the first flight over the North Pole in an airship with Roald Amundsen in 1926 and a previous attempt crossing Antarctica in 1933 with Wilkins as pilot of his Northrop Gamma. During his 1935 attempt, Ellsworth and co-pilot Herbert Hollick-Kenyon lost contact with their support team and the RAAF were deployed on a search and rescue mission out of Melbourne; the two men were found alive after almost two months stranded on the ice[7].

Unloading the Lockheed Vega I aircraft used by Hubert Wilkins from the William Scoresby in Antarctica in 1928. Wilkins had been knighted for his achievements in traversing the Arctic by air from Alaska to Spitsbergen in 1928, and in the same year, h

The formation of Australian National Antarctic Research Expeditions (ANARE) in 1947 paved the way for a regular RAAF presence on the continent. With Stuart Campbell as ANARE's first chief executive officer, its first voyage to Antarctica in 1947 transported a Vickers Supermarine Walrus to Heard Island for use in photography and survey. However, after just one week, the plane was destroyed in a wild storm. In the same year, a Sikorsky Kingfisher seaplane was successfully piloted by RAAF personnel for two one-hour reconnaissance flights near the

Ninnis and Mertz Glaciers on the main continent[8].

In 1949, ANARE came under the umbrella of the Department of External Affairs and physicist Phillip Law was appointed as its new Director. Law would oversee 28 Antarctic and sub-Antarctic voyages, the establishment of Australia's first permanent base on the continent, and exploration of 1.3 million square kilometres of territory. Law too, recognised the potential for aircraft flown by military pilots in Antarctic exploration. In 1955, flapless Auster Mark 6 aircraft were used to guide the ship *Kista Dan* into the site Law had chosen for the future Australian base at Mawson, although both were later damaged during a gale and a composite plane had to be cobbled together from the remaining parts. This aircraft was successfully flown by RAAF pilots on ANARE missions between 1955 to 1959[9].

The period 1956-60 ushered in a new era of Australian polar aviation operations out of the new Australian base at Mawson in east Antarctica. Single-engine de Havilland Beaver aircraft equipped with skis were used for sea ice-based operations in the southern hemisphere winter between April and November, ferrying research staff on short-range expeditions and providing a limited float-plane capacity during the summer. However, the year 1960 would represent a significant escalation in Australian Antarctic aviation ambition and capacity. And the boy would be at its head.

***

Jim Kichenside was leaving a lot behind for a chance at command below 60 degrees south. Much had occurred in the eight years since he had returned from Korea.

The Korean War was Australia's last involvement in conventional air warfare and provided the catalyst for the RAAF to enter the jet era. As the first war of the jet age, the conflict was the impetus for later development of third-generation jet fighters by both major Cold War adversaries. These included the American F-100 Super Sabre and F-105 Thunderchief aircraft as well as the Soviet's MiG-19 and MiG-21 types – aircraft capable of reaching Mach 2 (twice the speed of sound) and able to deliver nuclear weapons.

The mid-1950s also witnessed the emergence of the first gunless fighter aircraft such as the American F-86D and F-89, which carried a payload of heavy missiles which could be fitted with nuclear warheads[10]. It was a dynamic time for air development as the Cold War escalated toward what some viewed as inevitable outright conflict. And a group of battle-hardened young turks' who made it home from Korea would help to lead Australian military aviation into this new era.

After Korea, the boy stood at a crossroads in his flying career-one signpost pointed west, toward Malta and the possibility of further active engagement with Australia's Vampire-equipped squadrons. The other pointed north to RAAF Williamtown, to the newly formed No.2 Operational Training Unit (2 OTU): the new home of jet training in Australia[11]. While still a student pilot, Kichenside had been identified as 'capable and efficient at instruction duties with further service experience'. In Korea, too, Wing Commander Ron Susans had observed his poise and confidence. Now, at just 22 years of age, he was the youngest of 18 pilots selected for the 1953 Fighter Instructors Course at RAAF Williamtown. He finished the course in the top echelon with reports including, 'This sergeant possesses outstanding ability and can be thoroughly relied upon to carry out in the highest order any work entrusted to him.'[12]

He was earmarked for the No.9 Flying Instructors Course at East Sale from which he was commissioned as Pilot Officer. He was one of just four selected for the No.1 Jet Instructors Course to oversee the transition of student pilots from piston to jet aircraft. This quartet, which also included Max Outhwaite, was of intense interest to RAAF psychologists, and their personality characteristics and physiological processes under stress were documented throughout the 60-hour course. These were the new generation of Air Force instructors.

Jim Kichenside was promoted to Flying Officer in July 1954 and returned to Williamtown as a Category A fighter pilot: at the time, he was the only pilot at Williamtown with this rating and was offered a permanent commission immediately. In less than four years, he had risen from a trainee and a non-commissioned pilot to a commissioned officer, Qualified Flying Instructor (QFI), Instrument Rating Examiner (IRE), and Fighter Combat Instructor (FCI)[13].

He became a staff instructor at 2 OTU in 1955, where he would remain until March 1957. The year 1955 brought two other major additions to his life: his second son, named Kenneth for his tragic mate Smithy, and, at the age of almost 25, his first car drivers licence. Jim Kichenside had been a pilot for nearly five years but had rarely driven a car; his own father had never owned one. But in 1955, the boy took himself to Raymond Terrace police station and drove cleanly and sedately through the test, despite the fact he flew jets at 1000 kilometres per hour for a living.

While at East Sale, he had kept both Minnie-san's charm and Jack's silver dollar in a small box in his room until the box was stolen by persons unknown. But even without his lucky charms, his fortunes held in 1955 when he survived two forced landings in three days while training in Vampires. From his student pilot days, the boy was well aware of the Vampire's propensity for loss of control at the onset of the sound barrier[14]. Now, as an instructor, he would test fly aircraft to ascertain their compressibility characteristics before authorising any Mach runs for his students. He was one of the most skilled jet pilots in the country, with 200 Meteor hours and on target for 800 in the Vampire – he would soon become one of the first RAAF pilots to log 1000 hours on jets.

But on October 11, 1955, he was leading a student on a training exercise when the student radioed, 'You are on fire!' just after takeoff. The prospect of ejecting at low altitude was a grim one. He had twice parachuted out the back of a RAAF C-47 over Port Stephens in full flying suit and boots, but that was from 1000 feet over the sea, not 200 feet above a tarmac runway. So he held onto power for an agonising few seconds and went for height. As he hit 1000 feet, he cut the fuel, leaving just sufficient for a tight downwind turn and even tighter forced landing along the take-off path, all without damaging the aircraft.

Two days later, his Number Two reported fuel streaming just after take-off – the precursor to a deadly fire in the Vampire's light plywood airframe. With more speed this time, he was able to shut down the engine with plenty of time for a forced landing, but it was a further reminder that despite all the training and drilling and preparation, a classroom could never simulate the sensation of an airborne jet on fire – the heat, noise, loss of control, and the psychological impact of being strapped into a burning plane. But Jim Kichenside's famous luck had held once more – although with a strong element of fast thinking and skill.

Following his return from Korea in 1952, Jim Kichenside became a commissioned RAAF officer, Qualified Flying Instructor, Instrument Rating Examiner, and Fighter Combat Instructor. He was also one of the first RAAF pilots to log 1000 hours on jets [Kichenside family collection].

In 1957, Kichenside was promoted to Flight Lieutenant, and described by his superiors as, A capable instructor whose flying demonstrations and briefings (are) well carried out ... good knowledge of all subjects with above average in jet performance and high speed flight ... Will be a very sound leader, very good material.'[15] And shortly afterward, his first official chance to lead arrived.

No.21 (City of Melbourne) Squadron of the Citizen Air Force was based at Laverton in Victoria flying Vampire aircraft, and in 1957, its

CO, Korean veteran Vic Cannon, was posted to Staff College. Group Captain John Fullarton 'Ginty' Lush was a former flying boat and bomber pilot who had done his own jet conversion with the boy and had been impressed by his maturity and confidence with the tricky Vampire. He now proposed seconding Kichenside to 21 Squadron as temporary CO[16]. RAAF Headquarters Support Command in Melbourne felt that the boy, at age 26, was too young for the post, but Lush insisted, telling the boy, 'If you let me down, I'll kick your arse.' And so the appointment was made. The boy was responsible for all flying training, gunnery and instruction during Cannon's seven-month absence, achieving his childhood dream to lead a fighter squadron only six years after graduation.

Just months later, in April 1958, a further prospect for command arose. But the opportunity now before him was more complex – it was a three-year posting but there were no jet fighters, adjutants, or wood-panelled offices. However, the salary on offer was extra-generous: that meant a chance to anchor his growing family, which now included baby daughter Ann Cherie, into financial security. The hitch was – it was a posting to the coldest, most isolated outpost on earth.

CHAPTER 18

OUT IN THE COLD

Australians are not easy to command—a commander must earn their loyalty by looking after their welfare and sharing their risks. They always want to know the reason why.

—Air Vice-Marshal Joseph Hewitt

Western Bay, Mac. Robertson Land
Antarctica
March 25, 1960

'Gloves off, fellas.'

The ferocious wind snatched his words and flung them away like confetti. Flying slivers of ice peppered their faces. The watery sun, high in the sky that morning, was long gone; the weather was deteriorating fast. With the dark grey sea and lowering clouds as a backdrop, the orange tail of the Dakota was now the only bright spot of colour in the frozen monochrome landscape.

Resolutely, the boy tugged his own gloves off and positioned his bare hands on the frozen leading edge of the wing. 'On three, we lift from this side and get the top bolts in. I need two blokes on this side and two on the end; careful of the flaps!' He looked up, brushing blown snow from his goggles. 'Kev, are your boys right?'

'Yes, sir – ready!'

'Right—we're doing five-minute shifts. Get as many bolts in as you can, then we'll swap. Ready? On three: *lift* and *go!* Right on cue, the icy wind picked up and blasted them with a fresh sweep of snow and ice.

Each wing of the C-47, detached for the voyage south, was held together by three hundred small bolts which could only be inserted and tightened by bare hands. They had built up great banks of snow beneath the wings to manoeuvre them into position, but they still had to be manually heaved and shifted into place, and every bolt inserted with naked fingers in the-20°C chill.

After five minutes, the boy moved amongst his men, nominating another four blokes to lift, insert and tighten, checking all their fingers for the tell-tale blisters of frostbite then sending them inside the aircraft to re-warm their hands on the aircraft's auxiliary heating system. Kev Felton's hands were split and beginning to bleed, but the young man shrugged. 'We had worse than this in Korea, sir ... perhaps.' Through the snow caking his goggles and the hood of his parka, he was grinning.

It was a Friday, but after ten hours on the ice, they returned to their huts so cold they opted for the traditional Saturday night respite: Rumdoodle Punch. Four bottles of sherry, one pint of medicinal alcohol, one bottle fruit cordial, three tins of fruit salad, and four pints of water. 'Mix together and stand clear!'

***

In the 21st century, Antarctic expeditioners have email, Skype, buses with heated seats, hydroponically grown fresh vegetables, and Gore-Tex jackets to combat the fearsome elements and isolation on the continent. In 1960, the RAAF Antarctic Flight had a few prefabricated huts, a Ferguson tractor, a hangar for one plane and a space on the snow for the other, and woollen beanies knitted by anxious wives and mothers to warm their heads. Mawson Base, in Mac. Robertson Land in eastern Antarctica, is the oldest permanently occupied base south of the Antarctic Circle, but in 1960, it had stood for just six years, and the emphasis was as much on survival as on research and exploration.

In 1960, the boy was 29 years old, with combat experience and interim leadership of a fighter squadron under his belt. Now he was to lead the RAAF Antarctic Flight on what might be their most challenging year yet on the frozen continent. But leadership in polar environments was a much different proposition – he was facing primitive working conditions, isolation and extreme temperatures, coupled with an ambitious flying schedule, a new plane, and a larger staff than the RAAF had ever sent to the continent. Antarctic flying conditions are among the most hazardous in the world and his decisions would have immediate and life-threatening consequences.

He had come to Antarctica with two other pilots on his roster – Ken Assender and Graham Dyke—and the trio were facing an aviation environment that nothing in Australia could fully prepare them for. Whiteout – an optical phenomenon in which the lack of contrast from snow cover and overcast skies make it impossible to distinguish the horizon – means a potentially deadly loss of perspective and direction. Wind speeds during polar blizzards can exceed 300 kilometres per hour. The air over the interior of Antarctica is usually dry, but moisture near the coast can create deadly cloud formations. In 1979, an Air New Zealand McDonnell Douglas DC-10 jetliner on an Antarctic tourist flight ploughed into Mount Erebus near McMurdo Station in dense cloud and whiteout, killing all 257 people on board in what was both New Zealand and Antarctica's worst air disaster[1]. And in these early days, with no sophisticated radar and only rudimentary communications equipment, the 1960 Antarctic Flight were almost flying blind.

Jim Kichenside's Antarctic preparation began in 1958 when he completed the Antarctic Pilots Navigation Course at East Sale. It was also his introduction to the two aircraft he'd be flying in the south: the de Havilland DHC-2 Beaver and the Douglas C-47 Dakota. While the Beaver was a proven performer in Antarctic conditions, this was the first time the much larger dual-engine C-47 would be trialled on the continent, aiming to extend the range of ANARE expeditions and improve its photographic, search and rescue, and cargo-lift capabilities. However, both aircraft proved temperamental during the Course, and at the conclusion, Kichenside had only 5.5 hrs in the Beaver and 7 in the Dakota.

The day after Christmas in 1958, Kichenside boarded the chartered Danish ship MV *Thala Dan* as it sailed south from Melbourne to resupply the Australian Antarctic stations at Mawson and Davis. The 1959 RAAF Antarctic Flight were also on board. Ships can only approach the continental stations for a few weeks during the height of the southern summer, so it is at this period that staff are typically changed over, new equipment installed, and exploration of the coastline ramped up. Kichenside would spend eight weeks visiting the Australian polar bases and getting his first taste of true Antarctic conditions.

Just 24 hours into the voyage, as the ship approached King Island in the notorious waters of Bass Strait, *Thala Dan* suffered engine problems which necessitated a complete shutdown. The fickle weather had the ship rolling horribly, and the Flight lost 40 drums of Avgas overboard – fuel enough for 100 hours of flying. The RAAF's Beaver aircraft, A95-203, was lashed down on the forward decks and was fortunate not to follow. And this before *Thala Dan* had even entered the Southern Ocean, the most hostile wind and sea system in the world, where galloping low pressure systems and a prevailing westerly wind can strike fear into the most audacious mariner.

It was two weeks of shunting south before the first pack ice was sighted and a watch set for icebergs. On January 10, 1959, the ship berthed at Mirnyy, the Soviet base in east Antarctica. A Russian helicopter ferried a party of men, including Kichenside, from the ship to the station, where they were personally entertained by the Russian commander. This hospitality was reciprocated next day on board ship with warming toasts of Scotch and sherry[2]. The boy, who, less than a decade before, had flown in combat against Soviet pilots, was surprised but touched by the cordiality of the exchange, given the ongoing hostility of the Cold War. But in Antarctica, he concluded, you needed all the friends you could get.

The voyage was on the rocks again – literally – six days later on January 16, 1959, as *Thala Dan* approached the Australian base at Davis. It was a clear day, but she ran aground within sight of the station on an uncharted rock. The impact was so great that several men on the deck were upended, thankfully not over the side. The fracture in the hull had to be caulked with concrete before the ship could be refloated, meaning a five-day delay before they could sail the last 5 kilometres to Davis[3].

The boy had his first sight of Antarctica from the air when he and the OC of the incoming Antarctic Flight, James Conway Sandercock, flew the float-equipped Beaver from *Thala Dan* to Davis to drop mail then reconnoitre nearby Lake Stinear as a potential landing site. The boy thought the continent both beautiful and deadly-the ice was so dynamic; they could come back the very next day and find the place in whiteout or the lake frozen over or the local ice in a completely different configuration. Every day would be a discrete entity, requiring continual assessment, observation, and environmental evaluation.

On this voyage, Kichenside sailed alongside ANARE director Phillip Law. Law was not a big man – at five foot, nine inches, the boy was surprised to find himself on eye level with Law, whose confidence and charisma made him seem so much larger. Law rode the rolling ship easily – he had been a lightweight boxing champion at Melbourne University and was still a fitness fanatic, despite his 48 years. But Law also donned a jacket and tie for dinner each night, and would regale the expeditioners with his clarinet or piano-accordion with a glass of wine at his elbow.

The boy watched Law carefully throughout the voyage, He knew that, despite his many achievements, Law had never wintered on the continent, and he was curious about the response of the men to his command as a result. Antarctica in winter was a place of unique operational and planning challenges that surely had to be experienced to be understood. But most of the expeditioners seemed to hold Law in reverence, and the boy could see why – the man's enthusiasm, enormous work ethic, and hands-on involvement with all things related to expedition planning, funding, and staffing were impressive.

Some, however, such as the ship's captain Hans Christian Petersen, were not so deferential. The taciturn Petersen was blunt when it came to control of his vessel, refusing to take orders or suggestions from Law. Some of the ANARE men were taken aback by this, but the boy, with his own operational experience, knew this was simply the difference between *command* and *control*-a critical enabler for all military activities[4]. A captain who has signed for a ship, even with the head of ANARE, who had chartered the vessel, on board, retains operational control. While Law could give commands to his subordinates on board, Petersen had control over the ship's procedures, route and operation. The boy observed all of this but remained silent. He realised it was one thing for a leader to formulate a vision – another entirely to implement it.

On February 4, 1959, the *Thala Dan* arrived for a ten-day visit to Mawson: the critical juncture of the boy's voyage. Law's exploration program had long been frustrated by the inability to operate aircraft once the winter sea-ice in the harbour had broken up. In July 1959, Law proposed to the Department of Air to operate Beaver aircraft from an ice airstrip on the plateau above Mawson during the Antarctic summers, thereby potentially allowing for year-round aviation capabilities. The polar plateau at Mawson is 2,000 feet higher than the coast where the base is located, and some sections retain tough blue ice suitable for landing aircraft even through the Antarctic summer. Concerned about the structural impact on the little Beavers of landings on the dense blue ice, the Department suggested supplementing operations with a larger twin-engine aircraft such as a C-47, which would both extend the operational range and provide greater resilience[5]. In 1960, it would be Jim Kichenside's Flight who would first trial the bigger aircraft off both sea-ice and the plateau. In 1959, a runway site was chosen 2 kilometres inland from Mawson from which Sandercock would operate two Beavers off the plateau as a trial for the deployment of Kichenside's C-47 the following summer.

***

In June 1959, after Kichenside's return from his first visit to Mawson, the 1960 RAAF Antarctic Flight was officially raised at Point Cook. The boy was granted the acting rank of Squadron Leader[6]. At 12 strong, this was the largest contingent the RAAF had ever sent to the Antarctic. A draft cabinet submission estimated the cost of the C-47 scheme at £136,000, with the increased cost in personnel, clothing, food, and fuel[7]. Maintaining morale and congeniality among twelve men when they reached the isolation of the continent would be a demanding minute-to-minute responsibility, and as commanding officer, the boy was grateful for the chance to hand-pick at least some of his crew. First on his list was engine fitter Kev Felton, who had so carefully tended The Korean Kid, his Meteor jet in Korea. The young man's stamina, endurance, and unflagging good humour were just what Jim Kichenside wanted in his outfit.

With 12 members, the 1960 Antarctic Flight was the largest contingent ever deployed by the RAAF to the continent. The group are pictured in front of the C-47 transport sent to extend Australia's existing survey, exploration, and search and rescue capabilities [Kichenside family collection].

When he had learned Kichenside was going south, Felton had immediately put his hand up to go too. He was joined by pilots Graham Dyke and Ken Assender, navigator Ted Bloomfield, signaller N William Hanson, engine fitter Bert Carne, airframe fitters Mick Murphy and Bruce Harris, electrical technician John Arthur, instrument fitter Basil Rutter, and radio technician Donald Monks. Pilot Ken Assender was another who had applied after a favourable association with Kichenside: he had been a graduate pilot and the boy's adjutant during his secondment as temporary CO of 21 Squadron and now eagerly signed up to fly with him at Mawson.

In mid 1959, Kichenside and Dyke were attached to the Aircraft Research and Development Unit (ARDU) at RAAF Base Richmond for training on flying in cloud and icing conditions, before spending a week dropping supplies for the Army. The remainder of the crew were training in navigation, mapping, and C-47 servicing before the entire Antarctic Flight was sent to the winter ski resort of Mount Buller in Victoria for a ski and survival course.

On August 17, Dyke and Kichenside picked up the C-47 from No.1 Aircraft Depot, RAAF Base Laverton. Powered by two Pratt and Whitney 14-cylinder engines, with her carrying capacity of 3.8 tonnes and range of over 3300km, Douglas C-47 Dakota A65-81 was fifteen years old, having flown with the US Army Air Corps before its acquisition by the RAAF in March

1945. The aircraft was used by No.36 Squadron before it was sent to the de Havilland aircraft maintenance facility at Bankstown in Sydney's west in 1959 for Antarctic modifications, with 5,088 hours on the airframe[8]. Before it was handed over to the Flight in November, it was fitted with retractable skis, extra insulation, and a jet-assisted take-off (JATO) system to give it additional thrust[9]. But despite the diligent work of the ARDU, the Doppler radar did not function properly, and the months spent on modifications meant the Flight had had very little time with the aircraft before their departure.

On January 10, 1960, Kichenside's Antarctic Flight sailed for a year on the continent alongside 21 ANARE men, again out of Melbourne aboard the *Thala Dan*. The boy was leaving behind his three children – Gary and Ken as little boys in short pants, and Ann Cherie a toddler with her father's serious eyes. He was also leaving his young wife, and trying to suppress the little voice inside that suggested this whole endeavour was selfish. He settled with himself by acknowledging it probably *was*—but such a chance for command and adventure would probably never come again. And the money – with nothing to spend it on down on the ice, this venture would ensure the family's future financial security. But before they left, the boy had the C-47 officially christened *Ann Cherie*.

Jim Kichenside with the C-47 aircraft named after his daughter, Ann Cherie [Kichenside family collection].

***

Just a fortnight before their departure, the 1960 Flight received the disastrous news that both of Sandercock's Beaver aircraft had been destroyed in a four-day long blizzard on the plateau on December 28, 1959. Sandercock himself had almost saved one of them through his own fearlessness – with ferocious winds destroying two of its three-tonne tiedowns and threatening to fling the little plane away into the blizzard, Sandercock somehow scrambled on board, started the engine, and 'flew' the half-tethered aircraft into the gale for two hours before the anchors finally reefed out of the ice and the 190 kilometre per hour winds tore a wing off, forcing him to dive out. The other aircraft was also being blown away when two of the crew chased it down in a D4 tractor and dropped the blade onto one of the anchors; the big machine itself was then dragged across the ice before the Beaver finally broke free and disintegrated[10]. Mawson CO John Bechervaise called the loss of the aircraft 'a bitter blow which ... called a halt to a project which had taken a year's planning and hard work.'[11]

The Ann Cherie en route for Antarctica on the deck of the Danish charter ship, Thala Dan. The aircraft's wings, propellors, and elevators were removed for the trip and she was reassembled on the ice at Mawson base [Kichenside family collection].

A hastily organised replacement aircraft was now aboard the *Thala Dans* sister ship *Magga Dan,* which was *en route* for Davis base, while the *Thala Dan* was transporting the C-47[12]. But with her 29metre wingspan, *Ann Cherie* was far too large to ride on the ship's foredeck. Her propellers, rudder, elevators and wings were removed and fitted in crates on top of Number One hold before the fuselage was lifted on deck in a special cradle. This was an extremely delicate operation, with tricky winds hampering the ship's crane. Even when she was in place, *Ann Cherie* had only centimetres clearance. However, she rode well, with Captain Petersen skilfully turning the ship into the swell to reduce the strain of the rolling deck on her tiedowns.

The voyage was benign. The Flight played cards and practised lifeboat drills as *Thala Dan* ran rapidly west with the wind before entering the corridor of icebergs which led to Mawson. Such favourable weather and ice conditions at sea were frequently referred to by AN ARE men as 'Law Luck', and Petersen manoeuvred safely through the bergs and a belt of dense pack ice into calm open water, from where they could see the radio masts of Mawson standing out against the distant mountains on January 25, 1960[13].

A ritual among Antarctic expeditioners is to have their photograph taken with the first iceberg encountered en route for the continent. Jim Kichenside is shown here on the deck of the Thala Dan with his first iceberg in January 1960. One of the largest icebergs ever recorded, the Amery Berg, measured 9000 square kilometres in area and broke off from Antarctica in 1963, drifting for over 12 years before it finally broke up [Kichenside family collection].

The 33 expeditioners, in bright red and green woollen hats and bulky orange life preservers, were ferried ashore next day in an Army DUKW, that odd amphibious vehicle, bumping shoulder to shoulder over the little waves before they rolled up the stony beach. It was Australia Day. January is the warmest month at Mawson and temperatures were above freezing, averaging around 2°C. There was even some sparse vegetation in the form of mosses and lichens greening the black seaside rocks. Mawson Base was a scattered collection of huts and dongas on the stony shoreline of Horseshoe Harbour, a site Law had chosen as providing protection to ships from polar gales and allowing rapid unloading of stores and equipment. Behind the station were the great dark mountains and the polar plateau from which they would fly *Ann Cherie* in summer. But for now, priority for the Flight was unloading and reassembling the C-47 while the weather remained stable.

Unloading the C-47 occupied both the RAAF and ANARE contingents for five days. Until the plane was offloaded, no other cargo could be moved as the fuselage and wings blocked all three of the ship's hatches. Without a wharf, unloading from a ship riding at anchor onto a floating pontoon proved hazardous. The crane lifting one of the wings gave way and the wing crashed to the deck below, then the nose cone was dented against the deckhouse rail as it was being lifted.

This was only the beginning of *Ann Cherie'* s trials. She was brought ashore on January 30, 1960, landing on the western ice shelf of Horseshoe Harbour. It had taken four days to construct a 15x6m pontoon large enough to float the aircraft, and a further six hours to lower the plane onto it. *Thala Dan* had circled the harbour several times to break up the ice, and ANARE chief Henk Geysen and two assistants used plastic explosives to break up more of the floes. The 7.6 tonne weight of the plane left the pontoon with a draft of only 60 centimetres, forcing them to wait for calm conditions before attempting to tow the craft ashore.

Then came the next headache: the warm, secure hangar on the east arm of the harbour, constructed by the 1955-56 RAAF Flight, was too small for the C-47: a serious blow to plans to have the aircraft reassembled in time to start ANARE's aerial photography program in February. They had to accommodate *Ann Cherie* on the western foreshore, hand-digging pits in ice five feet deep to sink the railway sleepers which would act as anchors, and connecting them to the aircraft with 18-tonne wire ropes. They then bulldozed a snow road 400 metres up the slope from the beach, an operation which took two days, to be able to drag the aircraft to this mooring site[14].

With no wharf at Mawson base, unloading the C-47 from the Thala Dan required construction of a special pontoon to float the aircraft ashore and the use of plastic explosives to break up ice in the bay [Kichenside family collection].

It took three D4 tractors – one hauling, one holding and one static while either of the others changed position – and nine hours to drag the plane up the snow road before having to turn the aircraft around and lower it down a steep pinch to the tiedown area. Miraculously, the only damage was a slight knock to the tail wheel.

ANARE's proposed air photography program for 1960 included 200 hours of survey with the C-47, commencing in February. It would operate initially off the plateau and return to Mawson when the sea ice had consolidated in May, then fly again from the plateau at the end of November for summer operations. Such a scheme had never been attempted – from the start, it was plagued by problems and became a rapid learning curve on human endurance for its youthful leader.

Ann Cherie in her new home on the ice at West Bay, near Mawson base [Kichenside family collection].

Not only was the RAAF Antarctic Flight tasked with the reassembly of the C-47 in deteriorating weather conditions, all hands were needed at the main base to erect a new powerhouse, workshop, transmitter hut and stores sheds before the onset of winter darkness. The base powerhouse had gone up in flames in April the previous year, cutting electrical supplies by 60 per cent[15]. While some expeditioners joked it was good to have one's feet warm for a change, now a new site had to be levelled, concrete foundations poured and frames erected for both this shed and all the new buildings. There were no specialist tradesmen on the 1960 expedition: every man, from physicists to meteorologists, cooks to pilots, became a labourer. After *Thala Dan* departed, the party would be unlikely to see another human being for months – it was their first lesson in working together and getting along.

At Mawson, the scientific and aviation personnel lived together in small huts; there were five in the boy's hut, christened *Shackleton,* with each man having had their own partitioned space. Some wag christened the toilet as *Law Hut.* There was a separate building for kitchen and dining, with two years of supplies on hand in the event of a relief ship being unable to reach them next summer. The boy not only took his turn on a hammer and chisel: he donned an apron as potato peeler, dish washer, and sweep. He also good-naturedly took his turn at night watch and toilet cleaning, which was nobody's favourite job. The urinals had to be emptied down 'Piss Glacier' nearby to the main base, and the unfortunate man rostered on for this task often accompanied the contents down the slippery slope. But as the walls of new buildings rose out of the snow and men realised their latent skills in cooking and cleaning, Kichenside never let on to his Flight his anxiety about the C-47 – which was still sitting idle on its icy bed.

With no hangar to house the C-47, deep pits were dug in the ice to sink railway sleepers as anchors to prevent her being blown away by the notorious Antarctic blizzards. As Squadron Leader, Jim Kichenside recognised the importance of doing his share of the heavy manual work [Kichenside family collection].

The first blizzard of the season hit on March 1, 1960. Most building works had been completed and the new buildings were tied down with steel cables. The C-47-still not operational – was also firmly anchored to the ice. The storm left snowdrifts 3 metres deep in the lee of the huts which would remain unthawed until the following summer. It was March 23 before RAAF personnel were free to return to Western Bay, and after four days of hard work, both wings were re-fitted to the C-47, which was then promptly buried by another blizzard.

When they did excavate it and get the engines running in early April, Bert 'Canary' Carne and Kev Felton had their hands full with oil congealing in the lines as autumn temperatures continued to fall. Still working outdoors in increasing darkness, it was another month before *Ann Cherie* was ready to be moved to the sea ice on May 12. It was a disastrous day. With only one D4 tractor available, the plane was winched away from the tiedown area toward the beach; after being hauled about 80 metres, the plane was secured to compacted snow while the tractor was repositioned. It was at that unfortunate moment the aircraft brakes failed. Kichenside and Dyke at the controls managed to swing the aircraft around but it still hit the tractor broadside, tearing its starboard wing open. The crippled C-47 was taxied to the hangar, into which it could not fit, and tied down, whence it was buried again by 80 knots of blizzard. *Ann Cherie*' s future seemed in doubt before she had flown a single mission.

CHAPTER 19

DOGS IN A PLANE

When everything seems to be going against you, remember the airplane takes off against the wind, not with it.

—Henry Ford

While the Flight grappled with the challenges of the C-47, it was left to the sturdy little workhorse Beaver to support ANARE's field operations.

The de Havilland DHC-2 Beaver proved a sturdy and reliable workhorse in Antarctic conditions, which are recognised as some of the most challenging and dangerous in the world [Kichenside family collection].

The de Havilland DHC-2 Beaver weighed in at just 1.3 tonnes, with a wingspan of only 14.6 metres. Beaver A95-202 arrived at Mawson on February 1, 1960, from Davis station, where it had been delivered by *Magga Dan.* It was equipped with floats so as to land on the yet-unfrozen Horseshoe Harbour and piloted by Dick Cresswell, who had commanded 77 Squadron in Korea and now, as a civilian pilot, had a contract with de Havilland to fly the float plane on the ship. Phil Law was his passenger.

Three days later, the boy returned Cresswell and Law to the *Magga Dan,* now 110 kilometres out to sea, in the little orange plane.

Despite his familial loyalty to the fractious *Ann Cherie,* the boy was already half in love with the Beaver. It was certainly no Meteor, with a cruising speed of just 225 kilometres per hour, but its dour reliability and seeming indifference to the cold charmed him. On March 3, the Beaver was beached and changed from floats to skis as the sea ice rapidly set in. And in late April, he and his new love interest were called into service for one of its most novel but challenging missions of the season.

Law's fleeting visit to Mawson had included a meeting with ANARE surveyor Syd Kirkby, geologist Ric Ruker and radio officer Ken Bennett. The three had an ambitious plan to capitalise on the last of the good summer weather by surveying part of the interior of Enderby Land, 500 kilometres north of Mawson. They would expedite the journey by hitching a ride on the departing *Thala Dan* on February 16; the ship would deliver them to the Enderby coast from where they would sledge south then east to Edward VIII Gulf, carrying out astronomical and trigonometric surveys and studying the geology of the four-billion-year-old mountain outcrops, before being picked up by aircraft at the end of April[1].

Kirkby was extremely experienced in the polar regions, and had personally surveyed more Antarctic territory than any other explorer, including Scott, Shackleton and Mawson[2]. And Law was always eager to continue detailed analysis of Australia's vast Antarctic claim. At 6,500,000 square kilometres, the Australian Antarctic Territory (AAT) is the largest on the continent. In 1953, Foreign Minister Richard Casey described the Antarctic as of vital importance to Australia ... for strategic reasons, lying as it does so close to Australia's back door'[3]. The AAT became the responsibility of Australian government through the *Antarctic Territory Acceptance Act* in 1936, which mandated and prioritised scientific endeavour; while scientific progress was delayed by World War II, Law's tenure as head of ANARE since 1949 had seen thousands of kilometres of coastline mapped[4].

Law now approved Kirkby's field expedition, despite having overruled the initial proposal before leaving Australia for the south. Neither the boy nor Henk Geysen were in favour of the expedition. In addition to his appointment as CO of the RAAF Flight, the boy was also second in charge of Mawson base behind Geysen – the first RAAF officer to serve in such a cross-cultural role. Both Kichenside and Geysen were aware that, after the 1959 fire, every man was needed to assemble the new buildings at Mawson before the blizzard season began, and sending three of their 33 personnel out into the field could seriously harm these efforts.

They also recognised the danger of landing a party on an unmapped shore in Enderby Land. The boy had been on board *Thala Dan* when it ran aground at Davis in 1959, where at one stage it was feared the vessel was going to sink. There was also the problem of retrieving the field party in April: the boy was faced with assembling and testing the C-47, the only aircraft large enough to hold the party, with all of its equipment and sixteen dogs, within the six-week timeframe of Kirkby's return. He urged Law that there was no guarantee the aircraft would be available, but Law was as much a publicist for the Antarctic as he was an explorer, and he knew the achievements of an epic dogsledging expedition would be a significant stimulus to the public appetite for Australia's Antarctic efforts. Law overrode the objections and the expedition proceeded.

Kirkby, Ruker, Bennett and the dogs re-embarked *Thala Dan* for the voyage to Enderby Land on February 16. Their dogs were husky types, much like those which had been instrumental in Amundsen's 1911 successful quest for the South Pole[5]. While the 1960 Mawson party had D4 tractors to drag loads overland, dogs were lighter and faster and provided the safest way to cross sea ice and crevassed territory. And as handler Niels Lied later pointed out, you could not eat a tractor when it ran out of fuel, and dogs were much easier to start in the morning[6]. Kirkby loved the enormous shaggy creatures and called them 'great-hearted loveable lumps'. Kirkby and his colleagues would need every part of the dogs' great hearts for the fifty-three days of frightful conditions they were about to endure.

ANARE surveyor Syd Kirkby was a great admirer of the 1960 expeditions sled dogs, who endured six weeks on the ice in Enderby Land in blizzards of over 160 kilometres per hour [Kichenside family collection].

As the ship neared the landing site at Cape Boothby, Captain Petersen was anxiously watching the echo sounder. The short Antarctic autumn was a harbinger of gales, huge waves, freezing winds and plunging temperatures. And this was one of the first times a ship had entered the dangerous Edward VIII Gulf: with no charts, rapidly closing pack ice and unsounded depths, the potential for disaster was high. Petersen manoeuvred cautiously through the large floes for more than a day before reaching Kloa Point, where the sea floor suddenly shoaled vertically; Petersen signalled full astern just in time to avoid a huge submerged rock. Anxious to escape, Petersen landed the party hastily at the cape: not their preferred landing site, for the ice slope between the shore and the plateau was too steep for the dogs, meaning the three men had to bodily haul almost a tonne of equipment to the top before their trip could even start[7].

This was only the beginning of their trials. The late summer weather now seemed to plummet straight into winter: the men suffered through two weeks of freezing daytime temperatures and nights as cold as-30°C. Body heat melted the ice under their tents and their clothes and sleeping bags were never dry. The party took a month to struggle over the first 65 kilometres as the sledges sank so comprehensively in the snow the men had to help the dogs drag them, sinking knee-deep on every step. They slogged across the ice to the almost-unknown Napier Mountains and the ice plateaus of northern Enderby and Kemp Lands through impenetrable whiteout and blizzards of over 160 kilometres per hour.

The dogs suffered badly both in the wet conditions and from gastric upset from an experimental new dog food developed by the Antarctic Division. Nearing the end of the journey at Kloa Point, the dogs were so starved for fresh meat that they bolted upon sighting a seal: the men had to beat them off before it could be killed and butchered. But as Kirkby was proceeding to feed them, the dogs, maddened by the scent of blood, set upon him in a frenzy, forcing Ruker and Bennett to bodily drag the snapping, baying hounds off him. Kirkby later dismissed the incident as the dogs trying to 'love him to death'—but he could easily have been savaged or even killed[8].

At the end of six weeks, the group had sledged more than 240 kilometres, reaching Kloa Point on April 19, where the boy had flown in two days earlier with the Beaver to drop supplies. With the C-47 still earthbound, he now returned to collect them in the small plane – a risky proposition as the sea ice in the area was badly rafted. He flew over the area repeatedly, often so low the wheels almost touched the ice, searching for a safe touchdown among the sastrugi (wave-like ridges of snow caused by high winds). He had to repeat the trip seven times over the following three days with ice conditions continually changing with tides, currents, and wind. Station doctor Geoff Newton rode shotgun in the plane to tranquilise each dog before it was boarded, and there was so little cargo capacity in the small aircraft that the sledges and most of the scientific and camping equipment had to be left behind to be retrieved with the C-47 months later.

Rafted sea ice presented a significant challenge for pilots seeking a safe landing site in remote Antarctic locations [Kichenside family collection].

The Beaver reeked of wet, comatose dog and the aircraft had only a small fan to combat temperatures as low as-38°C, which could cause pilots and passengers to cramp up and water to freeze in the fuel lines. The boy and his fellow pilots had been given enormous padded Canadian flying suits which they spurned as being too heavy and cumbersome. Any exertion while wearing these outfits caused potentially deadly cold sweat to form under the heavy layers which could cause dehydration or, worse, a life-threatening chill. The boy preferred his old Korea ensemble of a string vest, shirt, light jumper, and a windbreaker – layers he could easily remove or replace during any physical work.

Jim Kichenside (right) and his fellow Antarctic pilots eschewed the heavy padded flying suits provided to them in favour of layers of lighter clothing which could be progressively added or removed to prevent heavy perspiration or dangerous chills [Kichenside family collection].

Dogs in a plane ...The expedition's doctor, Geoff Newton, was often required to sedate the sled dogs prior to a flight to prevent trouble in the small aircraft cabins [Kichenside family collection].

But the cold and the reek were not the reasons the Kloa Point retrieval troubled him. Despite the achievements of Kirkby and his companions over their six-week ordeal, the aircraft and both RAAF and ANARE personnel had been put at risk for a journey both Kichenside and Geysen had vetoed. The dogs were had not had sufficient running to condition them for the tough going, the weather had been terrible, and aircraft access at Kloa Point almost impossible[9]. Having three expeditioners absent for six weeks meant the remainder often had to double up on shifts and put aside regular duties to get the base buildings up. Differences between the RAAF and Law on issues of command, control and operational planning had arisen – not for the first time.

While he had agreed to use the Beaver to retrieve the dog teams, the boy and Geysen now placed a moratorium on any further long flights with the little plane until the back-up C-47 was available.

CHAPTER 20

THE TROUBLE WITH ANN CHERIE

Pilots take no special joy in walking.
—Neil Armstrong

Lambert Glacier, Mac. Robertson Land
Antarctica
May 22, 1960

Black mountain tops imprisoned in a frozen sea. A tsunami of ice slowly swallowing mountain ranges whole and subsuming the great horseshoe of Prydz Bay.

They puttered above those mountain tops like a languid orange bumblebee, buzzing slowly homeward, the little Beaver the only spot of colour among the frozen peaks. The boy glanced at the altimeter as they cleared the main outlet of the glacier, with its ice-streaked black cliffs: 6500 feet. The little aircraft was droning along steadily with the sea on his right and his two passengers dozing – Doc Newton in the copilot's seat, and Canary Carne snoring in the back, his big square chin and heavy grey beard resting on his chest. The boy, though, was glad to be awake and coasting among the stratus clouds through what might be the last glimpse of sunlight before winter truly closed in. Beneath them was the Lambert Glacier – the largest in the entire world. That simple fact thrilled him as though he were still a schoolboy: that he was flying over something so large nobody in the world could beat it.

In Antarctica, these jutting peaks represent mountains as high as those in the Alps which are subsumed by ice that may be millions of years old [Kichenside family collection].

And then she dived. Like a rodeo bronco out of a chute, the Beaver gave three terrible bucks which jerked the passengers out of their slumber with yells – then she began to plummet toward the ice, shaking and vibrating as though an invisible giant were trying to tear her apart.

'Hang on!' the boy bellowed over the cacophony. *Bloody hell-what was happening?* He hauled the stick to the right as they fell, trying to turn away from the yawing black cliffs, and thrust it forward to full power, the engine bellowing protest as it fought to keep the plane airborne against the downdraft. The stick shook, the fuselage shook, and as the altimeter spun backward and his passengers hollered in fright, he wondered crazily what would give out first – the wings, the prop, or would the whole thing just split apart like a pinata?

One thousand feet. The ice was coming up real fast now. 'Righto, you blokes,' he shouted, 'brace yourselves – we might hit pretty hard!'

Five hundred feet. The yelling had given way to Hail Marys.

Three hundred feet. Blue ripples of rafted ice, like acres of upturned crystal spears. But if he was going to be smashed apart upon them, he was going to die with the throttle full open and fighting every inch of the fall.

***

Antarctic weather conditions are among the most unique and challenging to aviation in the world. There are the visible phenomena –

blizzards, cloud, bizarre mirages and whiteout. The 1960 Flight painted drums black and set them out on the sea ice with lit oil wicks in them to define the Mawson runway during whiteout, but setting a rate of descent when the ground is invisible is little more than educated guesswork: waiting for the skis to hit the ground and landing by feel. Likewise, in cloud, the first glimpse of the runway came almost as the plane reached it. It was a matter of trusting the instruments and not allowing emotions to intervene, with the brain and eyes telling the pilot one thing and the instruments something else altogether. The resulting fear and conflict and confusion could sometimes end in a hell of a bang.

But Antarctic geography and meteorology also combine to produce invisible phenomena deadly to aircraft. Katabatic winds produce such severe and unseen turbulence as to punch an aircraft out of the sky in mere seconds. Radiative cooling over the Antarctic ice sheet produces very cold, dense air that flows downward away from the elevated areas and is replaced by subsiding air from above. The resulting wind accelerates downhill into the confluence of glacial valleys and low-pressure systems near the coast: roaring clear air gusting at over 300 kilometres per hour[1].

Douglas Mawson first noted the phenomena on the BANZARE expedition, flying a Gypsy Moth over pack ice in 1929. The Moth cruised at about 6000 feet and was caught in a downdraft on one sortie which instantly plummeted the aircraft over 1000 feet[2]. In 1960, ANARE commissioned two Hiller 12C helicopters for use on survey flights around Wilkes station; one was hit by 70 knot winds and violent turbulence off the polar plateau near Vincennes Bay. The machine was destroyed in the subsequent crash; fortunately, its two occupants escaped with only minor injuries.

The boy's own first unexpected encounter with the katabatic winds came just months later while flying over the gigantic Lambert Glacier, near the Prince Charles Mountains between Mawson and Davis. This sector contains the highest peaks in the Australian Antarctic Territory: peaks up to 13,000 feet high, although only 3000 or 4000 feet are visible, the remainder trapped in prehistoric ice. The glacier itself is 100 kilometres wide and 400 kilometres long, a slow-moving ancient ice train which may be millions of years old. Crossing this ice empire in May, the Beaver was, without warning, almost flung out of the air by the worst turbulence Jim Kichenside had ever experienced.

The aircraft, with base surgeon Geoff Newton and engine fitter Bert Carne on board, was returning from Davis where the doctor had been treating a sick expeditioner, when it was sent plummeting by a sudden downdraft. The only chance to break free was to apply full power to the frail plane. The Beaver had plunged from 6500 feet to just 300 feet, and all on board were preparing for a catastrophic impact when the aircraft was abruptly released, climbing airily away as though nothing had happened. The passengers were very green around the gills afterwards. The boy didn't panic, because that's what he had been trained for: constant reconnaissance, decision-making under extreme pressure, reacting to an ever-changing environment, and above all, keeping the aircraft intact – because, he said afterward, if you crash the aircraft, nobody down here could replace it: or you.

Nonetheless, in such extreme and unpredictable flying conditions, it was a great achievement that the RAAF had never lost a life in Antarctica.

***

Late in May, polar winter darkness began to descend upon the Antarctic. Winter sea ice extended a skirt of over 20 million square kilometres around the continent, forming first from pack ice in sheltered bays and reaching northwards across open ocean as the sea temperature decreased. The continual sunlight of summer fizzled away and temperatures on the coast dropped below-25°C. The auroral physicists were in their element, with near continual darkness to study the skies. But in between Beaver missions, slushie duties and ever-shortening days, the RAAF Flight were still grappling with the refractory C-47.

The disastrous attempt to tow the C-47 on May 12 meant another five weeks on the ice at Mawson for repairs in the most primitive conditions, with wind chill plummeting the temperatures to-40°C and forcing them to rivet components by hand as the air-compressors froze. Control surfaces had to be removed to clear the snow and ice build-up. The damaged skin sections were re-doped, but the frigid air dried the dope before the fabric was taut. Engine runs were terminated after pressure gauges failed due to moisture freezing in the lines. And the decree of 'short-range flights only in the Beaver while the C-47 was unserviceable had to be rescinded – the urgent call for the doctor at Davis in late May which had almost ended in disaster was backed by an unofficial commitment from the Russians to provide search and rescue capabilities if required: a deal unthinkable anywhere else in the Cold War-riven world.

By June 11, the wing was patched and another test flight attempted. But *Ann Cherie'* s brakes only worked intermittently, and even then only after 50 minutes of fruitless taxiing. An attempt to take off on June 13 was aborted when a hydraulic line ruptured and hydraulic fluid splattered into the cockpit. But the following day, after heating the undercarriage with hot air for five hours to ease the brakes, the C-47 finally got airborne with the boy in the pilot's seat. He landed her almost immediately to check the wing patch, then took off again for another 15 glorious minutes roaring along above the dark ice. His only comment on the trial afterward: 'Piece of cake.'

The C-47 was repeatedly buried by blizzards in her outdoor home at West Bay as the Flight struggled to prepare her for operational duty [Kichenside family collection].

Jim Kichenside at the controls of the C-47 as she prepared for her first take-off in the Antarctic on June 14, 1960 [Kichenside family collection].

With only a handful of daylight hours each day and continuing poor weather (including a temperature of-57°C recorded while refuelling the Beaver by hand), flying was abandoned for the remainder of June. The only exception was a grand fly-past of the base on Midwinter's Day, June 25. The winter solstice is a traditional time of celebration for polar wintering expeditions, and at Mawson, this meant a formal dinner, speeches and a fancy-dress party featuring many bearded ladies with improbably hairy legs. In the chink of light around midday, the RAAF crew pulled the Beaver out of the hangar, executed one buzzing circuit over the station, then put it away and headed for the feast amidst enormous cheers[3].

Winter solstice—the day of the year that has the fewest daylight hours—usually occurs in late June in Antarctica and is traditionally celebrated with a grand shindig. In 1960, the 33 expeditioners revelled in a fancy-dress party, with Jim Kichenside (left) and fellow pilot Graham Dyke (right) both getting into the spirit [Kichenside family collection].

But the merriment was short-lived. In July, the wrangle with *Ann Cherie* and its obdurate icing problems resumed. The undercarriage refused to retract, brake drums and shoes froze together, and frozen fluid jammed in the carburettor. To further complicate operations, the boy flew the Beaver to the Stanton Islands to pick up a sledging party on July 8 but during a heavy landing on the rafted ice, the tail wheel skid snapped, jamming the rudder and elevator controls; it was a fortnight before they could cobble together the replacement parts and resume flying[4].

But on July 9, with Graham Dyke in the chair, *Ann Cherie* successfully flew at 16,000 feet for the first time. It was the culmination of five painful months on the ice, walking over a kilometre each way to the aircraft each day (which could take an hour if a blizzard was up), and risking snow blindness, frostbite, and hypothermia from the extreme windchill.

***

There is no escape anywhere. You are hemmed in on every side by your own inadequacies and the crowding pressure of your associates.

—Richard Byrd

Perpetual darkness makes winter the most difficult time for many Antarctic expeditioners. The unvarying routines, lack of natural light and claustrophobic conditions can breed physiological and emotional reactions ranging from irritability to sleep disorders and depression. At Mawson in 1960, the isolation was close to total, meaning there was no real escape from each other or the base. The men had been away from home almost seven months with barely a word of news or exchange with loved ones. Douglas Mawson's 1911 Australasian Antarctic Expedition was the first to establish an Antarctic radio link, and in 1960, the Mawson radio staff, led by Graeme 'Chompers' Currie, were on shift 16 hours a day, with official messages to other Antarctic bases and Australia still sent by Morse code. But personal messages were restricted, and unless it was an emergency, most men had no or little contact with home.

While the restriction seemed austere, the boy agreed with Phillip Law's view that access to personal communications could cause more problems than it solved. Bad news from home was often stressful and unsettling for men not in a position to act upon it. Despite having never wintered on the continent, Law was conscious of the impact of both isolation and darkness on morale. He provided a good quality library and appetising food for the expeditioners, despite the extra cost. On Saturday nights, a screening of cine films was accompanied by chocolates, wines and ports (although most of the men preferred beer).

ANARE physicist George Cresswell (left) had his beloved Velocette motorbike loaded on the Thala Dan when he was unable to sell it before departing for Antarctica. The bike became a prime source of entertainment on recreation days in 1960. In this photograph, Jim Kichenside (centre) and Viv Hill (right) prepare to embark on a sled ride behind the bike [Kichenside family collection].

Darts were a popular form of recreation, although physicist George Cresswell wryly observed there was little point playing against the RAAF pilots, whose superior hand-eye coordination made them unbeatable. Weather observer Bill Dick produced a fortnightly newspaper, *Katabatic,* full of sly humour and fake news. And Sundays were usually a day of rest, an opportunity for trips to nearby penguin rookeries, islands or mountains, either aboard the old International army truck (which Henk

Geysen claimed 'jumped tide-cracks like a two-year-old'), or George Cresswel's motorbike bucketing across the corrugated ice. Cresswel's beloved 350cc Velocette had been winched aboard *Thala Dan* when he had been unable to sell it before their departure from Melbourne. Now, often with a dog sled and two or three expeditioners in tow, it was a principal source of entertainment on those precious free Sundays[5].

On their days off, the expeditioners and RAAF crews often took trips to nearby islands and glaciers. Jim Kichenside is pictured with an emperor penguin chick during a trip to Taylor Glacier [Kichenside family collection].

Inherent in the principles of operational planning are flexibility and morale. Jim

Kichenside's military career had taught him that morale and getting along together went beyond the provision of books, beer and chocolate bars. It is a complex issue for those facing the isolation of Antarctica. Sometimes personality traits, only revealed when the isolation and cold set in, complicated team dynamics. The psychological tests which the expeditioners had taken before departure had been rudimentary, and many men confessed to saying whatever they thought the doctors wanted to hear so they would be selected for the trip south.

Some polar explorers had specific characteristics in mind when selecting their teams: Amundsen had wanted men with a 'flamboyant fatalism to which risk appeals', Shackleton 'men able to live together in harmony', and Mawson 'dash and the recuperative powers of youth'[6]. The boy had sat on the selection panel for the 1960 Flight, and was aware of the wide range of personalities among the men in his small outfit, with their different levels of tolerance to pain and loneliness and disappointment. His best solution was to deal with them all as individuals rather than imposing the same system on everyone and expecting them to conform.

***

Improved weather and the tentative return of the sun in August brought hope of starting the summer flying program on the 25th. The C-47 made its first significant reconnaissance flight on August 16, a 1700kilometre round trip above previously unexplored territory to the south-west. Shortly afterward, seven of the contingent, including the boy, Graham Dyke, and Felton, departed for Davis Station with both aircraft, where they would remain for five weeks to conduct survey and photographic operations in that region.

The Australian base at Davis was established in 1957 during the International Geophysical Year, a collaborative effort by twelve nations to support research and better understand the Earth's climate and environment. Named in honour of John King Davis, who had captained Mawson's ship *Discovery* in 1929, it was a far smaller base than Mawson, with just eight men on station. They were led by 24-year-old law graduate Ian Douglas – another eminent name in the history of Australian Antarctic aviation. His father, Group Captain Eric Douglas, flew Gypsy Moths for Mawson during the 1929-31 BANZARE expeditions and had been a member of the 1935-36 RAAF Antarctic search and rescue expedition that located the missing Ellsworth; he gave his son the middle name Ellsworth in tribute to his subsequent friendship with the American explorer[7].

Jim Kichenside and six members of his RAAF Flight spent five weeks at Davis station in 1960, undertaking aerial photographic surveys. A particularly heavy snowfall buried some of the buildings at the base during their stay: Jim Kichenside is seen here emerging from a special hatch in the roof of one of them [Kichenside family collection].

Now, the younger Douglas went out of his way to welcome the RAAF men after their rigours on the ice at Mawson. He graciously lost most of his precious beer supplies to their impressive skill at bridge, and his consideration for their wellbeing had Douglas anointed as an honorary 'Mawson man'. Kichenside even flew him (unofficially) to Mawson for a night in mid-September while on a quick flit for spare parts, to repay his kindness and give the young man a brief respite. Douglas would later repay the boy twice over in his own time of need.

***

Unfavourable weather and continued unreliability of the C-47 meant only one flight between September 1 and 20, and even after returning to Mawson in October, the litany of frustrations continued, with a burnt-out starboard engine then days of unrelenting blizzards. The engine was changed but the aircraft was not cleared to fly again until November 13[8].

The continuing unreliability of the starboard engine of the C-47 forced a complete engine change in October 1960 as the summer flying season approached [Kichenside family collection].

CHAPTER 21

BEFORE THE STORM

The answer to every problem involved penguins.
—Rick Riordan

As November moved toward December, summer made its timorous approach over the white Antarctic horizon. Huts which had been half buried in snow now became scenes of frenetic activity, with preparations for intensive exploration, survey, and geological investigations. The flying rate at last accelerated, with photographic missions and depot operations in support of field parties in the Prince Charles Mountains and Enderby Land. And it was almost time to move the C-47 to her summer home in the North Masson Range for a revolutionary new phase in Antarctic air operations-summer flights from a blue-ice runway.

In the winter, sea ice in the frozen Horseshoe Harbour made a natural site for aircraft take-offs and landings. But the sea ice broke up in November, meaning aircraft could not exploit the best flying conditions of the year. Normally, loss of the ice would spell the end of aviation operations until the following autumn.

But Philip Law had an ambitious scheme for year-round operations out of Mawson by utilising the ice retained on the polar plateau behind the station to continue the pace of aerial exploration, survey and research.

The site for the summer ice runway in the Masson Range was some distance from the ice runway at Gwamm trialled by Sandercock's 1959 Flight, where their two Beavers had been wrecked by a summer blizzard. The new site, 16 kilometres south-west of Mawson, was chosen for the availability of rock to secure both a wind fence and the caravans that would form workshops and accommodation for the summer flight crews[1]. The 1960 Flight christened the site Rumdoodle, from the 1956 comedy novel by W.E. Bowman, *The Ascent of Rum Doodle*, which they had found a copy of in Law's expedition library.

The Masson Range, site of the Rumdoodle ice runway, was located 16 kilometres south-west of the main base at Mawson [Kichenside family collection].

The 16-kilometre trip took two hours to negotiate by tracked vehicle, even in good weather. Four caravans and a 6 KVA generator had been towed to the site back in February, and a party including the boy, Felton, and meteorologist Neil Streten lived in a caravan for several weeks to measure wind velocities, directions, and cloud ceilings, while the remaining RAAF staff worked on construction of a wind fence in the workshop at Mawson. Their first blizzard on the plateau in February was an early demonstration of the suddenness and violence with which plateau weather could turn as their caravans strained alarmingly against their guy ropes[2].

Kev Felton, John Arthur, Jim Kichenside, and ANARE meteorologist Neil Streten raise an Australian flag on their first visit to Rumdoodle, February 22, 1960 [Kichenside family collection].

The Flight had been able to do little at the site during winter, not only because of the ferocious weather and darkness but also the unreliability of the generator, which was finally replaced in November. The Flight could now turn their attention toward preparation of the blue-ice runway on which the C-47 would land with wheels, rather than skis. But as the temperature rose, Kichenside noted with concern the ice was losing its characteristic rippled winter surface, which provided a landing aircraft with critical traction. Ice observations from the Mawson plateau as early as 1955 had shown this rate of melt, or ablation, was highest in summer, increasing from around 0.08 centimetres per day to a peak of 2.75 centimetres per day in January, accompanied by disintegration of the top 10 centimetres of ice surface[3]. Not only did this pose a risk to the viability of the landing surface, but the aircraft tiedowns dug into the ice could also potentially be weakened.

It was just as the Russians from Mirnyy Base had warned. Soviet expeditioners transited through Mawson on four occasions in 1960, including landing an aircraft on the blue ice at Gwamm on March 6 at the end of the 1959-60 summer – only narrowly avoiding disaster on the slippery surface. Contact with the Russian expeditions was both intriguing and highly informative for the Australian airmen. The Mawson base radio operator, Oleg Zakharov, was of Russian descent and spoke that language fluently, facilitating much of the communication between the parties. The Russian aircraft captain, whom the boy knew only as Vladimir, in turn spoke excellent English as his wife was an English teacher in Moscow, and a camaraderie quickly sprang up between he and the boy, despite the presence of a *commissar* to supposedly police all the Russian interactions with their Australian hosts. Vladimir and Kichenside were close in age and, while he liked the big Russian for his frankness and hearty laugh, the boy also recognised this was a valuable opportunity to learn about cold weather aircraft operations from the experts.

The Russians were nervous about the proposed plateau scheme behind Mawson. In Soviet experience, areas of blue ice which had been swept clear of snow indicated strong local winds and turbulence which, in concert with ablation, made summer plateau operations untenable. Had Kichenside known it, the RAAF too, had been uneasy about stationing aircraft permanently on the plateau, even before

Sandercock's experience of the previous year. In April 1959, the Department of Air explicitly warned ANARE of the dangers of wind on the plateau, in particular that 'the turbulence and extremely high winds experienced there makes the mooring of an aircraft with a large wing area impracticable due to the stress imposed on the airframe.'[4] Law refuted the claim of winds in the order of 150 knots on the Mawson ice plateau – a claim which was supported by Bureau of Meteorology data[5]. He then advised the Department of Treasury on June 22, 1959, that he was 'prepared to accept (fiscal) responsibility for tethering the aircraft on the plateau during the summer months', and the plan went ahead[6].

Australian expeditioners at Mawson pictured with visiting Russians from the Mirnyy base in eastern Antarctica. Russian crews transited through Mawson on 4 occasions in 1960 and found a hospitable welcome. Jim Kichenside (front row, third from left) was eager to learn from their extensive experience of operations on blue ice runways [Kichenside family collection].

***

Kitchen hut, Mawson Station
Antarctica
November 14, 1960

It was always stifling in the cooking hut, and the man within always seemed to be in his shirt sleeves, regardless of whatever blizzard was howling outside. Ralph Dyer was not the boy's traditional idea of a cook. Despite his white apron, he was not chubby or jolly or red-faced, and he did not hit his underlings on the noggin with wooden spoons, even when their assistance was more hindrance than help. Dyer was lean, dark-haired and intense, and he was a man with plenty of problems to contend with, including dwindling supplies of fresh food and the constant need to devise new dishes from the same old rations.

ANARE cook Ralph Dyer (third from left) was rarely seen outside his beloved kitchen, but was persuaded by Jim Kichenside to take a flight on the Beaver in November 1960 – it was his first ever flight and an experience he never forgot [Kichenside family collection].

Dyer looked up from his floured board and saw the boy leaning on the kitchen doorframe. 'G'day, Jim.' He turned quickly to the big stovetop and picked up a tray of golden scones with a towel. 'Fresh out of the oven, 'fraid we used the last of the raisins yesterday for the fruit cake, but I put a bit of beer in these – they should be light as a feather.'

The boy smiled and, while not in the least hungry, took one and bit into it. It was perfectly fluffy inside. The man truly was a miracle worker, but he was seen so rarely outside his beloved kitchen that he was starting to look like a ghost from lack of sunlight.

The boy waved away the still-proffered tray and took up a dishtowel instead. 'Ralphie,' he said, starting on the soapy pots on the draining board, 'what do you think about penguins?'

***

Enderby Land, between Dronning Maud Land and Kemp Land on the east Antarctic coast, was discovered by Captain John Biscoe in 1831 and named after his employers, brothers Charles, Henry and George Enderby, who operated the London-based whaling and sealing firm British Southern Whale Fishing Company. The area had been one of focus during Mawson's 1929-31 BANZARE expeditions, and ANARE surveyor Syd Kirkby was also familiar with the place, given his experience with the dog teams back in April. By November 1960, Kirkby was keen to return to establish more astrofixes to continue mapping in the area. Before his own focus turned completely to Rumdoodle, the boy volunteered to take the Beaver and camp in the field with Kirkby to support his November expedition.

Ever-eager for action, Kev Felton also volunteered to go – 'to keep the plane in shape' – and, with room for one more on board, the boy, over another excellent dinner, thought of

Ralph Dyer squirrelling away in the kitchen with his ever-diminishing supplies. He could take Dyer up for a day's rest, and the cook could return in the C-47 when it came to deliver fuel. Dyer was frankly astonished at the offer—in fact, he still looked a little punch-drunk at his good fortune as they hoisted him into the Beaver at dawn on November 15 for the first flight of his life.

Kirkby made camp on the sea ice in the lee of Mount Christensen on Amundsen Bay, a sweeping cove discovered by Mawson in 1930. There was a flat area more than 8 kilometres long suitable for landing both the Beaver and C-47, with a metre of perfect smooth snow cover and ice up to 46 inches thick. Kichenside described the surface as the best I have landed on in Antarctica ... snow cover as smooth as a billiard top.'[7]

Jim Kichenside, Kev Felton, and ANARE surveyor Syd Kirkby spent ten days in the field in Enderby Land in November 1960, in simple tent accommodation with only a pedal wireless for communication back to Mawson [Kichenside family collection].

With the Beaver crew having scoped out a safe landing site, Graham Dyke delivered fuel in the C-47 on the afternoon of the 15th and transported Dyer back to Mawson. His few hours away from the base and the flight on the Beaver had brought a new high colour into Dyer's face. As he clambered on board the C-47, the cook paused, turned back and grasped the boy by the arm. 'The greatest experience of my life,' he said, and there was a suspicious brightness about his eyes. '*The greatest experience of my life,*'

The first three days' flying in Enderby Land were marred by unstable atmospheric conditions which effectively blacked out radio contact back to Mawson. The men passed the enforced downtime by fishing through the ice with bacon rind as bait. On one afternoon, they snagged around 100 trout-sized fish in two hours, which provided a welcome relief from tinned rations. But by the 19th, the trio were in the air and ranging as far inland as the distant western boundary of the Australian Antarctic Territory, taking astro fixes and aerial photography of previously untrodden landscapes.

A large group of emperor penguins was spotted from the air at Amundsen Bay in November 1960 and Kichenside, Kirkby, and Felton returned to the area on foot to count and observe them [Kichenside family collection].

As they returned to camp one day, they sighted a large aggregation of emperor penguins from the air on the east side of Mount Riiser-Larsen, near the mouth of Amundsen Bay. *Aptenodytes forsteri,* the world's largest penguin, stands up to one metre tall and is found only in the Antarctic. Emperors uniquely breed in winter to ensure fledglings leave the ice in summer when food is plentiful. Unlike their small and noisy cousin the Adelie penguin, which makes a nest of pebbles, male emperors nurse the egg in an abdominal pouch while females trek across the sea ice to feed; the males pack into huddles of up to 5000 birds and endure winter temperatures of-70°C and winds of over 200 kilometres per hour.

In 2009, there were more than 30 known emperor penguin colonies on the continent, with five breeding colonies on the Mawson coast including at Kloa and Taylor Glacier. Kirkby himself had noted a colony at Amundsen Bay in 1956[8]. After overflying this new sighting and estimating up to 2000 birds, the three walked back to the area from their camp. While Adelie penguins can be aggressive, the emperors were gentle and had no fear. Felton found an abandoned chick and carried the poor creature back to the camp, naming him "Perce". The men tried to tempt the chick with sardines and milk, but their kindly efforts were in vain; the little emperor died during the night. Mortality among emperor penguins is high – many eggs do not hatch and of those that do, 25 per cent of chicks perish within the first few months.

Syd Kirkby with "Perce" the abandoned emperor penguin chick. The expeditioners attempted to feed the little creature but he did not survive [Kichenside family collection].

The final flight of the Enderby Land expedition was for astrofixes in the Napier Mountains, where the party spent a night at 5400ft on November 26. Their afternoon radio sked with Mawson was crackly, but they got the message that Streten warned the weather was closing in. And he was right: an hour into the return flight to Mawson, potentially deadly cloud forced the aircraft to climb to over 10,000 feet. Ice began to form ominously on the tail, wings and windscreen, the engine was straining, and now Kichenside's quietly anxious eye turned to the dwindling fuel level. Much more of this and they might have to put down, meaning a long and very cold wait for aid. When they did finally land successfully at Mawson, happily in time for breakfast and a hot shower, there were just four gallons of fuel – one bucketful – left in the tank[9].

But while there was much admiration of the safe arrival, Kichenside had not left things to chance, He had left a drum of fuel at the Amundsen Bay camp in case they had had to turn back, and even if they had run out of gas during the flight, he had a clear contingency plan – to put down on the sea ice and radio in for a fuel drop. So while there had been little margin for error, he felt there was, in reality, no true danger – his operational planning had ticked all the boxes and brought his passengers back safely. Kichenside was, nonetheless, suitably gratified by the reliability of the Beaver in having stayed outside of its hangar for more than ten days and given no mechanical trouble. The endeavour was, however, as he noted in his field report, "successful provided (the aircraft) was based in a suitable area away from plateau slopes." The summer plateau flying season was approaching, and he was well aware of the stresses the aircraft could be exposed to on the exposed runway at Rumdoodle – katabatic wind, blizzards, and ice storms. It was a very different prospect to the smooth snows and mild coastal conditions of Enderby Land.

***

In 1965, a glacier 8 kilometres wide and 28 kilometres long, flowing north-east into the southern part of the Hannan Ice Shelf in Enderby Land, was officially named Kichenside Glacier by the Antarctic Names Committee of Australia[10]. The site, located at 67°76'S 47°6'E, was first charted by ANARE aircraft in 1956; the boy had unknowingly flown over it himself during Kirkby's Enderby Land expedition of November 1960. His surname, Kichenside, is thought to be a variant of the old north-eastern English name Catcheside, which coincidentally translates as 'cold cheer hill'.

The policy on naming of the Committee for Geographical Names in Australasia states that the names of living people are not conferred on landscape features unless that person had contributed significantly to the area where the feature was located, and even then, only in exceptional circumstances[11]. The honour now seemed a fitting reward for the boy's loyalty, operational planning and determination in the demanding year of 1960.

But as Kichenside, Felton and Kirkby flew back to Mawson from Enderby Land late in 1960, they were unaware their year of challenges was very far from over.

CHAPTER 22

BLOWN AWAY

We had discovered an accursed country.
We had found the Home of the Blizzard.
—Douglas Mawson

Rumdoodle camp, North Masson Range
Antarctica
December 8, 1960

'Baked beans *again?* The men poked morosely at the gloopy mess on the tin plates. 'Couldn't old Ralphie pack us anything else?'

'But if Kev here could at least warm them up without charring them black...'

'Aw, come on, you blokes – how about someone else take a turn on the stove if you're all going to whinge?'

The boy barely lifted his head as this banter went on about him. He was seated at the back of the caravan with Ken Assender, poring over a sheet of paper and looking perplexed. 'This report of Streten's says we could get hit, maybe tonight or tomorrow,' he said. He brushed the curtain back and peered outside at the overcast skies and softly falling snow. 'There's not a breath of wind.' He turned back to the forecast. 'He's usually pretty close to the mark though...'

'What do you want to do about a watch up on the runway?' Assender asked.

The boy glanced at the clock: it was nearly midnight. 'Look, if Streten's right and there's a chance the weather could turn bad, I don't want anyone up there tonight,' he said. 'If the radio link was working, it'd be a different story. But until we get it back up again, we're all staying put.'

Almost in answer, there came a soft yowl of wind from outside, and the caravan shook a little. Assender, who had half risen, sat down again. 'Jim, are you sure?'

The caravan rattled this time; the wind was louder, a gust instead of a puff. The other men, who'd pulled out a pack of cards, now paused too, watching him.

The boy squared his shoulders. 'No radio – no watch. Everything is tied down up there, so it'll be–' The caravan shook again, and all eyes turned out the window and up the dark slope, to where the two aircraft lay in the semi-dark, softly blanketed in snow. He had been going to say, 'It'll be right', but now he let the sentence trail away, unfinished.

***

December 8, 1960 was a significant date in 1960 Flight operations – the day both aircraft arrived at Rumdoodle to begin summer operations.

With the breakup of sea ice in November, the C-47 had already been flying out of the Masson Range for several weeks. It was now joined by the Beaver, the wind-fence was up, and the five caravans forming the RAAF camp – three for quarters, one for the radios, and one for catering – were guyed down in a rocky hollow below the plateau. There was a feeling of euphoria among the Flight – it had been a long year, much of it characterised by the struggle to keep the C-47 serviceable. But now their good humour was tempered by a report from Mawson meteorologist Neil Streten of the possibility of a blizzard that night or the next day.

Antarctica is the windiest continent on earth, where gale force winds can blow snow and grit for days at a time, reducing visibility to less than an arm's length, freezing eyelashes and exposed skin. The 1911-14 Mawson expedition experienced some of the worst weather conditions on record, unwittingly camping at one of the windiest places in the world at Cape Denison. Photographer Frank Hurley was almost carried away by a 193 kilometre per hour wind gust, despite lumping 36 kilograms of camera gear on his back at the time[1].

While the 1960 Flight had been through blizzards before, Kichenside had an ominous feeling on this first night on the plateau. Pressure on ANARE's limited resources meant the D4 tractors needed to supplement the planes' tiedowns behind the wind fence were away in the field with expedition parties – the Flight had only one of the three they needed. Securing the aircraft in such an exposed location as the Rumdoodle runway was of critical importance. After the loss of the Beavers at Gwamm the previous year, the boy had paid close attention during a February 11 visit to Mawson from a Russian aircraft transiting for fuel. The Russians had shared their techniques for tying down aircraft in high wind, including only using a single tiedown point for the aircraft nose and using wire rope of at least 20mm diameter. The Russians kept their tied aircraft on skis, not wheels, so they could slide sideways in high wind without damaging the undercarriage, and fitted wind-spoilers which allowed tied aircraft to survive winds of up to 200 kilometres per hour[2].

The wind fence constructed at Rumdoodle to break up the katabatic air flow and high winds which could damage aircraft tied down on the plateau. The fence remained intact during the blizzard of December 9, 1960, but was not enough to save the planes [Kichenside family collection].

Back in May, Kichenside's men had sunk six tiedown holes to a depth of over 1.2 metres into the Rumdoodle ice, and Ken Assender noted in his diary, 'If the Dak pulls these tiedowns out, I will be very much surprised. In fact, if anything short of an atomic explosion moves them, I'll be surprised.'[3] Windlift spoilers had also been fitted, but having a couple of 8 tonne bulldozers as additional anchor points would have put the boy's mind more at rest as the weather closed in[4].

His other problem was the stuttering radio link between the caravan up on the airfield and those in the hollow below—without it, he didn't want any of his men taking watch on the plateau that night. He elected to keep all of his personnel in the base camp, despite the wind remaining below 25 knots (46 kilometres per hour) in the evening, trusting their preparations on the plateau would hold. After all, there was nowhere else for them now to take the aircraft: there was no ice to land on at Mawson, and the only possible safe haven was the Russian base at Mirnyy, a trip which would have required refuelling at Davis, where they could land only between May and October when the sea ice was intact: it was out of the question now.

The storm hit at 2.30am on the morning of December 9. There was a sudden roar like an avalanche, then the wind crashed into the hollow, shaking the caravans like a dog with a rat. The old vans were fixed to rock with steel guy ropes, but the cables strained up to a metre at a time under the fearsome gusts. The boy quickly drafted the men into pairs and they pulled on crampons in the dark, struggling through blinding snow to tighten the guys as they were buffeted and blown over by the storm. He was relieved to count heads on the return and find all of the crew still present, although many had faces peppered red by flying shards of ice.

It wasn't until 8am next day, when visibility lifted slightly but flying snow continued to blot out the landscape, that he proposed an attempt to reach the aircraft. Kev Felton climbed onto their sole D4 tractor, and the boy, Dyke and airframe fitter Mick Murphy hunkered down on a sledge behind, still being pelted with chips of ice and bullets of snow in the 185 kilometres per hour blast. They were less than halfway up the slope when the storm closed down once more and the world disappeared into a wall of white, leaving them to crawl onward by dead reckoning alone.

On the plateau, they were met with a scene of catastrophe. The C-47 was gone. Nothing remained but its broken moorings, the two 15-tonne and one 7.5-tonne cables now flying in the blizzard like sad steel streamers. The Beaver had disintegrated around its own tiedowns: the wings were torn off and the fuselage had snapped in two, the front half flipped on its back. But there was no opportunity to stand and survey the heartbreaking scene. Even with crampons, the blizzard hurled the men off their feet and sent them sliding across the treacherous ice. The boy could not shout a retreat; he had to grab coats and shoulders and waists, dragging them bodily back to the D4. But conditions deteriorated so that even when they were back in the hollow, when Felton tried to re-guy one of the caravans again, he was picked up and thrown five metres across the ice before impacting a large rock, forcing him to crawl, winded and groaning, back to the caravan.

The remains of the Beaver after the 42 hour blizzard at Rumdoodle on December 9, 1960. Peak wind gusts of up to 300 kilometres per hour destroyed the aircraft – contemplating the remains of the faithful little plane was described by Kichenside as 'heartbreaking' [Kichenside family collection].

By now, their weather recording instruments were off the scale; Streten's subsequent analysis suggested peak wind gusts above 300 kilometres per hour[5]. All contact with Mawson disappeared as their radio aerials blew away; Don Monks bravely jury-rigged a mast, but the storm still carried off any attempt to reach the outside world. At midday, they made another attempt to return to the airfield to search for *Ann Cherie*.

The only part of the Beaver now remaining was the fuselage and starboard wing. The workshop caravan had disappeared too: the party followed the drag marks with the D4 until the force of wind became so great it threatened to stall the tractor. They had to turn back without finding the van.

At 4pm, 'Baz' Rutter looked out of the caravan in the hollow and saw 160-kilogram drums of fuel dancing across the ice on their ends. The Flight spent another sleepless night with their flimsy shelters being battered by the storm. And the risk of hypothermia set in next morning when, at 6am on December 10, drifts of snow cut their connection to the generator. It took four hours of digging against wind which flung the snow right back where it been dug from, before power was restored. The camp had now been under assault for 42 hours.

It was seven o'clock that night before the weather finally cleared enough to return to the airfield for a third time to fully survey the disaster. The Beaver lay on its side, broken, twisted and unrecognisable. Drums of fuel and oil were scattered about like a giant child's toys. Only the wind fence had somehow survived. Monks' ingenuity with the radio finally got a message through to Mawson, although the boy knew that brief communication could not possibly convey the scene of calamity before them.

Despite their sleepless and exhausting last two days, that evening, as the blizzard began to ebb, the boy led another search for *Ann Cherie.* The men slogged through blown snow for 8 kilometres before stumbling upon the remains of the old workshop caravan, smashed to pieces into a crevasse. But there was no sign of the missing aircraft. Exhausted, the boy, Ken Assender and Mick Murphy now faced a 16kilometre walk back to Mawson to report details of the disaster.

Mick Murphy (left) and Jim Kichenside on the long sad walk back to Mawson after their aircraft were destroyed on the Rumdoodle plateau [Kichenside family collection].

Henk Geysen, who later described the blizzard to Phil Law as the worst so far experienced ... and miraculous no-one hurt, had managed a short briefing on the scratchy radio sked and already dispatched base personnel into the field to join the search for *Ann Cherie*[6]. It was a sad reversal of roles that the C-47 had time and again located field parties with dogs: now dog teams were out looking for her. Shortly after the trio staggered into Mawson, radio operator Graeme Currie, following the prevailing winds on George Cresswel's motorbike, found the plane. The blizzard had hurled the 7-tonne aircraft more than 18 kilometres from Rumdoodle and now she was smashed into an ice cliff, hanging more than one hundred metres above the sea ice like a swatted fly.

When the remainder of the Rumdoodle party returned on the tractor, hauling the remains of their pitiful belongings on a sledge, they set salvaging what remained of *Ann Cherie*. On December 15, the boy and 14 men, equipped with dogs and the motorbike, commenced the tricky operation. They had to abseil down a 1-in-38 descent to salvage the Doppler navigation system, survey cameras, auxiliary power unit and radar altimeter, which were transported back to Mawson by dog sled. The carcass of the aircraft was left where it lay on the cliff. The weary men then had to once again trudge all the way back to the station, now burdened by the certainty the 1960 flying program was dead.

The C-47 was torn from its moorings by the blizzard at Rumdoodle and flung more than 18 kilometres by the strength of the storm, coming to rest atop an ice cliff more than 300 feet high [Kichenside family collection].

***

Meteorologist Neil Streten categorised the Rumdoodle blizzard as a deepening Southern Ocean depression which had been observed moving on a west-southwest to southwest course since December 6; by the time it reached Mawson, the barometric pressure had fallen to 944.7 millibars, comparable to conditions in a Category 4 hurricane[7]. Streten's data showed the interaction of Southern Ocean depressions with katabatic flows produced blizzards which could be up to 40 per cent more severe at Rumdoodle than at Mawson[8]. The destruction of the aircraft followed a similar pattern to that reported by Sandercock from the 1959 storm at Gwamm: the steel tiedowns, used in accordance with ANARE specifications, had been torn apart, but against such severe aerodynamic forces, the unsheltered airframes had also inevitably failed[9].

The destruction of the aircraft had immediate and significant implications for ANARE operations at Mawson. Geysen was extremely concerned the base was now without aerial search and rescue or medical evacuation capabilities, and requested permission to call in Russian assistance if required – a request denied by Australian authorities[10]. Field operations using the D4 tractors were curtailed through the inability to depot fuel. Geologist Ric Ruker called the loss of the aircraft a bitter blow to all of us, particularly Jim Kichenside and his men'[11]. The RAAF Antarctic Flight's final full year in Antarctica, in which they had battled continual equipment and facility problems and wild weather, was over.

The bones of the C-47 remained on the ice cliff for over 20 years before the ice crumbled away and *Ann Cherie* was committed to the sea.

***

Thala Dan arrived at Mawson again on January 27, 1961, and carried the Flight home, reaching Melbourne on March 22.

As they rode the grey waves out of Horseshoe Harbour, the black peaks around Rumdoodle stood out, cold and icy, against the sky behind Mawson. Someone produced a copy of *The Ascent of Rum Doodle,* pinched from Law's library at the base. The book had all the ingredients of their own adventure – missing and substandard equipment, things going wrong, but also soldiering on and making the best of who and what they had.

And the mystical and repetitive figure of 153, which appears numerous times throughout the book, now began to emerge in conversation on the windswept decks. Somebody piped up that *Ann Cherie* had been destroyed 153 days after its first test successful test flight. Someone else volunteered that while the airfield at Rumdoodle was 1600 feet above sea level, the main camp in the lee of the range lay at 1530 feet. And then they were all counting. When *Thala Dan* sailed away from Mawson, it was 153 days from the commencement of joint C-47 and Beaver operations. And as the ship reached 153 nautical miles from Mawson, they called for Petersen to pull her up briefly so the main mast could be doused in sherry: a toast to the year of 1960 and the lasting legacy of RAAF Antarctic Flight. The name Rumdoodle remains on the Antarctic map as a testament to their resilience and courage.

The number 153 came to hold a mythic fascination for the 1960 RAAF Flight with the eerie connection between the recurring number in W.E. Bowman's novel, The Ascent of Rum Doodle, and their own experiences in Antarctica [Kichenside family collection].

CHAPTER 23

FALLOUT

He who cannot put his thoughts on ice should not enter into the heat of dispute.
—Friedrich Nietzsche

The year 1960 remains significant in the legacy of RAAF involvement in Australia's Antarctic programs. Jim Kichenside was the final RAAF commander to winter on the continent, and the Flight's use of the C-47 had introduced a greater range and capacity for survey operations, search and rescue, and medical evacuation.

In March 1961, the Flight returned home from the great frozen silence to traffic and hustle and people and the forgotten white noise of life. And more challenges.

With four aircraft destroyed in two years, Australia's polar aviation operations were now under scrutiny. While still at Mawson, Kichenside had called for an immediate moratorium on plateau-based aviation operations at Mawson to permit detailed meteorological, technical and operational feasibility studies to be carried out for up to five years[1]. This he had sent immediately by Morse Code to Phillip Law in Melbourne in the aftermath of the blizzard on December 9. It was not well received.

Jim Kichenside's rapid call for an aviation embargo was based solely on preservation of life. Aircraft could be replaced – the fate of a second-hand C-47, he felt, was nothing compared to the safety of his crew. He also had to make the call swiftly because the 1961 Flight were just a month away from embarking for Mawson.

But despite its haste, Kichenside's recommendation was carefully worded as a moratorium, not a ban, and he presented Law with options to improve future aircraft and personnel safety on the continent: he suggested shifting aviation operations either to Enderby Land (which would require major infrastructure development) or to Davis, where logistical facilities were already in place and construction of a runway on the exposed rock surrounding the base would allow year-round operations in its milder weather conditions.

But Law was not so sanguine. His commitment to year-round research and survey was absolute, and without aircraft available in the summer months or during a significant hiatus for construction of new facilities, the brakes would certainly be applied to ANARE's ambitious program. ANARE's *Cabinet Submission on Antarctica* of March 28, 1960, had included a proposal for purchase of new Beaver aircraft, a second C-47 and a large helicopter for operations at Mawson – clear plans to extend its aviation operations, not curb them[2].

Law arrived at Mawson aboard *Kista Dan* for the personnel changeover in March 1961, and he and Kichenside met to discuss the incident on Rumdoodle, the boy's final report, and its implications. Law stuck fast to his plans for year-round aviation operations at the base he had personally established in 1954[3]. But the boy stood equally firm: based on known meteorological data and aircraft structural limitations, the safety of men and aircraft on the plateau could not be guaranteed, and his final report, with all recommendations, would remain unaltered. It was a stalemate. With *Thala Dan* and *Kista Dan* now both in harbour at Mawson, the boy and Law sailed home on separate ships.

Upon his return to Australia, the RAAF and Department of Air backed Kichenside's report on procedures at Rumdoodle and the impact of the blizzard, and endorsed his recommendation that aircraft not be based in the Mawson area unless adequate shelter could be provided[4]. The Rumdoodle incident drove a further wedge between the RAAF and Antarctic Division, on top of an already tense relationship over cost-sharing. RAAF had requested to the Department of External Affairs in October 1960 to be relieved of the duty of supporting ANARE, which it felt to be outside of its chief function of providing for the air defence of Australia[5].

On February 9, 1961, before Kichenside's Flight had even returned home, the RAAF declared they would not winter again at Mawson and any subsequent deployments would operate only during the summer season using ship-based floatplanes. The perceived risk to personnel and aircraft – and the fact no replacement aircraft had been ordered – meant the 1961 Flight was disbanded without leaving Australia. The absence of any aviation presence drew adverse press comment about safety and viability of the 1961 ANARE expedition, but the Air Board considered the risks of further polar operations too great to justify a return to the continent so soon. The two subsequent summers saw, as promised, RAAF operations restricted to ship-based light-plane operations in the summer months only. And in April 1963, the RAAF Antarctic Flight was officially disbanded, citing ANARE's increasing reliance upon helicopters and redirection of RAAF resources to the conflicts in Malaya and Vietnam[6].

In 1969, Jim Kichenside was awarded a Polar Medal, an imperial award instituted by King

Edward VII in 1904 to honour members of Robert Falcon Scott's Antarctic expedition, and now honouring those who provide outstanding service in conditions of extreme hardship in polar regions, whether explorers, scientists, officers or crew. Other recipients have included Ernest Shackleton, Sir Edmund Hillary and Sir Ranulph Fiennes[7]. The award is not without controversy: until 1958, every Australian expeditioner wintering in Antarctica received a medal, but now the selection process is highly secretive—while Kev Felton and Kichenside each received one, the other members of the 1960 Flight somehow all missed out[8].

Kichenside remained troubled by the animosity of his final encounter with Phillip Law. He had liked the man, in spite of his abrasive management style, and respected his enormous achievements on the continent. Years would pass before the two found themselves in the same room again. Law retired from the Antarctic Division in 1966 after 17 years as ANARE Director, having charted over one million square kilometres of polar territory and established Australian bases at Mawson and Davis. Multiple Antarctic operational sites and geographical features are now named in Law's honour, and he remained engaged with Australian Antarctic interests until his death in 2010, aged 97. The ashes of both Law and his wife, Nel, the first Australian woman to visit Antarctica, are interred at Mawson[9]. It was some 30 years after their final encounter in 1961, that Kichenside and Law met again at an ANARE reunion. Law took him aside and said quietly, 'I understand the Davis argument now, and I offer you a belated apology.'

Jim and Beryl Kichenside at Government House, Sydney, for the presentation of his Polar Medal for outstanding service in 1969 [Kichenside family collection].

***

The belated resolution with Law was not, however, the end of Jim Kichensides advocacy for aviation operations out of Davis Station.

In the 21st century, Antarctica's extreme climate and remoteness continue to pose challenges for year-round access for scientists and other personnel. Spending weeks aboard a ship to reach the continent is no longer considered practical when sea access is limited to summer months and charter is enormously costly[10]. Reliance on sea ice for landing aircraft restricts transit operations to winter months only. Demand for rapid access has driven moves to create year-round air links to the continent from Australia, with accompanying permanent aviation facilities below 60 degrees south.

The first direct flight between Australia and Antarctica occurred in September 1964, when a ski-equipped US Navy Hercules flying out of Melbourne landed at the United States' Byrd Station. Phillip Law was among the passengers for the historic 7110-kilometre, 15-hour flight[11]. That success prompted a round of Australian feasibility studies for development of permanent facilities to handle large passenger and cargo aircraft. Multiple options were identified across different locations, including blue ice glacial (plateau) runways, compacted snow-ice or permanent rock runways suitable for wheeled aircraft, and groomed snow skiways for ski-equipped planes[12].

Interest in constructing a runway at Australia's Casey Station stemmed from its geographical location being closest to Australia-some 2000 kilometres closer to Hobart than Mawson and within range of RAAF Hercules aircraft[13]. Casey was established in east Antarctica in 1957 as an American station; in 1959, Australia took over the site and, due to persistent and problematic snow drifting, relocated the station to nearby Newcomb Bay. While heavy snowfall and blizzards remained a feature of the local weather, an experimental compressed snow-ice runway was constructed 7 kilometres from the base in 1988 for trials of an intercontinental air link from Hobart[14]. Summer melt problems were soon evident, and following a two-year scoping study in the late 1990s, operations were moved to a compacted snow runway on glacial ice on the plateau at Lanyon Hills, 70 kilometres inland from the base[15].

Runways underpinned by glacial ice are dense enough to support heavy wheeled aircraft, but turbulent crosswinds in glacial ice regions are an operational hazard and the ice is vulnerable to summer melt. Before trials at the new Lanyon Hills site began, Jim Kichenside, with advice from his former Antarctic co-pilots Ken Assender and Graham Dyke, and former ANARE meteorologist Neil Streten and geologist Ric Ruker, wrote to both the authors of the scoping study and the office of the federal Minister for the Environment, offering the benefit of the 1960 experience of plateau-based operations. As the last Australians to engage in year-round air operations in Antarctica, and with Kichenside and Dyke (who went on to the rank of Air Commodore) later having careers in command, operational planning, and management, they expressed concern over the viability of operations at Lanyon Hills. There was no sea ice or rock formations for anchoring buildings and aircraft, and the hazards particular to plateau operations-ablation, katabatic wind, and turbulence – were all too well known to the 1960 expeditioners. Kichenside called for a pause in the runway development and for further consideration for aviation operations out of the region around Davis Station.

The development at Casey, however, proceeded. The first Airbus A319 from Hobart to Casey landed at the $46 million Wilkins Aerodrome at Lanyon Hills on January 11, 2008, with scientists and politicians, including Environment Minister Peter Garrett, aboard[16].

The runway was officially opened by Governor-General Sir Michael Jeffery two weeks later – but he was forced to conduct the ceremony by phone due to bad weather on the plateau[17].

Despite its advantages of geographical proximity to Hobart, operational challenges persisted at the site. Ablation of the glacial ice meant the runway sometimes accommodated only three intercontinental flights for the entire October-March season, far fewer than the 25 originally aimed for. To be approved by the Civil Aviation Safety Authority the runway had to be laser-levelled before each landing, requiring a crew of eight to maintain the levels and appropriate surface friction. In addition, the snow surface had to be re-prepared every season, shaving the surface back with snow groomers which lowered the ice base slightly on each occasion[18]. In 2012, flights to Lanyon Hills were suspended for a period due to excessive runway melt[19].

Jim Kichenside at Vestfold Hills near Davis station in 1960. He identified the area as a suitable landing site to reduce the effect of katabatic wind on aircraft during his sojourn at the base. The site is soon to house a permanent rock runway for year-round aviation access in Antarctica [Kichenside family collection].

The 2016 Commonwealth *Antarctic Strategy and Action Plan* announced intentions for development of an all-seasons paved runway near Davis Station to complement the ice runway at Wilkins[20]. Davis is known to expeditioners as the 'Riviera of the South': it is one of two ice-free oases in eastern Antarctica, and was first mooted as potentially suitable for year-round aviation operations in 1958[21]. The weather is comparatively mild, wind speeds are markedly lower than at Mawson and Casey, and the large areas of exposed rock reduces the effects of whiteout and snow accumulation and avoids ablation issues[22]. Following two years of geomorphology, construction feasibility, and environmental assessment, a site six kilometres from the main base at Davis, in the Vestfold Hills, was chosen for construction of a rock runway long to accommodate large passenger jets, to be operational in the decade after 2030[23]. In 1960, Jim Kichenside and his RAAF colleagues had stood on the same site and anointed it the perfect place to fly.

PART
FOUR
227

CHAPTER 24

KONFRONTASI

Australian jets on combat alert: Australian jet fighters stationed at Butterworth air base, northern Malaya, have been on a 24-hour alert in the two months of tension between Malaysia and Indonesia.
—*Canberra Times*, Saturday, November 23, 1963

In 1963, as Jim Kichenside and his Antarctic Flight re-established their lives in Australia after their polar adventures, the world was on edge. The Cold War threatened to spill over into outright nuclear conflict. The international missile crisis of October 1962 – when the United States discovered Soviet ballistic missiles stationed in Cuba in response to their own deployments in Italy and Turkey – was the latest in an ideological struggle which had already spread to Iran, Latin America, the Congo, Suez, and, of greatest concern to Australia, Indochina.

Following World War II, politics in South-East Asia was defined by the evolving powers of communism and nationalism. Developing nations including Vietnam, Pakistan and Malaya had pushed to shake off their colonial occupiers – moves seen as fertile ideological ground for the Soviet Union and China, which supplied both political and military support to Indochina but were also openly hostile toward one another over the occupation of Tibet.

In Australia, the perceived threat to domestic and international security posed by communism had figured in federal debate since the Menzies government were elected in 1949 on a platform of outlawing the Communist Party. The rapid deployment of Australian forces after the invasion of South Korea then formed part of the international effort to contain the spread of communism throughout east Asia, fuelled by a strategic readjustment in Australia forced by the devastating swathe cut by Japan in the region in 1941-42. Despite the traditional strong defence ties with Britain which had taken Australian air forces to the Middle East in 1952, Australian concerns about threats closer to home and the grave weakening of Brtain after the war led to a collective security arrangement with the US and New Zealand in 1951 known as the ANZUS Treaty, driven by the possibility of future Japanese expansionism and the rise of communism in South-East Asia.

At Australia's doorstep, tensions between Australia and Indonesia had been escalating since shortly after the cessation of World War II. In 1949, Indonesia declared independence from

Holland, but it was the territory of Irian Jaya which sparked initial unease when Australia supported the Dutch in what would become a twelve-year dispute over the region. However, it was the creation of the new nation of Malaysia in 1963 which threatened to push the already volatile region into open conflict and potentially drag surrounding nations, including Australia, into the fracas. The aggregation of the former British territories of Malaya, Singapore, and Borneo into the independent federation of Malaysia was condemned as a neo-colonialist British plot against Indonesia's geopolitical ambitions by Indonesian president Sukarno, who had led the independence struggle against Holland. The result was a new policy of *konfrontasi*, or confrontation – a violent undeclared campaign aimed at crushing the fledgling Malaysian nation through both propaganda and military attacks. The volatility of the region was now a distinct threat to Australian security. As early as 1963, both the UK and USA were pressing Australia for an active military commitment in Malaysia, with calls for Australian fighter squadrons to respond to threats to both Malaysia and northern Australia[1].

***

The 1960s heralded a program of massive expansion and development for the RAAF, with expenditure rising from $135 million in 1962/3 to $378.6 million in 1967/8. In 1963, the operational strength of RAAF consisted of 14 air squadrons, including five fighter units equipped with the CA-27, the Australian-built version of the American F-86 Sabre[2]. More than 110 Sabres were built by the Commonwealth Aircraft Corporation in Melbourne under licence from 1954[3]. They were powered by a new Rolls Royce Avon engine which provided 1500 pounds more thrust than the old General Electric J47. The CA-27 also had a greater nose-intake surface area, increased fuel capacity, a more ergonomic cockpit layout, and was armed with AIM-9B Sidewinder air-to-air missiles and cannons[4]. The two nose cannons were a major improvement on the USAF's 6 gun layout; the aircraft fuselage was also significantly enlarged in girth to accommodate the shorter engine, which had a greater diameter than the American version.

An Australian-built CA-27 Sabre Mk.32 over Melbourne in 1959, with the Melbourne Cricket Ground in the background. The Commonwealth Aircraft Corporation was based in Melbourne and built more than 110 Sabre jets, based on the design of the American F-86 [Australian War Memorial, accession no.070122].

The Sabre came into service at No.2 Operational Training Unit at RAAF base Williamtown in November 1954, where Vampire jets were still in use for instrument and air-to-air combat training. There was no dual-seat trainer for the Sabre, but Sabre pilots were provided with training in a rudimentary simulator before taking single-seater fighters into the air[5].

By the end of 1962, Jim Kichenside had become a Sabre pilot – but his path since returning from Antarctica had been far from smooth.

One thing Kichenside and Phillip Law had agreed upon in Antarctica was that the communications isolation was, in most part, a blessing in disguise. Keeping the men insulated from the day-to-day worries of their families in Australia – which they could do nothing about – relieved them of much stress and anxiety[6]. Since their marriage in 1952, Jim and his wife Beryl had lived solely on his modest airman's wages. The boy had taken his appointment to the Antarctic Flight primarily as an opportunity for command, but also with an anticipated financial reward, with good Antarctic pay and nothing to spend it on while at the frozen continent. But in 1961, he arrived home from more than a year virtually *incommunicado* to a shock: a tremulous wife and an empty bank account. All the money he had saved during his sojourn below 60 degrees south was gone.

During her husband's long year in the Antarctic, Beryl Kichenside had been left alone with three small children in an Air Force house in stultifying suburban Melbourne. Her mother in Sydney had died and her father, also in Sydney, had a new partner to occupy him, leaving her with even less support. Beryl was a trusting soul and her isolation left her desperate for friendship – the kind of desperation which attracts parasites and weasels. Money had been borrowed from her and never repaid. And now there was nothing left.

Jim Kichenside's immediate reaction was to blame himself. He'd been selfish to leave her – in going away for so long, he had left her prey to all the wrong kinds of people. But it was still a demoralising situation. He had to sell of all his belongings, including car and furniture, to settle the debts. Ian Douglas, the young barrister who had been CO at Davis in 1960, also stepped in to return an old favour: he organised a network of his legal contacts to consolidate any further debts *pro bono*.

The best move now seemed to send the family, including his children aged eight, six and four, back to Sydney, where Beryl's father and his own parents still lived and could provide her with more support. The boy had to remain in Melbourne: if he stayed for the remainder of 1961 and renewed his instrument rating examiners ticket, the RAAF would then arrange a posting to Williamtown, closer to his family.

It was the beginning of two very difficult years. He stayed on at Point Cook in 1961 on the No.10 Officers' Advanced Administrative Course, finishing the course ranked second in Public Speaking and Leadership. The course convenors noted, 'Flight Lieutenant Kichenside is a bright officer with a ready sense of humour ...

He admits that while flying is his main interest, he should prove most reliable in any position requiring initiative and sense of responsibility.'[7]

He was then posted, as agreed, back to RAAF Williamtown, where he spent 12 months as head of the air combat training on Vampires before his own Sabre conversion at the end of 1962, when he was promoted to the rank of Squadron Leader and joined No.76 Fighter Squadron. The move back to Williamtown had brought him closer to his children, who were living with their mother in Palm Beach in northern Sydney. He was able to see them every few weeks, although his relationship with Beryl remained unresolved.

But as 1963 progressed and tensions threatened to spill over in the Indonesian archipelago, pressure mounted for Australia to provide an active military commitment to the region. While ground troops were not deployed until April 1964, Australian fighter jets were already in the region following the 1948-1957 Malayan internal civil war: No.78 Wing RAAF (made up of Nos.3 and 77 Squadrons) were flying missions against insurgent Communist forces in the tropical hills and jungles, and now would take a new defensive role from their base at Butterworth in the west of the fragile new nation of Malaysia.

At the end of 1963, the boy was posted from Williamtown to Butterworth as senior Flight Commander with No.77 Squadron: the squadron he had flown his first combat missions with in 1952 in Korea. Before his departure for Malaysia, he was contacted by the Department of Air and asked to make a decision on whether his family would accompany him on the deployment. It was a tipping point. Suddenly he knew he could not go without Beryl.

***

Australia had been engaged in strategic defence in the South-East Asia region since the 1948-1960 Malayan Emergency a guerrilla insurgency led by the radical Communist Party of Malaya sparked by the British-led creation in 1948 of the Federation of Malaya. The South-East Asia Treaty Organisation (SEATO), formed in September 1954 and of which Australia was a founding member, aimed to defend both the territories of member organisations and so-called protocol states including as Laos, Cambodia, and South Vietnam from growing unrest in the region. By 1955, Australian air, naval and ground forces were in Malaya as part of the joint British, Australian and New Zealand Far East Strategic Reserve (FESR)[8]. No.77 Squadron were deployed to Malaya in August 1958, one year after the Federation of Malaya achieved independence from Britain. But it was not until 1960 that an official end to the Emergency was declared.

The respite was brief. Just three years later, regional tensions reignited with the Indonesian declaration of aggression against Malaysia. Australia was now walking a tightrope between traditional political and strategic ties with Britain (and therefore Malaysia) and the aggravation of a well-armed and volatile neighbour to the immediate north with whom the federal government was anxious to avoid an open rift.

***

Beryl Kichenside and her three children took their first ever plane flight at the end of 1963 when, after a ten-day sea voyage to Singapore, they flew on to Butterworth RAAF base in western Malaysia with the boy. It was a truly exotic destination, with the airfield carved from thick forests and palm plantations and flanked by sharp mountain peaks wreathed in cloud. The base was the largest peacetime installation maintained by Australia outside its borders, its buildings shining white in the hot tropical sun and rows of jets, bombers, and fighters standing ready on the heat-rippled runways.

Most single men lived on the base itself, but as a family, the Kichensides were provided a furnished house in Georgetown on the nearby island of Penang, a short ferry ride away. The steaming city of Georgetown was overlooked by the Pagoda of One Thousand Buddhas and old forts with their cannon-topped walls as a reminder of its British colonial past. In 1963, the streets were jostling with taxis, trishaws, and buses, with Air Force wives bartering in stores and bazaars over handicrafts, fruits, and brightly printed cloths.

But amid the parrots and palm trees and white sandy beaches, 77 Squadron were in a high state of alert. Four Sabres were on standby seven days a week as Nos.77 and 3 Squadrons remained on operational readiness for 12 hours every day, handing over to the British No.60 Squadron for night duties. The Indonesian Air Force (*Tentara Nasional Indonesia-Angkatan Udara* or TNI-AU) had acquired Soviet fighter and bomber jet aircraft and their base at Medan in Sumatra was less than 200 kilometres from Butterworth[9].

In Malaysia, Jim Kichenside was reunited with many old faces from Korea, now all senior RAAF officers – Max Outhwaite, Bruce Gogerly, who had shot down a MiG in Korea, Gordon Harvey, who had spent 32 months as a prisoner of war, and Ray Trebilco, who had taken the fateful call in Iwakuni which sent 77 Squadron to war in 1950. Now, the veterans flew together again in the first operations with live ammunition undertaken by RAAF fighters in a combat zone since Korea, striking against communist camps in the tropical wilderness of Malaysian and Borneo[10].

Incursions by Indonesian ground troops to the southern Malay peninsula in August 1964 prompted an escalation of security on the northern Australian coast, including fresh anti-aircraft measures. Likewise, RAAF personnel were evacuated from Penang to the main base at Butterworth as the Malaysian government declared a state of emergency.

On December 12, 1964, Jim and Beryl Kichenside's fourth child, a son named James Andrew, was born amid the uncertainty and instability in Malaysia.

***

As the belligerence intensified between Indonesia and Malaysia in the early 1960s, civil strife and communist insurgency were also threatening the stability of other South-East Asian nations, including Vietnam, Thailand and Laos. Both Thailand and the former French protectorate of Laos were battling internal communist insurrection, with the security situation in Laos – one of the poorest nations in mainland southern Asia – now emerging as of key importance in maintaining a buffer against its powerful northern neighbour, China. Recognising the implications of the increasing instability for its own security, Australia, joined by the US, urged a previously unwilling SEATO to respond to the growing tensions. SEATO had tempered its own reaction over fears of provoking a wider conflict, but in 1962 the organisation endorsed support for Thailand and South Vietnam, and in May, Australia agreed to redirect a portion of its RAAF fighter strength from Butterworth to the defence of northern Thailand.

Ten Sabres from No.78 Wing at Butterworth were formed into No.79 Squadron and stationed at Ubon, near the Laotian border in northeastern Thailand, where a Royal Thai Air Force base was already shared by the US 13th Air Force. The arrangement, however, was diplomatically delicate as Malaysia was not a SEATO member and the terms of the Anglo-Malayan Mutual Defence Agreement did not allow for SEATO operations within its borders. The RAAF were warned by the Department of Defence to avoid any public connection between air operations in Thailand and those in Malaysia, at risk of prejudicing the Malaysian government's logistical support at

Butterworth[11]. Rotation of personnel between the two bases was carefully stage-managed: two Sabres from Ubon would meet two from Malaysia (escorted by a No 2 Squadron Canberra bomber) at the Thai border and the five aircraft would mingle to confuse any watching ground or radar observers, before the Sabres from Ubon would return to Butterworth and the Butterworth Sabres proceed to the Thai base[12].

Jim Kichenside (with an accompanying primate) outside the flight hut at RAAF Ubon, Thailand, in 1964 [Kichenside family collection].

On May 1, 1964, the boy flew to Ubon for a seven-week stint as detachment commander of the RAAF contingent[13]. While the airstrip had a 2100-metre concrete runway suitable for jets, the base was rudimentary, with timber and iron huts and hangars hacked out of the jungle and concrete revetments to protect aircraft from ground or aerial assault. It was hot and sticky and basic, but the high degree of tension on the Laotian border outweighed the tropical discomforts. While airborne assets of the USAF and Marines were authorised to attack or destroy any hostile aircraft and engage in 'hot' pursuit across both the Laos and Cambodian borders, No.79 Squadron was confined to Thai territory and authorised only to use force for self-defence, in air defence of Thailand (when instructed by the Air Board), or if requested by Thai authorities[14]. Between border patrols, RAAF pilots flew navigation exercises and simulated strikes, including one on the famed bridge on the Kwai River. Australian Sabres would also 'intercept' USAF F4 Phantoms returning from strikes over South Vietnam and fly sorties against the USAF F-100 Super Sabres.

Life in Ubon was much different to the spit and polish of Butterworth. In addition to the usual jungle maladies such as dengue fever, No.79 Squadron were assailed by a plague of feral dogs which caused several near misses on the Ubon runway (one Sabre was forced to overshoot to avoid a pair of mating mutts). Monsoonal storms dumped up to five inches of rain at a time: the kind of torrential rain which forced its way into aircraft cockpits and electrics, causing a Squadron unserviceability rate of up to 60 per cent. But there was humanitarian work too – on June 3, 1964, Kichenside and Wing Commander Bradford presented gifts to children at a local orphanage on behalf of the Australian government[15].

The tropical heat at RAAF base Ubon was challenging for ground crews and pilots alike. Members of No.79 Squadron, stripped to the waist, manually manoeuvre a CA-27 Sabre into position on the runway prior to take-off [Australian War Memorial, accession no. P02835.041].

No.79 Squadron were awarded the Duke of Gloucester Cup in January 1965 as the most efficient squadron in the RAAF. Making the presentation was Minister for Air Peter Howson (left), with Wing Commander Ross Glassop and Squadron Leader Jim Kichenside [Kichenside family collection].

The boy felt an intense affiliation with the Thai people. His personal faith had been shaken during a brief visit home to Marrickville before his departure for Malaysia in late 1963. The widow of his old neighbour Rowly in Roseby Street, Georgina Rowlands, was dying, and the boy learned a local priest had refused her the last rites because she had committed a sin against the church by marrying a Protestant.

The boy's anger and helplessness had rattled his Christian faith almost to breaking point. But here in Thailand, he found no such austerity or prejudice. This seemed exemplified by a local teen the RAAF boys christened "Smithy", who worked at the Ubon base behind the bar. On his second tour to Ubon, Kichenside found that the boy was no longer there, and enquiries revealed Smithy was doing his national service: not with a gun, but with a saffron robe and begging bowl as a Buddhist monk. The Thai humbleness, the unofficial national philosophy of *mai pen rai*—of forgiveness, pliancy, and good humour – warmed something in him that the cold asceticism of the Christian church had threatened to freeze out.

Kichenside spent two further stints as detachment commander at Ubon in December 1964 and the period July to September, 1965. The highlight was the presentation of the Duke of Gloucester Cup for the most efficient squadron in the RAAF to 79 Squadron on December 9, 1964. Minister of Air Peter Howson flew into Ubon to present the Cup, and along with Ubon base OC Ross Glassop (who himself had been a Meteor pilot in Korea), the boy accepted the award on behalf of the other detachment commanders in the 79 Squadron rotation[16]. Prince Henry, the Duke of Gloucester for whom the award was named, had been Australia's first royal Governor General in 1945[17]. No.77 Squadron had won the cup while in Korea in 1950; No 36 Squadron has won the award a record seven times[18].

***

The new year of 1965 brought an escalation in tensions as the United States expanded its military presence to prop up the struggling South Vietnam government again the communist Viet Cong. Three squadrons of USAF F-4C Phantom fighter-bombers arrived at Ubon, and the Australian pilots became increasingly frustrated at their nonparticipant status and inability to cross the Mekong – they could only assist by refining the combat skills of the American pilots to counter a growing threat from MiG-17 fighters now flown by the Soviet-trained North Vietnamese Air Force. But on January 12, 1965, the RAAF pilots were sobered by the news that three of six USAF F-100 Super Sabre aircraft which had refuelled at Ubon that day *en route* to North Vietnam had been shot down; the conflict seemed to take a dark stride closer.

On January 29, 1965, Kichenside returned from his second tour at Ubon to a heightened security situation in Malaysia. Indonesia had responded to the appointment of Malaysia to the UN Security Council in late 1964 by both withdrawing from the UN and pouring troops into Sumatra and Kalimantan. This provocation prompted Australia to dispatch ground troops to reinforce British forces, the amplified threat outweighing any potential diplomatic breach with Indonesia.

Despite their pressing operational schedule, all RAAF pilots continued to undertake scheduled half-yearly proficiency assessments while in South-east Asia. On July 6, 1965, the boy's flying test report rated him as 'exceptional—a 'Category A' fighter pilot.'[19] *Exceptional* is just that – only for the best. After joining the RAAF as a trainee in 1949, Jim Kichenside's dreams had finally been achieved – he was officially at the top; what today would be considered a 'Top Gun' pilot.

But celebrations would have to wait. From October through December, he deployed with 77 Squadron as one of six Sabre pilots on Labuan island off the north-west coast of Borneo, patrolling the Indonesia-Kalimantan border under special rules of engagement from the FEAF, alongside Hawker Hunter aircraft of the RAF's No.20 Squadron. Unlike at Ubon, direct armed combat was now authorised against the Indonesian Air Force, aided by Australian Army ground forces attacking Indonesian airfields with heavy artillery. Flying conditions were deadly, with almost continuous cloud over the rugged hilltops and gaps of sometimes only 50 metres in the saddles of the hills for a jet to dive through[20].

Australian Sabre pilots at Labuan Island, October 1965. Many are wearing laced-up G-suits designed to ameliorate the high physiological loads of subsonic flight. Jim Kichenside is fourth from left [Kichenside family collection].

***

No.79 Squadron were deployed to Thailand for more than six years before the political situation in Laos stabilised sufficiently for SEATO intervention to be withdrawn. In mid-1968, the tenure of 79 Squadron at Ubon concluded. While the terms of operation had prevented any direct engagement with hostile forces, the deployment remains significant in maintenance of Australia's strategic partnership with the US. That same alliance, however, also led to pressure on Australia for a joint partnership with the US on fighter operations in Vietnam. In 1963, the US twice sought RAAF support as they strove to regain the upper hand against Viet Cong forces in South Vietnam. The Australian federal government refused on both occasions over the political sensitivity of active engagement and unwillingness to send the ageing Sabres into the front line when American air superiority seemed already established.

The US changed tack in December 1965, calling for the RAAF to either support combat operations in Vietnam or vacate the base at Ubon, a move again resisted as potentially complicating the relationship with Thailand. In December 1966, Deputy Chief of Air Staff Air Vice Marshal Brian Eaton supported deployment of both Canberra bombers and Sabre fighter aircraft to Vietnam, sensing that a large part of

South-East Asia could follow if Vietnam fell (the so-called *domino theory*). But while the Cabinet of new prime minister Harold Holt approved the deployment of No.2 Squadron, it rejected the Sabre element being sent. No Australian fighter jets were ever deployed to the conflict in Vietnam, although a number of RAAF pilots did serve on exchange with US units[21].

The Indonesian-Malaysian conflict had declined after an attempted coup in Indonesia on October 1, 1965, in which several army generals were kidnapped and murdered by the *Partai Komunis Indonesia* (Indonesian Communist Party, or PKI). The Indonesian army, led by General Suharto, repressed the coup within a day, but President Sukarno resigned over his association with the PKI and Suharto assumed power in March 1966. Konfrontasi ended on August 12, 1966, when Indonesia signed a peace treaty with Malaysia[22].

In 1969, No.77 Squadron returned to Williamtown following ten years' service in Malaysia (some 40,000 flying hours). The Sabres were replaced soon after with the supersonic French Dassault Mirage III-O fighter[23]. Butterworth remained a RAAF base until 1988, when it was handed over to the Royal Malaysian Air Force. The RAAF, however, continues to maintain a presence at RMAF Butterworth as part of Australia's commitment to the Five Power

Defence Arrangements (FPDA), a series of nonbinding multi-lateral defence agreements between the UK, Australia, New Zealand, Malaysia, and Singapore created in 1971[24].

CHAPTER 25

FLY LOW, LAND SHORT

A leader is one who knows the way, goes the way, and shows the way
—John C. Maxwell

Officers Mess
RAAF Base Richmond
June 1969

He'd told the driver to go slow and the young adjutant obliged: from the moment the staff car rolled quietly beneath the brick triumphal arch emblazoned with *RAAF Base Richmond,* he had literally kept the car in second gear. They cruised past the staff quarters, the big warehouses, the neatly mowed lawns and immaculate gardens, giving the old man time to take it all in – the immensity, the meticulous order.

They drove beneath shady bunya pines and Port Jackson figs to the Officers' Mess. The unassuming low-slung building appeared at first not to impress, but he saw the old man's eyes widen briefly as they went in – the bright polished timber floors, the plush chairs in air-force blue, and the formality of the top table, with its central chair set aside for the boy as President of the Mess.

They drove down to the hangars and the grandeur of the 2100-metre runway, where the gigantic C-130A Hercules' squatted on the tarmac like ungainly buzzards. The old man walked slowly around one of the Caribous resident in the yellow-brick hangar of 38 Squadron, and the boy thought of trying to explain how this big bird needed only 350 metres of runway to get into the air, how it could lump 32 troops or 14 stretcher casualties or three and a half tonnes of cargo ... but he decided to keep quiet and just let the old man look.

Then he nodded to his Warrant Officer and the young man ushered them to the CO's office, just off the tarmac. The men on the taxiway saluted as they passed, making the old man jump. The boy had instructed the adjutant to get the silver service out for morning tea and he'd done himself proud – the big spacious office was neat as a pin, the service was polished, there were cakes and hot tea and delicate little china cups. The deferential young man poured two cups, saluted smartly, and disappeared.

The boy stood behind his desk, waiting for his father to sit in the big leather chair the adjutant had provided to replace the usual hard upright ones. But the old man did not sit. He continued to look slowly around, at the wood panelling and the wide desk and the windows with a view of the busy airfield. Then he slowly lifted his hand and touched his own forehead in a kind of awkward salute. 'Well done, son,' he said – and there were tears in the old dark eyes.

***

In 1966, it seemed Jim Kichenside's flying days were over. He was 36 years old – senior, for a fighter pilot. Despite the glowing reports from Butterworth, perhaps his reflexes were not quite what they had been.

But the RAAF did not want to let Kichenside go. He had over 3700 flying hours to his name, including almost 1500 as an instructor, and command experience in combat and extreme climatic conditions. That kind of experience cannot be bought off a supermarket shelf. Upon his return from South-East Asia, he was nominated to attend RAAF Staff College at RAAF Fairbairn, Canberra, based on recommendations such as that of No.77 Squadron CO, Wing Commander Les Reading (another Korea veteran), who commended his 'high proficiency in planning and directing'.

Wing Commander Jim Kichenside, Commanding Officer of No.38 Squadron RAAF, in 1969 [Kichenside family collection].

Staff College admission is based primarily on an assessment of an officer's potential for promotion and/or command, and aims to prepare selected officers for operational and management roles. But the boy found it hard, being earthbound. Cars were slow and traffic irked him. Walking made his feet feel heavy and his soul heavier. Nonetheless, he threw himself into the training as he always did and was made captain of No.22 Staff Course, where once more he was a classmate of Max Outhwaite[1]. In 1968, he was rewarded with promotion to Wing Commander, and at the end of that year, he received the only flying posting of the No.22 Course graduates[2]. He had his wings back!

For there was trouble with No.38 Squadron at RAAF Base Richmond.

RAAF Richmond has until recently been the RAAF's primary transport hub, a large base in northwestern Sydney providing airlift capabilities for logistics and transport, combat support, and disaster relief. In 1969, it was the home of No.38 Squadron. The tactical transport unit was raised in 1943 and equipped first with Lockheed Hudson Mk-IVs then Douglas C-47 Dakotas for transport of casualties, paratroops, and freight in Papua New Guinea and the Pacific. After World War II, the Squadron operated a courier service to Japan to support BCOF and spent three years in Singapore supplying Commonwealth forces in the Malayan Emergency. In 1964, the squadron re-equipped with the Canadian-built de Havilland DHC-4 Caribou and served as the RAAF's operational conversion unit for that aircraft[3].

During the 1950s and early 1960s, No.38 Squadron also developed a reputation as a cowboy' unit with lax flying standards[4]. There were issues with expense accounts and discipline. Someone with tact was needed to take a firm leadership role, someone with the command experience to engender both respect and change.

Jim Kichenside, now 38 years old, was appointed Commanding Officer of No.38 Squadron on December 9, 1968. The military are somewhat notorious for the perception of summary justice and harsh discipline. But during his first month in charge, he simply watched, listened and noted. It appeared most of the anti-social problems were occurring in the hangars, but there were also discipline issues in the air. Experience told him that unjustified harshness generates only anger and resentment without the self-reflection which leads to behavioural change. The boy, who Vic Cannon had noted 'handles subordinates firmly but wisely', brought a consultative approach to the problem. First, he armed his squadron with knowledge: he made it clear what the rules were, so everybody knew exactly where they stood. He empowered his junior officers by trusting their ability to solve problems before he got involved. And above all, he prioritised fairness and consistency: most men were willing to accept discipline if they could see a fair process and one applied without favour. Air Commodore Horton 'Spike' Marsh, Officer Commanding at RAAF Base Richmond, was impressed: he reported the boy as having 'the respect and support of his squadron and a firm control over his squadron's activities ... (maintaining) discipline and a high standard of morale.'[5]

But it was not just the respect of crews and the officers he gained. The boy had seen little of his father since leaving for Point Cook as a student pilot 15 years earlier. And while their relationship was cordial, a certain strain always arose at any mention of the Air Force. Now in 1969, his father took a train from Marrickville to Richmond for his own inspection of the squadron and its youthful CO. The boy ensured everything was laid on – silver service, guided tour of the huge facility, staff car. To a man who had grown up during the Depression, who had had to struggle for every dollar, this was so far outside his experience that Charles Kichenside could barely process the splendour. But he was clearly proud, even if he didn't say much. That was the icing on the cake: it seemed the boy was, to quote the No.38 Squadron motto, 'equal to the task' at last.

***

Discipline and morale issues aside, Kichenside was also at Richmond to fly. After two years out of the saddle, he renewed acquaintances with C-47s at East Sale in December 1968 before his formal conversion on the No.11 Caribou course at Richmond in early 1969. His natural endeavour, so critical to earning the respect of his new charges, impressed the instructors, who reported, 'Considering a long period off active flying duties and his entry into a completely new sphere of Tactical Transport operations, Wing Commander Kichenside worked very hard to achieve an overall second result.'[6]

Domestic tactical transport operations from Richmond included ferrying cargoes from brass bands to jeeps, rugby teams, paratroops and cadets from as far afield as Adelaide, Hobart, and Townsville. But in 1969, as the Vietnam War raged on, 12 Australian Caribou aircraft were transferred to RAAF Transport Flight Vietnam (later No.35 Squadron), operating close to the front line on short unprepared strips that would deter any other aircraft of similar size. The brief of No.38 Squadron was expanded to provide pilots to Vietnam who were equipped to fly in tropical and mountainous conditions. In 1965, No.38 Squadron established a Flight known as Detachment A or Det A in Papua New Guinea to conduct this training, operating out of Port Moresby with two Caribous. All aircraft captains were required to complete at least one two-month deployment with Det A before serving with No.35 Squadron in Vietnam[7].

The crews in Papua New Guinea operated throughout the territory on both military and civil operations from survey to medical evacuation and heavy-lift logistics. High mountains, volatile weather, poor infrastructure, and lack of reliable map references made flying conditions among the most dangerous in the world. The Caribou is a low-level twin-engine tactical transport, rugged and STOL-capable (Short Take-Off and Landing), requiring only a short approach to get airborne and capable of a near-zero ground roll when landing[8]. But it is underpowered for an environment like Papua New Guinea, with a ceiling height of 14,000 feet, flying in terrain where peaks can exceed 16,000 feet. Pilots risk being caught in deadly narrow valleys, faced with airstrips where there is no option to go around on a false landing, and where cloud, monsoon storms, and even volcanic eruptions are routine airborne hazards.

The boy devised a classification system for his pilots based on experience, decision-making abilities, reaction under pressure, and understanding of the aircraft to assess each pilots' readiness for conditions in Papua New Guinea. There were no accidents on his watch in 1969. He would go north himself for a week every few months, landing at grass strips across Papua New Guinea to familiarise himself with the conditions his pilots were facing in one of the world's most extreme and dangerous aviation environments[9].

With Papua New Guinea gaining independence from Australia in 1975, Det A was disbanded, although the squadron continued periodic training deployments in that nation[10].

***

Caribou A4-285 on the apron at Canadian Forces Base Downsview, Ontario, November 1969 [Kichenside family collection].

Despite the adrenaline and challenges of flying in Papua New Guinea, the final flying job of his posting to Richmond proved the most spectacular. Accompanied by a second pilot, navigator, and loadmaster, Kichenside flew to Canada in November 1969 to pick up a new Caribou, A4-285, from de Havilland at Canadian Forces Base Downsview, Ontario[11]. To transport the aircraft back to Richmond would mean a completing a total circumnavigation of the globe. The regulation return route was back the way they had come, west across the Pacific, but December wind conditions in the northern hemisphere dictated an eastern return route instead, via the Mediterranean, Africa and southern Asia, hopping through 13 countries in 16 days.

Personnel from No.38 Squadron RAAF in Canada to deliver Caribou A4-285 back to Australia. L-R: Wing Commander Jim Kichenside, Flying Officer Jack Rydstrom, Sergeant Alan Fraser, Flight Lieutenant Ron Ewing [Kichenside family collection].

After two weeks spent on checks and acceptance tests, and with long-range fuel tanks fitted, the big bird lifted away from the Canadian snows *en route* for the sun, sand, and glamour of Bermuda on December 8, 1969. Things began to go wrong almost immediately. Leaving Bermuda for the long haul across the Atlantic to the Azores, they ran into extremely strong headwinds which forced them to turn back or risk running out of fuel over the ocean. This put their already tight itinerary a day behind – but it was impossible to be too concerned by a forced return to the beautiful Caribbean.

Two days later, with the jewel-bright Mediterranean just 8,000 feet below them, they buzzed slowly from Gibraltar to Malta and on to the bright whiteness of Athens. The schedule tightened like a ligature here, however, with a strict diplomatic clearance required to enter Suez: they needed to reach Egypt at 6am next morning, plus or minus only five minutes, or their clearance would be void. This meant taking off at midnight in Athens into a raging thunderstorm, an experience which rattled both the nerves and the teeth of all four men. But the bone-shaking trip was worthwhile when they cleared Suez and flew down the Valley of the Kings along the Nile at dawn.

There were stops at Bahrain, Karachi, Dhaka, and his old haunt of Butterworth before they reached Darwin on Christmas Eve. They eased the Caribou into Richmond before the Christmas turkey could go cold the next day, after 128 hours in the air. Jim Kichenside's flying career was, at last, closed.

***

Since joining the RAAF as a 19-year-old trainee in 1949, Jim Kichenside acquired 4464 hours during his 21 years of flying. Of that, 1750 hours were in Vampires, 650 in Sabres, and approximately 200 in Meteors. He spent more than 60 per cent of his career in jet aircraft, including as a pilot in the first ever war fought between jets. It is difficult to accumulate a lot of hours in jets because most operations are short due to the high fuel usage, so Kichenside's 2600 hours in jet aircraft is significant, as are his 1175 hours as a jet instructor. The remaining hours came from Beaver (210 hours) and C-47 Dakota (242) operations in Antarctica, and from his final deployment on Caribous at Richmond and in Papua New Guinea (649).

CHAPTER 26

BILLY THE BROOM BOY

You can be a rooster today and a feather duster tomorrow.

—Adage

Department of Trade and Resources
Canberra, 1977

'Now, these are to go upstairs,' she said, dumping a pile of manila folders on the desk in front of him. '*These* are to be posted,' she said, indicating a wire basket containing stamped letters. 'And these are to go across to Policy and Planning.' He was handed another armload of files with coloured paper tabs fluttering off the tops like tiny flags. 'They'll need them by eleven o'clock too.' And with that broad hint, she turned and tottered away, all tight skirt and red lipstick and all of about twenty years old.

The boy sat back in his chair, poker-faced, until she was out of sight, before he allowed a broad grin to spread across his face. He had been ordered about in the past by the very best – by bellowing drill sergeants, snappish and exacting flight instructors (*why, he had been one himself!*), and overbearing commanding officers who needed reports done yesterday. But being ordered about by a room full of typists and mail girls was something entirely new in his experience.

He shook his head – it was like being the new boy at school again, where academic or sporting prowess counts for little because even the kid at the bottom of the class knows his way around better than you and understands the class pecking order better than you. It's the time when anybody can push you about with impunity because you've got nothing to hang your hat on yet. And right now, even the girls who typed the minutes, Class 2s at best, were bigger fish than he. It made him smile, shake his head ruefully, and gather up the folders with their officious little flags.

As he rose, a man glanced through the window of his cubicle as he passed in the corridor outside. He seemed to do a double-take, for he stopped, came around the partition and looked hard at the boy. 'Don't I know you?' he said.

***

In the RAAF, the flying part is the simple part. It's on the ground that things can get complicated.

The boy seemed set for a solid upward rise in the staff ranks after his stint at No.38 Squadron. He spent a further six months at Staff College in Canberra in 1971, with its emphasis on geopolitics and management skills. 'Lively and confident, he can usually get order into his facts and is not easily put off by obstacles,' came the official report. 'Suitable for a Joint Services staff appointment.'[1] And in July 1971, he started at the new Defence Central at the Russell Offices in Canberra, as Head of Joint Warfare Staff. The role aimed to develop coordination between the three defence Services and maximise economy of effort and cost in training, exercises, policy and future planning[2].

At Joint Warfare, Kichenside was reunited with a member of No.77 Squadron who had been an icon to many of the young pilots in Korea, even if just in name (for his tour was over and he had already departed for Malta when the boy arrived in 1952). John Irwin 'Bay' Adams was a genuine legend of RAAF fighter operations. He had flown Hawker Tempests in Europe in World War II, shooting down two V1 flying bombs and credited with three aircraft kills. He was said to 'fear neither God nor the Devil' and had been praised admiringly in Korea by no less than UN air commander General Stratemeyer as 'the best shot in the FEAF'[3]. Adams was powerfully charismatic, with his square chin and air of invincibility. He was now an Air Commodore and Director of Joint Operations and Planning, a powerful one-star executive at Joint Warfare.

The three young representatives of each of the defence services at Joint Warfare, with Kichenside as their nominal head, were corralled into a single office, each with a desk and a filing cabinet but lacking the critical privacy for confidential discussions or interviews. Adams was lukewarm on the issue, but Kichenside remained unhappy with the perceived disparity between the facilities provided at Russell for the civilian administrators (plush) compared to those for military staff (substandard, in his view). So he produced a two-page document calling for equality, a call which reached the ears of a two-star Army general who then raised the matter with Adams and Air Member Personnel. Adams was not impressed with what he saw as Kichenside usurping his authority.

While Kichenside's call was never intended as a challenge to Adams, the problem only escalated when the three reps were subsequently each assigned new offices and Kichenside, as the senior member, got the biggest one. This minor issue nonetheless drove a wedge between himself and his colleagues which only deepened over what Adams perceived as the boy's failure to fulfil the social obligations befitting his rank of Wing Commander.

Appearances at social drinks, golf games, and dinner parties were *de rigueur* for Defence executives, but Kichenside, who had always done things his way, didn't see it like that. It had already been noted on his record that 'he has decided opinions and is not easily dissuaded'. He had spent years away from his family and now declared his weekends reserved for his wife and children. But declining the Department's social invitations proved to be a career-killing move. The result – the first mediocre report of his life: a report which put his promotions aspirations into a tailspin.

The PP29 report provides a performance rating on factors ranging from fairness, toughness and objectivity, to social mien. Adams' report was not negative, but it was average, and average reports do not buy promotion. The boy transferred to Joint Warfare at Air Force Headquarters Operational Command at Penrith in 1974 as Staff Officer Air Support – a Group Captain level position although he was still a Wing Commander – and his performance assessments were outstanding. But the second-rate report followed him, and when the promotions board met in 1975 to consider making the rank appointment substantive, he had tumbled from top spot in 1972 to fourteenth in line – from a rooster to a feather duster.

Jim Kichenside (left) with Sir Roden Cutler VC, Governor of New South Wales (centre), and Air Vice Marshal Fred Robey (right) at Air Force Headquarters Operational Command, Penrith, 1974 [Kichenside family collection].

The Whitlam government announced early retirement options for senior Defence Force executives in the early 1970s, and in 1975, Jim Kichenside decided to go, dispirited by the complicated internal politics associated with life on the ground. A Wing Commander could take notional retirement at 45, so in March 1975, his

Air Force career concluded[4]. Before he left, Bay Adams called to say he was sorry to lose him.

J.C. 'Sam' Jordan, the first RAAF navigator to be promoted to Air Vice Marshal, wrote a glowing testimonial to the boy's 26 years of service: 'You should reflect with pride on the splendid degree of resourcefulness, initiative and cheerful cooperation that you displayed in your many flying and staff appointments ... I should especially like to mention your fine work during your tour as Commanding Officer of 38 Squadron. Your wide experience as a pilot and your excellent managerial ability were reflected in the high level of proficiency your Squadron achieved and by the esteem in which you were held.'[5] Air Commodore Leonard Williamson echoed the sentiments, praising his outstanding cooperation with others and 'complete honesty and fairness'[6]. And the boy thought back suddenly to 1946, to his days as a prefect at Sydney Technical High School and endless recitation of the school motto: 'Manners maketh the man'. Now, he felt he truly knew what that meant.

***

Jim Kichenside was 45 years old and – for the first time – he had unlimited time. It was a little intimidating to have the entire world open to him. He decided to start small, at the sleepy holiday village of Brunswick Heads on the NSW north coast, where he had taken a happy fishing vacation the previous year. Now, he bought an old two-storey motel on the beach, converting the top storey into a three-bedroom residence for his family and refurbishing the three units below as holidays lets. Soon after, his father came for a six-week stay. Charles Kichenside was now 81 years old and had suffered a series of strokes, but the sharp sea air brought colour to his face and warmth to his cold limbs. He and his son talked for what seemed the first time in decades.

Just weeks later, on January 1, 1976, Charles Kichenside died-perhaps at peace at last[7].

Three generations of Kichenside fishermen: (L-R): James Kichenside jr. with son Jack Kichenside, and Jim Kichenside [Kichenside family collection].

***

The beach idyll was never going to be enough to sustain a man as ambitious and driven as Jim Kichenside. And he had promised himself the move to the north coast would not compromise the education of his youngest son, 13-year-old James. So in 1977, after two years of sandy-legged, suntanned ease, the family returned to Canberra to renew acquaintance with school blazers and office timesheets.

It was the first time since he was 16 that he'd had to find a job outside the military. The job market in academic middle-class Canberra was challenging for a mature-aged applicant without the university degree the higher echelons of public service demanded, but with a Staff College and command background that overqualified him for the lower. He took the Public Service entrance exam, finishing in the top 5 per cent, and on the basis of his RAAF credentials, was awarded a certificate of Associate Fellowship at the Australian Institute of Management.

He received an offer from the Department of Trade & Resources, but it was a lowly start. As a C/A-l, he was given a cubicle, a cap and appointment as 'Billy the Broom Boy'—part errand boy and part taxi driver, couriering documents and staff between divisions. He was ordered about by bossy secretaries, which he found hilarious, but his diet of humble pie was to last less than three weeks. The quiet dark-haired man with the military bearing and meticulous attention to detail stuck out like a sore thumb. He was in his stuffy cubicle one morning when a face glanced through the window, stopped, stared, and said, 'What the hell are you doing here, Kichenside?' It was an old colleague from the Department of Defence who was now a Division Head at Trade & Resources. Within hours, the boy had been moved upstairs as the department's new paymaster.

But that appointment, too, was short-lived. The head of security at Trade & Resources was nearing retirement, and the boy's Division Head came to him again with the proposal that, as he had top-secret clearance and service experience, he apply for the security role. It was a leap up to Class 8 level, but his record of having hundreds of men at his command and his spotless service history, he secured the role.

He was briefly tempted by the opportunity to take a post with the Trade Commissioner in Indonesia in 1978 – *adventures and exotic locations again!*—but he knew Beryl would hate the noise and pollution of Jakarta, and his youngest son would hate being sent to a boarding school. So this time, he put his own ambitions aside.

***

Dick Thompson was one of the most respected servants of the Antarctic Division in the 1950s and 60s. As a World War II navy man and senior administrative officer to Phillip Law, Thompson took part in six ANARE relief expeditions, travelling over 83,000 kilometres in expedition ships[8]. By 1980, Thompson had left the Department of External Affairs for a role in management at the Department of Transport, Air Transport Group (formerly the Department of Civil Aviation). He and the boy had sailed together twice on Antarctic voyages and found a great mutual respect. Now he invited Kichenside to apply for a security position at Transport as the department sought to increase their intelligence capacity in response to terrorism threats emerging from the Middle East, the Balkans and the Soviet Union.

In 1980, Kichenside was appointed as Assistant Director of Security and Intelligence (Class 9) based on his strong aviation and security background. Of primary concern to Australian air security officials was the growing use of hijacking as a terrorist *modus operandi:* in the late 1970s, there were airline hijacking incidents in New York, India, and Sydney, where on June 29, 1979, a lone terrorist demanding to be flown to Moscow hijacked Pan American World Airways flight 815 with a home-made beer can bomb before being shot dead by police[9]. Kichenside's role was in assessment of airport security from 'last port of calf destinations, including Hong Kong, Tokyo, India, Singapore, and Papua New Guinea. His passport quickly filled with exotic stamps again – although he had to be cautious about who he had a beer with in the local bars.

He played a part in the Australian government's assessment of air travel permissions for South Africa during the apartheid era of the early 1980s. In March 1983, Minister for Aviation Kim Beazley announced South African air services to Australia would be curtailed to one flight per week. While this was a question of demand rather than of security, two months later Foreign Minister Bill Hayden announced a review of Australian relations with the pariah nation and its apartheid regime, including an arms embargo, ban on sporting contact, and review of economic and diplomatic relations, including air services[10]. Kichenside travelled to South Africa and Zimbabwe to assess potential aviation security risks as part of this review. In 1984, Beazley announced the Australian government would take no steps to change the *status quo* of air services to southern Africa: Qantas would continue to operate a once-weekly service to Zimbabwe, with connections to other points in southern Africa, but not fly directly into South Africa in accordance with the existing embargo[11].

In 1985, aged 55 and after five years of almost continual international travel, Jim Kichenside was weary of jetlag and endless political and diplomatic niceties. There came an opportunity to progress up to Class 11 and into the bureaucratic heart of Transport, and he considered it right up until the morning of the interview: then he phoned Thompson to thank him and to say no. He'd grown from Billy the Broom Boy to a representative of the Minister for Aviation. He had kept his promise to his son. Now to enjoy life.

CHAPTER 27

RETURN TO THE 38th PARALLEL

What you remember saves you.
—W.S. Merwin

West Street
Gundagai, NSW
June 2010

He was dozing in his favourite chair on the porch, dimly aware of the winter sun on his face and the nearby hum of the highway. He had been feeling vaguely unwell, and the sandwich Beryl had brought him remained untouched on the table.

'You've got a letter, Jim.'

He shucked himself more upright in his chair and rubbed his eyes, then turned the missive over curiously. It was a heavy embossed envelope with a gold seal at the top. His eightieth birthday was in a couple of weeks – was it something to do with that? But from whom?

He pulled out the letter and unfolded it. It was an invitation, but not to a grand birthday party. The curly signature at the bottom read Lee Myung-Bak, President – South Korea. It was an invitation to return.

He had thought the weight of almost sixty years had dulled the memories. But he would still occasionally wake during a storm, imagining the whine of wind was the swoop of a flock of MiGs. A red dawn was still the great sheet of flame from a jet slamming into a hillside. When he saw food being scraped from plates at the end of a meal, he thought of the gaunt-faced columns of refugees amid the smoking ruins of Seoul. And he would never, ever forget Col King's voice in the darkness of that musty old tent, hoarse and torn with grief, saying, 'Smithy's gone in.'

With a slight groan, he smoothed the letter across his knee and read it again more slowly. The words were pretty, in black ink on fancy heavy paper. The Korean people wished to pay tribute to war veterans, to their 'selfless sacrifice in fighting tyranny and aggression ... courage in enduring the unimaginable horrors of war ... commitment in protecting liberty and freedom.' But the essence of the message was unchanged: the door was open for a return to Korea.

***

March 8, 2018: The world watched as US President Donald Trump met with North Korean national security adviser Chung Eui-yong and National Information Director Suh Hoon at the White House in Washington DC.

The North's envoys had brought news of an upcoming interKorean summit with the South in April – and issued an invitation from North Korean president Kim Jong-un for a follow-up meeting between the United States and the North. How would the mercurial US leader respond? This was, after all, the President who had mocked Kim as 'Little Rocket Man' on social media in 2017[1]. Acceptance of the invitation would make Trump the first sitting US president ever to meet with a North Korean leader. Could Trump, the belligerent, the bombastic, succeed where Clinton, Bush and Obama had not?

President Trump endorsed the North Korea-United States summit just an hour after the invitation was issued. Suddenly Korea was back in mainstream world news and conversation.

But had it ever really left?

Despite the armistice signed on July 27, 1953, North Korea and the South remain technically at war: the first conflict of the Cold War remaining as its last. Since 1953, Korea has lurched in and out of world consciousness, with sporadic security threats and the North's own set of calamities, its self-described 'Arduous March' of famine, drought and catastrophic floods. Even as the global security focus shifted to Vietnam, Afghanistan, Iraq, and the caliphate of the so-called Islamic State, Korea was always there, simmering in the background – and in 2018, Donald Trump and his rollercoaster relationship with Kim Jong-un made Korea newsworthy again.

East Asia is a tinderbox of old enmities and new ambitions, nuclear posturing and territorial shunting. The US still maintains more than 20,000 thousand troops in South Korea. North Korea has enough atomic weapons to decimate the Pacific and the reputed capability to deliver its nuclear payload as far away as the United States or Australia. The future shape and form of east Asia remains a pressing concern for Australia strategic policy planners, with the multiple uncertainties of China, Hong Kong, Taiwan, and the South China Sea, and the unfathomability of the North Korean relationship with both its southern counterpart, Japan and the United States[2]. And while the war on the peninsula lingers at a diplomatic and security level, for many survivors, it remains at a personal one.

***

Until the year 2000, life in retirement for Jim Kichenside had been peaceful and easy. Inspired by the 1988 Australian Bicentennial, he spent ten years compiling a detailed family history while dividing his time between the pretty NSW coastal town of Tathra and a mobile home in Nambucca Heads. He and Beryl revisited old haunts in Penang and Singapore, and vacationed in Hollywood, Las Vegas and Mexico, where a Tijuana street hawker produced some 1886 silver dollars identical to the one given him as a lucky charm in Korea and later stolen at East Sale. He bought four – one for himself and one each for his three sons.

Jim and Beryl Kichenside enjoying retirement in 2008 [Kichenside family collection].

Jim Kichenside with his family: (back row): sons Gary and Ken, Jim, son James; (front row): daughter Ann, wife Beryl [Kichenside family collection].

But early in 2000, the boy was feeling ill more and more often. When he finally had to lay his beloved family history aside, he decided it might be time to see a doctor. The diagnosis: bowel cancer. The surgeon said if he'd left it one week later, he would not have survived.

For a time, Jim Kichenside was a very sick man – he suffered three heart attacks, endured radiation treatment for prostate cancer and four surgeries for bowel cancer. A 2003 study on the incidence of cancer in Korean War veterans found a 23 per cent increased risk compared to the general Australian community; data released in the same year showed Korean ex-service personnel experienced a 21 per cent higher mortality rate than the non-serving male population, with a 71 per cent higher incidence of prostate cancer[3].

His own, and now Beryl's, health problems forced them to leave their beloved south coast and move to the small town of Gundagai in southern NSW in 2006, where their daughter Ann Cherie resided with her own family. They rented a pretty villa and it was here that the President's letter found him four years later.

The boy had been aware of the Korea Revisit program for veterans since its inception in 1975. But it was a Pandora's box he was not sure he wanted to open. He had rarely spoken of his Korean experience, even with his family – to the world, he was the quintessential fighter pilot, the 'Top Gun', gung-ho and invincible, all knife-edge creases, sharp salute and firm handshake. But Australia's Korean veterans continue to suffer significant psychological ill health, with rates of post-traumatic stress disorder (PTSD), anxiety and depression up to six times higher than other Australians[4]. Jim Kichenside's own decades of silent struggle against PTSD had been a part of his decision to take early retirement from the RAAF in 1975, although he had never told his family that. And now, with age and ill-health advancing, and with 2010 as the 60th anniversary of the outbreak of hostilities in Korea, he decided it was now or never.

The ten-hour flight to Inchon on October 12, 2010, all paid for by the South Korean government, ended with the group of octogenarian veterans passing VIP-style through South Korean immigration. A two-hour bus trip brought them to one of Seoul's finest five-star hotels, the Lotte, with its marble halls and grand chandeliers. Bus number 5 was to remain the regular transport for the 27 Australian, Canadian and South African veterans, with courteous attendants and an on-call doctor on board.

What a change they witnessed in the South Korean skyline. Ten million people now lived in glass and steel high-rise towers where there had been tidal mudflats and bomb craters. There were Hyundai cars in place of the ox carts, Samsung washing machines instead of buckets of dirty water, and – most tellingly – commercial aircraft full of happy holiday-makers where there had been the scream of low-flying fighter jets.

He fought briefly against a flood of technicolour memories – then sat back in the bus seat, closed his eyes, and just let them come.

Jim Kichenside is presented with the Ambassador of Freedom medal at a banquet for Australian, South African, and Canadian Korean War Veterans at the Lotte Hotel, Seoul, during the 2010 Korea Revisit program [Kichenside family collection].

It was the beginning of six days of tributes by the Korean people, including a formal dinner and military guard of honour hosted by the chief of the South Korean airforce, where the veterans were showered with praise and gifts. They were presented with the Ambassador of Freedom medal by President Lee Myung-Bak himself during a banquet in the Lotte's crystal ballroom, and officially proclaimed Ambassadors for Peace'.

Bus 5 also took them to the treaty village of Panmunjom and the Demilitarized Zone, that heavily fortified no-man's land still keeping the two Koreas at arm's length. On October 16, they forsook the bus for a fast train to the old port of Pusan, now known as Busan and Koreas second largest city. Here, they spent three hours in communion with the dead at the United Nations Memorial cemetery. So many familiar names here, names he had, for decades, tried not to think about but tried not to forget. Ian Cranston, Blue Colebrook, Bill Purssey, Lionel Cowper, Don Robertson ... and Smithy. The boy laid a wreath on behalf of the RAAF, 60 years after 77 Squadron first took to Korean skies.

Australian Korean War veterans at the memorial dedicated to Australian sailors, soldiers, airmen and nurses, within the grounds of the War Memorial of Korea, Seoul. Jim Kichenside stands third from left, back row [Kichenside family collection].

The gratitude, generosity and sincerity of the South Korean nation was unflagging, right through to priority boarding for the flight home on October 18. So it was a shock in Sydney when the weary veterans were made to shuffle in a two-hour queue through Customs.

But even in Australia, the Korean diaspora do not forget. In 2019, Col King, now 89 years old, encountered a Korean waiter in a Sydney restaurant who ran excitedly for his manager when he discovered his patron was a Korean War veteran. The two bowed before King and offered him everything he could eat without charge, thanking him again and again for what he had done for their homeland, almost seventy years before.

Jim Kichenside lays a wreath on behalf of Australian veterans at the at the United Nations Memorial Cemetery, Busan, in 2010 – 60 years after No.77 Squadron first flew in Korean skies [Kichenside family collection].

***

The boy is an old man now, in body at least. Many decommissioned Vampire and Meteor jets are now mounted on poles and plinths in parks around Australia as monuments to the early jet age and the first conflict of the post-World War II era. The boy's children would get very excited on family holidays while passing these stationary reminders, and the boy would sometimes consult his old logbook to see if he had once flown in any of them. But he still dreamed of his 207 days of service in Korea – of bullets and flames, but also of soaring wings and flowing contrails and civilians living in bomb craters who smiled and waved and called out thanks.

Australia continues to search for their lost airmen in Korea. In 2015, Foreign Minister Julie Bishop launched a diplomatic push to convince North Korean authorities to open access to sites along the DMZ in an attempt to recover the bodies of missing Australian service personnel[5]. A Memorandum of Understanding was signed with the United States on September 19, 2018, to share DNA and other identifying information from recovered remains. But forty-two Australian servicemen, of which eighteen are RAAF members, remain listed as missing in action in North Korea, including pilots Ken Smith, Don Robertson, Blue Colebrook and Lionel Cowper[6].

For Jim Kichenside, the 2010 Revisit brought closure to some of the challenges that confronted him more than five decades before. But he still asks the question, 'Why him, not me?' And his memory remains undimmed of all those moments when his luck might have run out: flame-outs over the Williamtown coast, substitute aircraft in Korea, bullets which never quite pierced the controls, a screaming blizzard which carried off a seven-tonne aircraft but left their flimsy tin-can of a caravan untouched. Luck, or fate, or destiny – those indefinable nebulous entities – has always been on his side.

ACKNOWLEDGEMENTS

I am beyond grateful that Jim Kichenside has trusted me with the story of his extraordinary life. Through his experience, I have developed a profound and enduring admiration for all service personnel who heeded the call in Korea, and beyond to Antarctica and South-East Asia. I also extend my thanks to the late Beryl Kichenside and their daughter Ann, for encouraging both Jim and myself in the two years we worked together on this book.

I am fortunate to be supported by a wonderful team at Big Sky Publishing, and have been the beneficiary of many information professionals during the course of my research: my thanks to staff at the National Archives of Australia, National Film and Sound Archive, Australian Antarctic Division library, National Library of Australia, State Library of New South Wales, Temora Aviation Museum, and the Australian War Memorial.

A special acknowledgment to Air Commodore John Meier, Director-General History and Heritage – Air Force for his support and approval for use of the RAAF badge to be included on the cover. I am also grateful to Group Captain David Fredericks, Director History and Heritage Services, History and Heritage – Air Force for reviewing my manuscript, believing in it and providing technical assistance and support in gaining approvals. To Wing Commander Jason Easthope, Commanding Officer 77 Squadron RAAF, thank you for taking the time to read my manuscript and for providing the Foreword.

One of the delights which outweighs the labour of research and writing is the planned (and chance) meetings with many of the players in this story who so generously shared their own experiences. I would like to thank Ian Douglas, Owen Zupp, Col King, George Cresswell, and the family of the late Don Robertson (Don Culvneor, Judith Culvenor, and Leanne Norris) for your support and kindness. Your contributions have brought the critical human element to this story that it deserves: the courage, the sacrifice, the mateship and endeavour.

Finally, to my writing friends: Jenny Glazebrook, Debra Clewer Williams, Freda Nicholls, Helen Castles, Vivien Thomson, Joy Coggan, April Glaser-Hinder and Michael Murphy-you understand. And to my family: Andrew, Vicki, Bob, Rowdy and Frody – you are irreplaceable.

ENDNOTES

Chapter 1:

[1] City of Sydney, 2019, *Sands Directory 1930 to 1933: Part 20: Classification of Trades and Professions Directory [Alphabetical] – Accountants to Furniture Warehousemen*, Sydney, cited June 30 2019, https://www.cityofsydney.nsw.gov.au/learn/search-our-collections/sands-directory/1930-1933. Marrickville Heritage Society, 2015, *History Lost: The Warren*, Sydney, cited June 6 2019, http://marrickville-heritage.blogspot.com/2014/08/history-lost-warren.html. State Library of NSW, 2019, *[Marrickville Subdivision Plans] [Cartographic Material] 1875-1939*, Sydney, cited June 30 2019, http://www.sl.nsw.gov.au.

[2] Gall, J., *From Bullocks to Boeings: An Illustrated History of Sydney Airport*, Australian Government Publishing Service, Canberra, 1986, p.48.

[3] Fitz-Gibbon, B. & M. Gizycki, 2001, *The 1890s Depression*, Reserve Bank of Australia, Canberra, cited June 28 2019,

https://www.rba.gov.au/publications/rdp/2001/2001-07/1890s-depression.html.

[4] NSW Registry of Births Deaths & Marriages, 1930, *Death Certificate: James Rutherford [Registration No.18756/1930]*, Sydney, cited February 1 2019, https://familyhistory.bdm.nsw.gov.au/.

[5] In 1935, there were more than 130 manufacturing operations in the suburb. Many families spent their whole lives within walking distance of the local factories. Meader, C., 2008, *Marrickville*, The Dictionary of Sydney, Sydney, NSW, cited March 21 2019, https://dictionaryofsydney.org/entry/marrickville.

[6] Ville, S. & G. Withers, *The Cambridge Economic History of Australia*, Cambridge University Press, UK, 2014.

[7] Barwell, D., 2018, *Heritage Bid to Save Car Plant*, Inner City West Courier, cited July 2 2019, http://newslocal.smedia.com.au/iw-courier-city/shared/ShowArticle.aspx?doc=NLIWCC%2F2018%2F07%2F10&entity=Ar00908&sk=B771890A. Inner West Council, 2018, *Local Notes: General Motors-Holden Assembly Plant Restarts 1934*, Petersham, cited July 2 2019, http://localnotes.net.au/?s=general+motors.

[8] The device, similar to a typewriter, communicated directly between offices instead of via the General Post Office, with messages automatically transcribed to the receiver by electrical impulses from each key. 'Every Man Can Now Be His Own Telegraphist', *Smith's Weekly,* Saturday October 7 1933, p.4.

[9] 'Radio Men Join A.L.P.', *Labor Daily,* October 27 1933, p.8.

'Ten Per Cent Cut: Wages to Be Reviewed', *Sydney Morning Herald,* October 13 1933, p.11.

[10] Offices Abolished, Created etc.:. Postmaster-General's Department: NSW. *Commonweath of Australia Gazette No.56 (Thursday October 12),* Australian Government Publishing Service, Canberra, ACT, 1933.

[11] 'Police Courts: Street Betting', *Sydney Morning Herald,* June 3 1933, p.10.

[12] Ancestry.com, 2010, *Australia, Electoral Rolls, 1903-1980 [Database on-Line],* cited June 29 2019, search.ancestry.com.au/.

[13] Craftsman, 'Among the Trade Unionists', *Australian Star,* December 23 1899, p.10.

[14] Hornsby Shire Council, 2019, *History of Beecroft,* cited July 5 2019, https://www.hornsby.nsw.gov.au/library/catalogues-and-resources/local-history/historyresources/suburb-histories/beecroft.

Chapter 2:

[1] State Library of New South Wales, 2020, *Aviation in Australia: Vickers Vimy,* Sydney, cited January 15 2020, https://www.sl.nsw.gov.au/stories/aviation-australia/vickers-vimy.

[2] Molkentin, M., *Flying the Southern Cross: Aviators Charles Ulm and Charles Kingsford Smith,* National Library of Australia, Canberra, 2012.

[3] Bird, N. & N.B. Walton, *My God! It's a Woman: The Inspiring Story of One Woman's Courage and Determination to Fly,* Harper Collins, Pymble, 2002.

[4] Macintyre, S., *Australia's Boldest Experiment: War and Reconstruction in the 1940s,* NewSouth Publishing, Sydney, 2015.

[5] National Archives of Australia & National Digital Learning Resource Network, 2010, *Air Raid Precautions at Sydney G.P.O.,*

Canberra, cited August 8 2019, http://vrroom.naa.gov.au/print/?ID=18844.

Chapter 3:

[1] Unemployment in the postwar decade averaged around 1.9 percent. McLean, I.W., *Why Australia Prospered: The Shifting Sources of Economic Growth,* Princeton University Press, New Jersey, 2016.

[2] Australian Military Forces, *Boyter Jack Edwin: Service Number – Nx 109930: Date of Birth-31 Mar 1919: Place of Birth – Coraki NS. W: Place of Enlistment – Unknown: Next of Kin – Boyter Edwin [Series No. B883],* Canberra, 1941.

[3] Geeves, P., 1976, *Saywell, Thomas (1837-1928),* Australian Dictionary of Biography, Canberra, cited August 1 2019, http://adb.anu.edu.au/biography/saywell-thomas-4540.

[4] 'Aircrew Trainees Wanted', *The Sydney Morning Herald,* April 26 1949, p.8.

[5] The base was located in the present suburb of West Lindfield, Sydney. The base was closed shortly after World War II in 1946. A memorial was opened at the site in 2006. Monument Australia, 2020, *Bradfield Park Royal Australian Air*

Force Station, Halifax, cited August 8 2019, http://monumentaustralia.org.au/themes/conflict/ww2/display/21859-%22spiral-ascent%22bradfield-park-royal-australian-air-force-station.

[6] RAAF service record, *Kichenside James Charles: Service Number 033628: Date of Birth 28/7/1930. Place of Birth: Marrickville NSW Conflict—Korea,* National Archives of Australia, Canberra, ACT, 1954-1998.

Chapter 4:

[1] Campbell-Wright, S., *An Interesting Point: A History of Military Aviation at Point Cook 1914-2014,* Air Power Development Centre, Commonwealth of Australia, Canberra, 2014.

[2] Stephens, A., 1995, *RAAFPolicy, Plans and Doctrine 1946-1971,* Air Power Development Centre, Canberra, cited September 26 2019, www.airpower.airforce.gov.au.

[3] O'Neill, R., *Australia in the Korean War 1950-53: Volume I: Strategy and Diplomacy,* The Australian War Memorial and the Australian Government Publishing Service, Canberra, 1985.

[4] King, C.G., *Luck Is No Accident: Flying in War and Peace,* Australian Military History Publications, Loftus, 2001.

[5] 'Two Die When Wirraway Crashes into the Sea', *West Australian,* March 30 1951, p.1.

[6] Odgers, G., *Remembering Korea: Australians in the War of1950-53,* Lansdowne Publishing Pty Ltd, Sydney, NSW, 2000.

[7] Newton, D., 1996, *Drummond, Vance (1927-1967)* Australian Dictionary of Biography, Canberra, cited March 27 2018, www.adb.anu.edu.au/biography/drummond-vance-10054.

[8] 'R.A.A.E Fighter Unit to Help U.S. In Korea', *The Age,* Saturday July 1 1950, p.1.

Chapter 5:

[1] Guile, M., *Culture in North and South Korea,* Reed International Books, Port Melbourne, 2003.

[2] Cumings, B., *North Korea: Another Country,* New Press, New York, 2004. Hastings, M., *The Korean War,* Guild Publishing, London, 1987.

[3] Cumings, B., *North Korea: Another Country,* New Press, New York, 2004.

[4] Hurst, D., *The Forgotten Few: 77RAAF Squadron in Korea,* Allen & Unwin, Crows Nest, 2008.

[5] Department of Veterans' Affairs, *Korea: A Cold War Conflict 1950-1953,* Australian Government, Canberra, 2016.

[6] UN military contributor nations: Australia, Belgium, Canada, Colombia, Ethiopia, France, Greece, Luxembourg, Netherlands, New Zealand, Philippines, South Africa, South Korea, Thailand, Turkey, UK, USA. UN medical contributor nations: India, Italy, Norway, Sweden. North Korean military contributor nations: China, North Korea, Soviet Union. North Korean medical contributor nations: Bulgaria, Czechoslovakia, East Germany, Hungary, Mongolia, Poland, Romania.

[7] Hurst, D., *The Forgotten Few: 77RAAF Squadron in Korea,* Allen & Unwin, Crows Nest, 2008.

Chapter 6:

[1] Brown, W., A. Cork, C. Faggo, & A.E. Donselaar, *Swift to Destroy: An Illustrated*

History of 77 Squadron RAAF 1942-2012, Norman Morris Pty Ltd, Newcastle, NSW, 2012.

[2] Hurst, D., *The Forgotten Few: 77 IAAF Squadron in Korea,* Allen & Unwin, Crows Nest, 2008.

[3] Evans, B., *Out in the Cold: Australia's Involvement in the Korean War 1950-1953,* Department of Veteran's Affairs, Canberra, ACT, 2000.

[4] O'Neill, R., *Australia in the Korean War 1950-53: Volume I: Strategy and Diplomacy,* The Australian War Memorial and the Australian Government Publishing Service, Canberra, 1985.

[5] Hurst, D., *The Forgotten Few: 77RAAF Squadron in Korea,* Allen & Unwin, Crows Nest, 2008.

[6] Odgers, G., *Remembering Korea: Australians in the War of 1950-53,* Lansdowne Publishing Pty Ltd, Sydney, NSW, 2000.

[7] Brown, W., A. Cork, C. Faggo, & A.E. Donselaar, *Swift to Destroy: An Illustrated History of 77 Squadron RAAF 1942-2012,* Norman Morris Pty Ltd, Newcastle, NSW, 2012.

[8] Forbes, C., *The Korean War: Australia in the Giants' Playground,* Pan Macmillan Australia Sydney, NSW, 2010.

[9] Hurst, D., *The Forgotten Few: 77RAAF Squadron in Korea,* Allen & Unwin, Crows Nest, 2008. Brown, W., A. Cork, C. Faggo, & A.E. Donselaar, *Swift to Destroy: An Illustrated History of 77 Squadron RAAF 1942-2012,* Norman Morris Pty Ltd, Newcastle, NSW, 2012. 'An Inspirational Leader in Two Wars', *Sydney Morning Herald,* January 6 2007, p.18.

[10] Odgers, G., *Remembering Korea: Australians in the War of 1950-53,* Lansdowne Publishing Pty Ltd, Sydney, NSW, 2000.

[11] Hurst, D., *The Forgotten Few: 77RAAF Squadron in Korea,* Allen & Unwin, Crows Nest, 2008.

[12] Craig, B., *The Chosin Few,* Turner Publishing Co., Paducah, 1993.

[13] Forbes, C., *The Korean War: Australia in the Giants' Playground,* Pan Macmillan Australia Sydney, NSW, 2010.

Chapter 7:

[1] 'Miracle Plane of the RAAF?', *Argus,* November 30 1951, p.3.

[2] Odgers, G., *Remembering Korea: Australians in the War of 1950-53,* Lansdowne Publishing Pty Ltd, Sydney, NSW, 2000.

[3] Ibid.

[4] Odgers, G., Atwj *the Parallel,* William Heinemann Ltd, London, 1952.

[5] King, C.G., *Luck Is No Accident: Flying in War and Peace,* Australian Military History Publications, Loftus, 2001.

[6] Davidson, P., 2007, *Beyer, Ihomas David (1906-1982),* Australian Dictionary of Biography, Canberra, cited July 30 2018, http://adb.anu.edu.au/biography/beyer-thomas-david-12206.

[7] Melbourne Cricket Club, 2019, *M.C.C. Cricket,* Melbourne Cricket Club, Melbourne, cited December 9 2019, https://www.mcc.org.au/mcc-cricket/mcc-cricket.

[8] O'Neill, R., *Australia in the Korean War 1950-53: Volume II: Combat Operations,* The Australian War Memorial and the Australian Government Publishing Service, Canberra, ACT, 1985.

[9] Menzies, R.G., *Proposed Order for Meteor Aircraft from United Kingdom for Re-Arming No.77 Squadron,* Prime Minister's Department, Canberra, 1950.

[10] Isby, D.C., *Fighter Combat in the Jet Age*, Harper Collins, London, 1997.

[11] Committee on Defence Preparations, *Defence Preparations Committee – Requirements of Meteor Aircraft for No 77 Squadron, Korea [National Archives of Australia Reference A4933, DPC52/35]*, Fourth and Fifth Menzies Ministries: Folders of Cabinet Committee Papers, Canberra, 1952.

[12] Hurst, D., *The Forgotten Few: 77RAAF Squadron in Korea*, Allen & Unwin, Crows Nest, 2008. Brown, W., A. Cork, C. Faggo, & A.e. Donselaar, *Swift to Destroy: An Illustrated History of 77 Squadron RAAF 1942-2012*, Norman Morris Pty Ltd, Newcastle, NSW, 2012.

[13] O'Neill, R., *Australia in the Korean War 1950-53: Volume II: Combat Operations*, The Australian War Memorial and the Australian Government Publishing Service, Canberra, ACT, 1985.

[14] King, C.G., *Luck Is No Accident: Flying in War and Peace*, Australian Military History Publications, Loftus, 2001.

[15] 'First Look at New "Wings"', *Argus*, August 3 1951, p.3. 'RAAF Pilots Are Given Wings', *Evening Advocate*, August

10 1951, p.6. 'They're Full Fledged Pilots Now', *Herald,* August 2 1951, p.1.

Chapter 8:

[1] Commonwealth Aircraft Corporation Pty Ltd, *Starting & Operating Instructions: Nene II V.H. Aust. Turbo-Jet Aero-Engines in Vampire Aircraft [Issue No.1, December 1948]*, CAC, Melbourne, VIC, 1948.

[2] King, C.G., 2003, *Through Korean Skies: Early Days of 5 Course'Pilots 77Squadron RAAF in Korea 1950-1953*, RAAF Air Force Association NSW, cited June 20 2019, https://www.raafansw.org.au/index.php.

[3] Royal Australian Air Force, *RAAF Unit History Sheets (Form A50) [Operations Record Book-Forms A50 and A51] Number 77 Squadron Jul 50 – Mar 52 [A9186103]*, National Archives of Australia, Canberra, 1995.

[4] King, C.G. & R.D. Guthrie, *Escape from North Korea: The Ron Guthrie Story,* Meteor, NSW, 2002.

[5] O'Neill, R., *Australia in the Korean War 1950-53: Volume II: Combat Operations,* The Australian War Memorial and the

Australian Government Publishing Service, Canberra, ACT, 1985.

[6] King, C.G., *Luck Is No Accident: Flying in War and Peace,* Australian Military History Publications, Loftus, 2001.

[7] United Services Club Queensland, 2016, *Roll of Honour: Korean War. Flight Lieutenant Ian Goodwin Swan Purssey Dfc,* United Service Club History & Heritage Notes, Brisbane, cited September 2 2019, https://www.unitedserviceclub.com.au/files/9614/5610/1491/People._Members._Honour_Roll._Korean_War._Purssey._Revised_Jan_2016.RM.pdf.

[8] Forbes, C., *The Korean War: Australia in the Giants' Playground,* Pan Macmillan Australia Sydney, NSW, 2010.

[9] Odgers, G., *Remembering Korea: Australians in the War of 1950-53,* Lansdowne Publishing Pty Ltd, Sydney, NSW, 2000.

[10] Hurst, D., *The Forgotten Few: 77 RAAF Squadron in Korea,* Allen & Unwin, Crows Nest, 2008.

[11] RAAF Museum Point Cook, 2019, *A79 DHA Vampire,* Royal Australian Air Force, Point Cook, cited September 20 2019, https://www.airforce.gov.au/si

tes/default/files/minisite/static/7522/RAAFmuseum/research/aircraft

[12] King, C.G., *Luck Is No Accident: Flying in War and Peace,* Australian Military History Publications, Loftus, 2001.

[13] O'Neill, R., *Australia in the Korean War 1950-53: Volume II: Combat Operations,* The Australian War Memorial and the Australian Government Publishing Service, Canberra, ACT, 1985.

[14] Hurst, D., *The Forgotten Few: 77RAAF Squadron in Korea,* Allen & Unwin, Crows Nest, 2008.

Chapter 9:

[1] May Florence Sjoberg (nee Adamson) died suddenly a year later. 'Deaths', *Sydney Morning Herald,* August 26 1953, p.28.

[2] 'Three Women Drowned', *Evening News,* October 8 1912, p.8.

[3] Tobbes Familje Sidor, 2020, *Johan Frans Leopold Sjoberg,* The Next Generation of Genealogy, Sweden, cited September 29 2019, http://akerman.me/tng/getperson.phpPpersonID=I4814&tree=tree1.

[4] Kichenside, J.C. & S. Owen, 'The Lottery of Life: The Kichenside/Sjoberg Story [Unpublished Manuscript]', Tathra, 2000.

[5] 'Groves – Outhwaite', *Singleton Argus,* July 4 1951, p.2.

Chapter 10:

[1] Hurst, D., *The Forgotten Few: 77RAAF Squadron in Korea,* Allen & Unwin, Crows Nest, 2008.

[2] Susans, R.T., *Tactical Report – Period 15th January – 15th February 52. In: Commanding Officers' Reports – Monthly Reports and Unit History Sheets (A50) – No 77 Squadron Nov 1944 to Dec 1962 with Gaps [NAA A9435,37],* Vol. Appendix G. No.77 (I/F) Squadron, Kimpo, Korea, 1952.

[3] Department of Veterans' Affairs, 2019, *Nominal Roll of Australian Veterans of the Korean War: Cranston, Ian Rew (033821),* Australian Government: Department of Veterans' Affairs, Canberra, cited September 2 2019, http://www.koreanroll.gov.au/veteran.aspx?id=1213592.

[4] 'RAAF Pilots Are Given Wings', *Evening Advocate,* August 10 1951, p.6. 'All Blacks Win Sydney Rugby', *Age,* June 21 1951,

p.14. RAAF service record, *Cranston Ian Rew: Service Number 033821: Date of Birth 03/10/1927. Place of Birth: Willoughby NSW. Conflict – Korea [A12372 R/3382HH]*, Royal Australian Air Force, Canberra, 1952.

[5] King, C.G., *Luck Is No Accident: Flying in War and Peace*, Australian Military History Publications, Loftus, 2001.

[6] Hurst, D., *The Forgotten Few: 77RAAF Squadron in Korea*, Allen & Unwin, Crows Nest, 2008.

Chapter 11:

[1] Royal Australian Air Force, *RAAF Unit History Sheets (Form A50) [Operations Record Book-Forms A50 and A51] Number 77 Squadron Jul 50 – Mar 52 [A9186103]*, National Archives of Australia, Canberra, 1995.

[2] Odgers, G., *Remembering Korea: Australians in the War of 1950-53*, Lansdowne Publishing Pty Ltd, Sydney, NSW, 2000.

[3] Hastings, M., *The Korean War*, Guild Publishing, London, 1987.

[4] King, C.G., 2003, *Through Korean Skies: Early Days of '5 Course'Pilots 77Squadron*

RAAF in Korea 1950-1953, RAAF Air Force Association NSW, cited June 20 2019, https://www.raafansw.org.au/index.php.

Chapter 12:

[1] King, C.G., *Luck Is No Accident: Flying in War and Peace,* Australian Military History Publications, Loftus, 2001.

[2] RAAF service record, *Colebrook Maxwell Edwin: Service Number 05895: Date of Birth 08/05/1926. Place of Birth: Perth. Conflict-Wa, Ww2, Korea [A12372 R/33821/H],* Royal Australian Air Force, Canberra, 1949-1952.

[3] Royal Australian Air Force, *RAAF Unit History Sheets (Form A50) [Operations Record Book-Forms A50 and A51] Number 77 Squadron Jul 50 – Mar 52 [A9186103],* National Archives of Australia, Canberra, 1995., RAAF casualty/repatriation file, *Colebrook Maxwell Edwin (Pilot Officer): Service Number A5895/05895: File Type – Casualty/Repatriation; Aircraft – Meteor 8 A77-627; Place – Korea; Date – 13 April 1952,* Royal Australian Air Force, Canberra, 1949-1952.

[4] Royal Air Force, *Gloster Meteor Mk.7 Pilot 's Flight Operating Instructions (4th Ed.)*, Royal Air Force London, 1957, p.113.

[5] Royal Australian Air Force, *RAAF No 77 [Fighter] Squadron – Unit History Sheets 1952-1958 [Covers Operations in Republic of Korea (South Korea), Japan and Williamtown, NSW Aircraft Flown: Meteor Mk 8] NAA Series Number A9186*, National Archives of Australia, Canberra.

[6] United Services Club Queensland, 2016, *Roll of Honour: Korean War. Flight Lieutenant Ian Goodwin Swan Purssey Dfc*, United Service Club History & Heritage Notes, Brisbane, cited September 2 2019, https://www.unitedserviceclub.com .au/files/9614/5610/1491/People._Members._Honour_Roll._Korean_War._Purssey._RevisedJan_2016.RM.pdf. RAAF casualty/repatriation file, *Purssey Ian Goodwin Swan (Flight Lieutenant): Service Number 011561: File Type – Casualty/Repatriation, Aircraft – Meteor Eight A77-189, Place-North Korea, Date – 22 April 1952 [Call No. A12372//32536/H]*, Royal Australian Air Force, Canberra, 1952.

[7] Aviation Safety Network, 2019, *ASN Wikibase Occurrence #85914*, Flight Safety

Foundation, cited October 1 2019, https://aviation-safety.net/wikibase/85914. Zupp, O. & M. Edwards, 2019, *Australian & New Zealand Military Aircraft Serials & History: RAAFA77 Gloster Meteor F.3, E8, T.7, Nf.II and U.21a,* ADF-Serials, cited October 1 2019, http://www.adf-serials.com.au/2a77.htm.

[8] Bennett, J., 'RAAF Aircraft Markings since 1950. Squadron Markings – Part 3 – the Meteor.', *ADF Serials Telegraph News,* vol.7, no.3, 2017: pp.3-55.

[9] Kichenside, J.C., 'The Life and Times of J.C.K. [Unpublished Manuscript]', Gundagai, 2016.

Chapter 13:

[1] 'Royal Australian Air Force College', *Commonwealth of Australia Gazette No.47,* July 3 1952, p.3007. King, C.G., 2002, *The Korean Episode: Historical Anecdotes – 77 Squadron RAAF in Korea 1950-1953,* RAAF Air Force Association NSW, https://www.raafansw.org.au/docPDF/77SQN_KOREA_1950-53_COL_KING.pdf. RAAF service record, *Robertson Donald Neil: Service Number 032536: Date of Birth 26/06/1929. Place of Birth: Melbourne*

Vic. Conflict—Korea [Call No. A12372//32536/H], Royal Australian Air Force, Canberra, 1952.

[2] 'RAAF College Graduate Lost', *Age*, May 17 1952, p.4. Aviation Safety Network, 2019, *ASN Wikibase Occurrence #85656*, Flight Safety Foundation, cited October 1 2019, https://aviation-safety.net/wikibase/85656.

[3] 'The League and Korea Men: Public Apathy Deplored', *Western Mail*, May 22 1952, p.51.

[4] 'Dead Airman's Father Writes to Peace Council', *Tribune*, May 6 1953, p.4. Australian Imperial Force, *Robertson Leonard John: Service Number 3012: Place of Birth: Mount Gambier Sa. Place of Enlistment: Melbourne Vic. Next of Kin: (Father) Robertson John*, Australian Imperial Force, 1914-1919.

[5] 'Deaths', *West Australian*, March 6 1941, p.1.

[6] 'Dead Airman's Father Writes to Peace Council', *Tribune*, May 6 1953, p.4. 'A Father's Letter', *Argus*, May 21 1952, p.2.

[7] Murphy, J., *Harvest of Fear: A History of Australia's Vietnam War*, Routledge, London, 2019.

[8] 'Peace Council Call: Ten Thousand Letters for Peace in Korea', *Tribune*, October 3 1951, p.11.

[9] 'Readers Join Issue on Korea: Quote from Father's Letter Starts Debate', *Mountain District Free Press*, June 12 1952, p.5. 'Korea', *Argus*, July 2 1952, p.2.

[10] O'Neill, R., *Australia in the Korean War 1950-53: Volume I: Strategy and Diplomacy*, The Australian War Memorial and the Australian Government Publishing Service, Canberra, 1985. 'Middle East Move Is Example of Sound Strategy', *Daily Telegraph*, March 7 1952, p.8.

[11] O'Neill, R., *Australia in the Korean War 1950-53: Volume I: Strategy and Diplomacy*, The Australian War Memorial and the Australian Government Publishing Service, Canberra, 1985.

[12] Devereaux, D.R. & C. Schrecker, *The Formulation of British Defense Policy Towards the Middle East, 1948—56*, Palgrave Macmillan UK, London, 1990.

[13] Parliament of the United Kingdom, *House of Commons Official Hansard: Defence, Vol 467, P431-560, 5 March*

1952, Vol.467. Parliament of the United Kingdom, London, 1952.

[14] 'RAAF Jets for Mid-East', *Sun,* March 5 1952, p.1.

'They're Off to the Middle East: Brides Going, Too – on Honeymoon', *Sunday Herald,* June 29 1952, p.5.

'Top RAAF Fliers Going to Malta', *Courier-Mail,* July 4 1952, p.5.

Lowe, D., *Menzies and the 'Great World Struggle': Australia 's Cold War, 1948-1954,* UNSW Press, Sydney, 1999.

[15] Bongiorno, F., 'The Price of Nostalgia: Menzies, the 'Liberal' Tradition and Australian Foreign Policy', *The Australian Journal of Politics and History,* vol.51, no.3, 2005: pp.400(18). Commonwealth of Australia, *House of Representatives Official Hansard: Wednesday 5 March. 20th Parliament – First Session: Third Period,* Commonwealth of Australia, Canberra, 1952.

[16] Commonwealth of Australia, *House of Representatives Official Hansard: Wednesday 6 August. 20th Parliament – First Session: Fifth Period,* Vol.32. Commonwealth of Australia, Canberra, 1952.

[17] No.77 Squadron played a small but important part in persuading the US to ratify the ANZUS treaty. With United Nations forces in Korea were under severe pressure during the treaty negotiations, 77 Squadron made a vital contribution in preventing American forces from being over-run. The achievement was influential in the US concluding the pact with Australia and New Zealand. Stephens, A., 1995, *RAAF Policy, Plans and Doctrine 1946-1971,* Air Power Development Centre, Canberra, cited September 26 2019, www.airpower.airforce.gov.au.

[18] O'Neill, R., *Australia in the Korean War 1950-53: Volume I: Strategy and Diplomacy,* The Australian War Memorial and the Australian Government Publishing Service, Canberra, 1985.

[19] 'Air Chief Forecasts Changes in RAAF', *Sydney Morning Herald,* April 28 1952, p.1.

[20] No.2 RAAF Operational Training Unit at Williamtown had sent 20 pilots to Korea in the last 2 months and had 10 more ready to leave for conversion, and were expecting 12 more to begin

training. 'Jet Pilots Undergo Intensive Training', *Courier-Mail,* Monday July 7 1952, p.2. Jim Kichenside kept a copy of this clipping in his logbook. 'RAAF Pilots 'Not Overworked'', *Advertiser,* June 19 1952, p.2.

[21] 'Denies Pilots Pushed', *Courier-Mail,* June 19 1952, p.1. 'Minister Cuts Korea Air Duty', *Courier-Mail,* June 27 1952, p.1.

[22] 77 Squadron CO Ron Susans finished his tour on May 26 and was awarded the DSO for his work refocussing the squadron after they were withdrawn from aerial combat late in 1951. Susans had led the squadron on 110 sorties, of which 100 were rocket and strafing, and turned a rapidly-deteriorating situation of morale and utilisation single-handedly around. Odgers, G., *Remembering Korea: Australians in the War of1950-53,* Lansdowne Publishing Pty Ltd, Sydney, NSW, 2000.

[23] 'Inquiry on RAAF Training', *Daily Telegraph,* June 6 1952, p.7. 'RAAF Men Fly Most Missions', *Herald,* June 4 1952, p.3.

[24] Chamberlain, F., 'Cabinet Summoned over Mid-East', *Courier-Mail,* June 11 1952, p.1. 'RAAF Wing for Malta',

Canberra Times, June 9 1952, p.5. 'Strain on Pilots', *Brisbane Telegraph*, June 18 1952, p.15.

[25] 'Minister Cuts Korea Air Duty', *Courier-Mail*, June 27 1952, p.1. 'Shorter Time in Korea for RAAF Pilots', *Age*, June 27 1952, p.4. 'Too Much from Too Few', *Courier-Mail*, June 19 1952, p.2.

[26] 'British Pilots Join RAAF Squadron', *Advertiser*, July 22 1952, p.3.

[27] Committee on Defence Preparations, *Defence Preparations Committee – Requirements of Meteor Aircraft for No 77 Squadron, Korea [National Archives of Australia Reference A4933, DPC52/35]*, Fourth and Fifth Menzies Ministries: Folders of Cabinet Committee Papers, Canberra, 1952.

[28] Stephens, A., *The Australian Centenary History of Defence: The Royal Australian Air Force (Volume 2)*, Oxford University Press, Melbourne, 2001.

[29] O'Neill, R., *Australia in the Korean War 1950-53: Volume I: Strategy and Diplomacy*, The Australian War Memorial and the Australian Government Publishing Service, Canberra, 1985. 'The RAAF's Malta

Deployment 1952-1954', *Pathfinder: Air Power Development Centre Bulletin,* vol.192, no. January 2013, 1.

[30] Births Deaths and Marriages Victoria, *Deaths in the District of Melbourne in Victoria: 13 June, 1960 – Leonard John Robertson,* Births Deaths and Marriages Victoria,, Melbourne, Vic, 1960, p.1.

[31] Hurst, D., *The Forgotten Few: 77RAAF Squadron in Korea,* Allen & Unwin, Crows Nest, 2008.

Chapter 14:

[1] Bennett, J., 'RAAF Aircraft Markings since 1950. Squadron Markings – Part 3 – the Meteor.', *ADFSerials Telegraph News,* vol.7, no.3, 2017: pp.3-55. Australian War Memorial, 2019, *Gloster Meteor Mk 8 Jet Fighter: 77 Squadron RAAF,* cited April 5 2019, https://www.awm.gov.au/collection/C242652.

[2] King, C.G., *Luck Is No Accident: Flying in War and Peace,* Australian Military History Publications, Loftus, 2001.

[3] Quilp, 'Clare & District Personalities', *Northern Argus,* July 16 1952, p.10. 'S.A. Pilot Posted Missing', *Chronicle,* July 17 1952, p.7.

Chapter 15:

[1] Hurst, D., *The Forgotten Few: 77RAAF Squadron in Korea,* Allen & Unwin, Crows Nest, 2008.

[2] Jever Steam Laundry, 2007, *Wing Commander OlafM O Bergh AFC,* No 122 Wing, RAF Jever, Germany, cited August 1 2019, http://www.rafjever.org/93sqnper008.htm.

[3] King, C.G., 2002, *The Korean Episode: Historical Anecdotes – 77 Squadron RAAF in Korea 1950-1953,* RAAF Air Force Association NSW, https://www.raafansw.org.au/docPDF/77SQN_KOREA_1950-53_COL_KING.pdf.

[4] Evans, B., *Out in the Cold: Australia's Involvement in the Korean War 1950-1953,* Department of Veteran's Affairs, Canberra, ACT, 2000. Australian War Memorial, 2019, *Australian Prisoners of War – Korean War,* Australian War Memorial, Canberra, cited August 1 2019, https://www.awm.gov.au/articles/encyclopedia/pow/korea.

[5] Thornton, J.W., *Believed to Be Alive,* Naval Institute Press, Annapolis, 2004.

[6] Jever Steam Laundry, 2007, *Wing Commander OlafM O Bergh AFC,* No 122

Wing, RAF Jever, Germany, cited August 1 2019, http://www.rafjever.org/93sqnper008.htm.

[7] Odgers, G., *Across the Parallel,* William Heinemann Ltd, London, 1952.

[8] Hurst, D., *The Forgotten Few: 77 RAAF Squadron in Korea,* Allen & Unwin, Crows Nest, 2008.

[9] 'First Look at Baby', *Mercury,* September 26 1952, p.14. Polkinghorne, A., 'Sydney Diary', *Sun,* September 27 1952, p.5.

Chapter 16:

[1] Stack, L., 'Korean War, a 'Forgotten' Conflict That Shaped the Modern World', *New York Times,* January 1 2018, p.23.

[2] Evans, B., *Out in the Cold: Australia's Involvement in the Korean War 1950-1953,* Department of Veteran's Affairs, Canberra, ACT, 2000.

[3] Lyman, G.B., *The Significance of Australian Air Operations in Korea,* Air Power Development Centre, Canberra, 1992.

[4] Hurst, D., *The Forgotten Few: 77RAAF Squadron in Korea,* Allen & Unwin, Crows Nest, 2008.

[5] US Air Medal gazetted 30 October 1953, for 'meritorious achievement while participating in aerial combat as the pilot of a Meteor aircraft. Mention in Dispatches: Commonwealth Gazette No 17, March 3 1953, for '148 operational sorties in Meteor aircraft against enemy ... many attacks against heavily-defended areas and always display(ing) a great devotion to duty. This example is in keeping with the highest traditions of the RAAF.' Commonweath of Australia, 1953, *Commonweath of Australia Gazette No.17 (Thursday March 19),* Australian Government Publishing Service, Canberra, www.nla.gov.au. Royal Australian Air Force, *Governor-General's Offce, Honours and Awards File: RAAF: Sergeant James Charles Kichenside A33628 [A.W.M.88 RAAF K/311],* National Archives of Australia, Canberra, 1952-53.

[6] Lane, S., 2011, *Gillard Marks Anzac Day in Korea,* ABC News, Canberra, cited October 2 2019, https://www.abc.net.au/news/2011-04-25/gillard-marks-anzac-day-in-korea/2605018.

Chapter 17:

[1] Bechervaise, J., *Antarctica, the Last Horizon,* Cassell Australia, North Melbourne, 1979. Trewby, M., *Antarctica: An Encyclopedia from Abbot Ice Shelf to Zooplankton,* David Bateman Ltd, Auckland, 2002.

[2] Huntford, R., *Shackleton,* Hodder & Stoughton, London, 1985.

[3] Australian Antarctic Division, 2012, *100 Years of Australian Antarctic Science,* Australian Government Department of the Environment and Energy, Kingston, cited January 6 2019, http://www.antarctica.gov.au/magazine/2011-2015/issue-22-2012/science/100-years-ofaustralian-antarctic-science.

[4] Trewby, M., *Antarctica: An Encyclopedia from Abbot Ice Shelf to Zooplankton,* David Bateman Ltd, Auckland, 2002.

[5] Australian Antarctic Territory became responsibility of Australian government (Antarctic Territory Acceptance Act) on August 24, 1936. Bowden, T., *The Silence Calling: Australians in Antarctica 1947-97,* Allen & Unwin, St Leonards, 1997.

[6] Australian Antarctic Division, 2018, *History of Australian Antarctic Aviation,*

Australian Government Department of the Environment and Energy, Kingston, cited Saturday January 6 2018, http://www.antarctica.gov.au/about-antarctica/history/transportation/aviation. Byrd, R.E., *Little America: Aerial Exploration in the Antarctic, the Flight to the South Pole,* GP Putnam's Sons, New York, 1930. Marks, K., 'Antarctic's First Plane Found in Ice', *Independent,* January 4 2010, p.6. Wilson, D., *Alfresco Flight: The RAAF Antarctic Experience,* Royal Australian Air Force Museum, Point Cook, 1991.

[7] Swan, R.A., *Australia in the Antarctic,* Melbourne University Press, Parkville, 1961.

[8] Wilson, D., *Alfresco Flight: The RAAF Antarctic Experience,* Royal Australian Air Force useum, Point Cook, 1991. Wilson, D., 2007, *Campbell, Stuart Alexander Caird (1903-1988),* Australian Dictionary of Biography, Canberra, cited August 1 2019, http://adb.anu.edu.au/biography/campbellstuart-alexander-caird-12290.

[9] Bowden, T., *The Silence Calling: Australians in Antarctica 1947-97,* Allen & Unwin, St Leonards, 1997.

[10] Isby, D.C., *Fighter Combat in the Jet Age,* HarperCollins, London, 1997.

[11] RAAF Association (NSW Division), 2019, *No 2 Operational Conversion Unit*, RAAF Association, NSW, cited August 28 2019, https://fsb.raafansw.org.au/2ocu.php.

[12] RAAF service record, *Kichenside James Charles: Service Number 033628: Date of Birth 28/7/1930. Place of Birth: Marrickville NSW. Conflict – Korea*, National Archives of Australia, Canberra, ACT, 1954-1998.

[13] *Commonweath of Australia Gazette No.59 (Thursday September 30)*, Australian Government Publishing Service, Canberra, 1954. *Commonweath of Australia Gazette No.8 (Thursday February 16)*, Australian Government Publishing Service, Canberra, 1955.

[14] Goebel, G., 2019, *[1.0] Vampire Variants*, Air Vectors, cited October 5 2019, http://www.airvectors.net/awampj.html. Laming, J., 'Aircraft and Other Stuff, *The RAM (online)*, no.58, 2017: pp.16.

[15] *Commonweath of Australia Gazette No.19 (Thursday March 28)*, Australian Government Publishing Service, Canberra, 1957.

[16] RAAF service record, *Lush John Fullarton: Service Number – 0369: Date of Birth-17/09/1915:] Place of Birth – Hawthorn, Vic: Conflict – Ww2/Vietnam,* Royal Australian Air Force, Canberra, ACT, 1931-1970.

Chapter 18:

[1] Burke, D., *Moments of Terror: The Story of Antarctic Aviation,* New South Wales University Press, Kensington, 1994.

[2] Wilson, D., *Alfresco Flight: The RAAFAntarctic Experience,* Royal Australian Air Force Museum, Point Cook, 1991.

[3] Geysen, H., *Mawson Station Log 1960 [PI556],* Antarctic Division, Department of External Affairs, Canberra, 1960.

[4] Royal Australian Air Force, *Command and Control in the Royal Australian Air Force,* Air Power Development Centre, Canberra, ACT, 2009.

[5] Department of External Affairs, *Part 1: Civil Aviation – Antarctica: 1957-61 [A1 838 716/55/6/1],* Department of External Affairs, Canberra, 1962.

[6] *Commonweath of Australia Gazette No.50 (Thursday August 13),* Australian Government Publishing Service, Canberra,

1959. Royal Australian Air Force, *RAAF Unit History Sheets (Form A50) [Operations Record Book – Forms A50 and A51] RAAF Antarctic Flight Sep 57 – Mar 63 [A9186449]*, National Archives of Australia, Canberra, ACT.

[7] Australian National Antarctic Research Expedition, *Antarctica-ANARE1959-1960 Expedition: 1960 Relief Expedition to Mawson—Report by Assistant Director Don Styles*, ed, Canberra, Vol. A1838 1495/3/4/7/14 Department of External Affairs, 1960.

[8] Wilson, D., *Alfresco Flight: The RAAF Antarctic Experience*, Royal Australian Air Force Museum, Point Cook, 1991. Ruker, R. & I. Bird, 'Mawson Midwinter 1960: Record of the 50th Anniversary Reunion', Hobart, TAS, 2010.

[9] 'Dakota Gets a Boost', *Beverley Times*, Thursday December 10 1959, p.11. Wilson, S., *Dakota, Hercules and Caribou in Australian Service*, Weston Creek, Aerospace Publications, 1990.

[10] Cablegram regarding the loss of Beavers at Mawson 1959 from J. Sandercock to the Department of Air. Antarctic Division, *Report on Loss of Dakota and Beaver Aircraft at Mawson,*

December 1960 [A703, 400/1/10/P1], Department of External Affairs, Canberra, ACT, 1961.

[11] Bechervaise, J., *Mawson Station Log 1959-1960 with Brief Note on Field Trips Not Included in Surveyors or Biologist's Log*, Antarctic Division, Department of External Affairs, Canberra, 1960.

[12] Law, P., 'New ANARE Landings in Australian Antarctic Territory 1960', *The Geographical Journal*, vol.128, no.2, 1959: pp.174-183.

[13] Styles, D.F., *Thala Dan – Voyage 3 – 1959-1950–1960 Relief Expedition to Mawson-Report by Assistant Director Antarctic Division[3 Copies]*, ed, D.O.E.A. Antarctic Division, Canberra, ACT, 1960.

[14] Geysen, H., *Mawson Station Log 1960 [PI556]*, Antarctic Division, Department of External Affairs, Canberra, 1960.

[15] Peake-Jones, K., *Mawson 1959-1960 Fire Officer's Report [P1556]*, Antarctic Division, Department of External Affairs, Canberra, 1959.

Chapter 19:

[1] Geysen, H., *Mawson Station Log 1960 [P1556]*, Antarctic Division, Department of External Affairs, Canberra, 1960.

[2] Australian Antarctic Division, 2019, *Sydney L Kirkby (1933-)*, Australian Government Department of the Environment and Energy, Kingston, cited August 20 2019, http://www.antarctica.gov.au/about-antarctica/history/people/syd-kirkby.

[3] Beck, P.J., *The International Politics of Antarctica*, Routledge, London, 2014.

[4] Australian Antarctic Division, 2010, *Vale: Phillip Garth Law Ac, CBE, 1912-2010*, Australian Government Department of the Environment and Energy, Kingston, cited September 10 2019, http://www.antarctica.gov.au/magazine/2006-2010/issue-18-2010/vale/vale-phillip-garth-law-accbe-1912-2010.

[5] Australian Antarctic Division, 2019, *Huskies*, Australian Government Department of the Environment and Energy, Kingston, cited August 20 2019, http://www.antarctica.gov.au/aboutantarctica/history/transportation/ground-transportation/huskies.

[6] Bowden, T., *The Silence Calling: Australians in Antarctica 1947-97*, Allen & Unwin, St Leonards, 1997.

[7] Styles, D.E, *ANARE Reports: Narrative: Coastal Exploration of Kemp and Enderby Lands, Antarctica,* Vol.1. Antarctic Division, Department of External Affairs, Canberra, 1964.

[8] Ruker, R. & I. Bird, 'Mawson Midwinter 1960: Record of the 50th Anniversary Reunion', Hobart, TAS, 2010.

[9] Geysen, H., *Report on Dogs: Mawson 1960 [P1556]*, Antarctic Division, Department of External Affairs, Canberra, 1960.

Chapter 20:

[1] Yu, Y. & X.-M. Cai, 'Structure and Dynamics of Katabatic Flow Jumps: Idealised Simulations', *Boundary-Layer Meteorology,* vol.118, no.3, 2006: pp.527-555.

[2] Wilson, D., *Alfresco Flight: The RAAFAntarctic Experience,* Royal Australian Air Force Museum, Point Cook, 1991.

[3] Kichenside, J.C., *Antarctic Flight 1960 Log Summary: In: Mawson 1960 50th Anniversary Reunion,* ANARE Club, Hobart, 2010.

[4] Department of Air, *Incident to Beaver A95-202 – Pilot: Kitchenside J.V.C. (033628) [A705, 32/18/1638]*, Commonwealth of Australia, Canberra, 1960.

[5] Australian Antarctic Division, 2015, *Two-Wheeled Antarctic Adventures*, Australian Government Department of the Environment and Energy, Kingston, TAS, cited September 5 2019, http://www.antarctica.gov.au/magazine/2011-2015/issue-29-december-2015//history/twowheeled-antarctic-adventures.

[6] Trewby, M., *Antarctica: An Encyclopedia from Abbot Ice Shelf to Zooplankton*, David Bateman Ltd, Auckland, 2002. Courts, L.A., *4 Leaders. First to the Poles: The Leadership Challenge*, Brolga Publishing Pty Ltd, Melbourne, 2012, p.

[7] Wilson, D., 2007, *Douglas, Gilbert Eric (1902-1970)*, Australian Dictionary of Biography, Canberra, cited August 1 2019, http://adb.anu.edu.au/biography/douglas-gilbert-eric-10038.

[8] Geysen, H., *Mawson Station Log 1960 [P1556]*, Antarctic Division, Department of External Affairs, Canberra, 1960.

Chapter 21:

[1] Australian National Antarctic Research Expedition, *Antarctica—ANARE 1959-1960 Expedition: 1960 Relief Expedition to Mawson—Report by Assistant Director Don Styles*, ed, Canberra, Vol. A1838 1495/3/4/7/14 Department of External Affairs, 1960.

[2] Kichenside, J.C., *Antarctic Flight 1960 Log Summary: In: Mawson 1960 50th Anniversary Reunion,* ANARE Club, Hobart, 2010.

[3] Crohn, P., *Observations on Plateau Ice and Nevee, Mawson, Antarctica [P1556, Mawson 1955]*, Australian National Antarctic Research Expeditions, Melbourne, 1955.

[4] Antarctic Division, *Report on Loss of Dakota and Beaver Aircraft at Mawson, December 1960 [A703, 400/1/10/P1]*, Department of External Affairs, Canberra, ACT, 1961.

[5] Notes from the ANARE Executive Planning Committee meeting 27 April 1959. Ibid.

[6] Correspondence from the Department of Treasury, November 2, 1961. Ibid.

[7] Kichenside, J.C., *Amundsen Bay Flying Camp: In: Mawson Field Trips 1960 [Pl556]*, Antarctic Division, Department of External Affairs, Canberra, 1960.

[8] Wienecke, B., 'Emperor Penguin Colonies in the Australian Antarctic Territory: How Many Are There?', *Polar Record,* vol.45, no.235, 2009: pp.304-312.

[9] Kichenside, J.C., *Amundsen Bay Flying Camp: In: Mawson Field Trips 1960 [Pl556]*, Antarctic Division, Department of External Affairs, Canberra, 1960.

[10] Australian Antarctic Data Centre, 2019, *Gazetteer: Kichenside Glacier,* Australian Antarctic Division, Hobart, cited October 5 2018, https://data.aad.gov.au/aadc/gaz/display_name.cfm?gaz_id=583. United States Geological Survey, 1965, *Antarctica Detail: Kichenside Glacier,* USGS, Reston, cited October 5 2018, https://geonames.usgs.gov/apex/f?p=gnispq:5:0::NO::P5_ANTAR_ID:7916.

[11] Australian Antarctic Names and Medals Committee, 2013, *Australian Antarctic Names and Medals Committee Policy,* Australian Antarctic Division, Hobart, www.data.aad.gov.au_gaz_antarctic_place_names_policy_dec2013.

Chapter 22:

[1] Trewby, M., *Antarctica: An Encyclopedia from Abbot Ice Shelf to Zooplankton*, David Bateman Ltd, Auckland, 2002.

[2] Australian National Antarctic Research Expedition, *Antarctica-ANARE1959-1960 Expedition: 1960 Relief Expedition to Mawson—Report by Assistant Director Don Styles*, ed, Canberra, Vol. A1838 1495/3/4/7/14 Department of External Affairs, 1960.

[3] Cresswell, G., 'Antarctic Pilot: Extracts from the 1960 Diary of the Late Ken Assender', *Wings: Journal of the Air Force Association*, vol.70, no.1, 2018: pp.8-12.

[4] Antarctic Division, *Report on Loss of Dakota and Beaver Aircraft at Mawson, December 1960 [A703, 400/1/10/P1]*, Department of External Affairs, Canberra, ACT, 1961. Kichenside, J.C., *Antarctic Flight 1960 Log Summary: Ln: Mawson 1960 50th Anniversary Reunion*, ANARE Club, Hobart, 2010.

[5] Notes on meteorology at Mawson in 1960 (NA Streten). In: Ruker, R. & I. Bird, 'Mawson Midwinter 1960: Record of the 50th Anniversary Reunion', Hobart, TAS, 2010.

[6] Signal D530 9/12/60 – 14/12/60 from Henk Geysen, OIC Mawson to PG Law. In: Antarctic Division, *Report on Loss of Dakota and Beaver Aircraft at Mawson, December 1960 [A703, 400/1/10/P1]*, Department of External Affairs, Canberra, ACT, 1961.

[7] Signal D530 9/12/60 – 14/12/60 from Henk Geysen, OIC Mawson to PG Law. Ibid. National Hurricane Center and Central Pacific Hurricane Center, 2019, *Saffir-Simpson Hurricane Wind Scale*, cited October 10 2019, https://www.nhc.noaa.gov/aboutsshws.php.

[8] Ruker, R. & I. Bird, 'Mawson Midwinter 1960: Record of the 50th Anniversary Reunion', Hobart, TAS, 2010.

[9] In the analysis of aircraft lost on the plateau, Sandercock contended even if the deadmen and cables had held in the 1959 blizzard, both aircraft would still have been wrecked. In Signal D530 9/12/60 – 14/12/60 from Henk Geysen to Law, Geysen reported: All tiedowns used were in accordance with ANARE instructions ... The severity of this blizzard would have made any aircraft tied down on the plateau unsafe.' Antarctic Division, *Report on Loss of*

Dakota and Beaver Aircraft at Mawson, December 1960 [A703, 400/1/10/P1], Department of External Affairs, Canberra, ACT, 1961. Cresswell, G., 'Antarctic Pilot: Extracts from the 1960 Diary of the Late Ken Assender', *Wings: Journal of the Air Force Association*, vol.70, no.1, 2018: pp.8-12.

[10] Wilson, D., *Alfresco Flight: The RAAFAntarctic Experience*, Royal Australian Air Force Museum, Point Cook, 1991. Antarctic Division, *Report on Loss of Dakota and Beaver Aircraft at Mawson, December 1960 [A703, 400/1/10/P1]*, Department of External Affairs, Canberra, ACT, 1961.

[11] Ruker, R. & I. Bird, 'Mawson Midwinter 1960: Record of the 50th Anniversary Reunion', Hobart, TAS, 2010.

Chapter 23:

[1] Report on the loss of Australian National Antarctic Research Expedition Dakota and Beaver Aircraft – 9th December 1960 – JC Kichenside. In: Antarctic Division, *Report on Loss of Dakota and Beaver Aircraft at Mawson, December 1960 [A703, 400/1/10/P1]*,

Department of External Affairs, Canberra, ACT, 1961.

[2] Department of External Affairs, *Antarctica—Long Range Plans 1959-60, 1960-61, 1963-67 [A1838 1495 314127 Part 1,2,3]*, Department of External Affairs,, Canberra, 1967.

[3] Law to Department of Air, 22 June 1959: 'I have consistently during the last 5 years sought to find some methods of operating from the Antarctic Plateau behind Mawson in order to permit flying during the Antarctic summer when a sea-ice airfield is not available.' In: Antarctic Division, *Report on Loss of Dakota and Beaver Aircraft at Mawson, December 1960 [A703, 400/1/10/P1]*, Department of External Affairs, Canberra, ACT, 1961. Australian Antarctic Division, 2018, *Mawson Station: A Brief History*, Australian Government Department of the Environment and Energy, Kingston, cited September 10 2019, http://www.antarctica.gov.au/about-antarctica/history/stations/mawson.

[4] Minute sheet 400/1/10: 4 May, 1961: senior RAAF staff discussed Kichenside's report with specialists from Department of Air Engineering, who agreed that

Kichenside's conclusions were valid. 15 May 1961: Department of Air Secretary AB McFarlane to Law: 'the recommendation that aircraft should not be based in the Mawson area unless adequate shelter can be provided is endorsed by this Department. It also seems reasonable that this should apply to other Antarctic bases if we are to avoid recurring damage to aircraft. It is suggested that a close study of any selected area, with special regard to likely wind velocities, should be made before deciding on future air operations.' Antarctic Division, *Report on Loss of Dakota and Beaver Aircraft at Mawson, December 1960 [A703, 400/1/10/PI]*, Department of External Affairs, Canberra, ACT, 1961.

[5] Cabinet Submission on the Antarctic 1495/3/4/27, Department of External Affairs, 17/10/1960. In: Part 1: Department of External Affairs. (1967). And Cabinet Minute from the Minister for External Affairs, 16/02/1961: Future Australian activities in the Antarctic. In: Part 3: Department of External Affairs. (1967). In: Department of External Affairs, *Antarctica – Long Range Plans*

1959-60, 1960-61, 1963-67 [A1838 1495131412 7Part 1,2,3], Department of External Affairs,, Canberra, 1967.

Law, P., *Draft Section of Cabinet Submission on Future TIN ARE Work: 1. Future Antarctic Policy: Future Participation by the RAAF in ANARE Expeditions. Ln: Phillip Law Collection: Ms9458: Box 21: Correspondence Subject File: Antarctica: ANARE Reports on Voyages and Stations,* National Library of Australia, Canberra, 1961.

[6] Australian Antarctic Division, 2018, *History of Australian Antarctic Aviation,* Australian Government Department of the Environment and Energy, Kingston, cited Saturday January 6 2018, http://www.antarctica.gov.au/about-antarctica/history/transportation/aviation. Wilson, D., *Alfresco Flight: The RAAFAntarctic Experience,* Royal Australian Air Force Museum, Point Cook, 1991.

[7] Parliament of the United Kingdom, 2018, *About the Polar Medal,* UK Parliament, London, cited January 21 2018, https://www.parliament.uk/about/living-heritage/building/culturalcollections/medals/collection/polar-medal/history/.

[8] Bowden, T., *The Silence Calling: Australians in Antarctica 1947-97*, Allen & Unwin, St Leonards, 1997.

Cohen, N., 1994, *Icy Hush Falls on Polar Medal Quango*, London, cited June 18 2019, http://www.independent.co.uk/news/uk/home-news/icy-hush-falls-on-polar-medalquango-1423669.html.

Commonwealth of Australia, *Commonweath of Australia Gazette No.106 (Thursday December 18)*, Australian Government Publishing Service, Canberra, ACT, 1969.

[9] Australian Antarctic Division, 2010, *Vale: Phillip Garth Law Ac, CBE, 1912-2010*, Australian Government Department of the Environment and Energy, Kingston, cited September 10 2019, http://www.antarctica.gov.au/magazine/2006-2010/issue-18-2010/vale/vale-phillip-garth-law-accbe-1912-2010.

[10] £625 per day in 1961, or around $9,000 Australian dollars in 2019. Burke, D., 'Air Link with Polar Bases Is Needed', *Sydney Morning Herald*, mApril 19 1961, p.9.

[11] Department of External Affairs, *Antarctica – Flights to Antarctica 1952-67/1967-68 [A1838 1495/3/4/4*

Part 2,3], Department of External Affairs, Canberra, 1968.

'Today's Polar Flight a New First', *Canberra Times*, October 1 1964, p.7.

[12] Mellor, M., *Notes on Antarctic Aviation*, U.S. Army Cold Regions Research and Engineering Laboratory, University of California, Berkeley, 1993. Riffenburgh, B., *Encyclopedia of the Antarctic*, Taylor & Francis, London, 2007.

[13] Department of External Affairs, *Antarctica-Air Communication 1956-67 [A1838 1495/1/3]*, Department of External Affairs, Canberra, 1967.

[14] Bowden, T., *The Silence Calling: Australians in Antarctica 1947-97*, Allen & Unwin, St Leonards, 1997.

Commonwealth of Australia, *House of Representatives Official Hansard No 168: Parliamentary Debates, Wednesday August 30, 1989*, Commonwealth of Australia, Canberra, ACT, 1989.

Commonwealth of Australia, *Senate Official Hansard No 138, 1989: Wednesday December 6, 1989[35th Parliament, First Session, Fifth Period]*, Commonwealth of Australia, Canberra, ACT, 1989.

[15] Australian Antarctic Division, 2002, *Antarctic Runway Work to Begin*,

Australian Government Department of the Environment and Energy, Kingston, cited October 6 2019, http://www.antarctica.gov.au/news/2002/antarctic-runway-work-to-begin.

Commonwealth of Australia, *Official Committee Hansard: Senate – Department of the Arts, Sport, the Environment, Tourism and Territories: Estimates Committee C: September 4*, ed, Consideration of Budget Estimates, Canberra, 1991.

Commonwealth of Australia, *Department of Environment and Heritage Annual Report 1999-2000*, ed, D.o.t. Environment, Canberra, 2000.

Hill, R., *Media Release: Antarctic Air Link a Step Closer*, Minister for the Environment and Heritage, Canberra, 1999.

Shevlin, J. & J. Johnson, *Antarctic Air Transport Scoping Study*, The Australian Antarctic Division of Environment Australia, Canberra, 1999.

[16] Mulvey, P., 'Antarctic Flight Opens New Frontiers', *Age*, Saturday January 12 2008, p.7.

[17] Commonwealth of Australia, 2008, *Media Release: Bad Weather Delays Governor-General's Visit to Australian Antarctic Territory (January 22, 2008)*,

Governor-General of the Commonwealth of Australia, Canberra, cited September 2 2019, http://parlinfo.aph.gov.au.

Commonwealth of Australia, 2008, *Department of the Environment, Water, Heritage and the Arts Annual Report 2007-08*, Commonwealth of Australia, Canberra, ACT, cited September 2 2019, https://www.environment.gov.au/about-us/accountability-reporting/annual-reports.

[18] Commonwealth of Australia, 2013, *Official Committee Hansard: Senate – Environment and Communications Legislation Committee: Estimates: Monday November 18*, Consideration of Budget Estimates, Canberra, https://parlinfo.aph.gov.au.

Sebastian, S., 2010, *From Oz to Ice: Flight Operations of the Australia Antarctic Division*, cited September 4 2019, https://airlinerworld.keypublishing.com/.

[19] ABC News online, 2012, *Melting Runway Puts Antarctic Flights on Ice*, ABC News, Hobart, cited October 8 2019, https://www.abc.net.au/news/2012-10-24/melting-ice-runway-puts-freeze-on-antarcticflights/4331770.

Darby, A., 'Frozen $46m Runway Melting', *Sydney Morning Herald,* October 24 2012, p.13.

[20] *Australian Antarctic Strategy and 20 Year Action Plan,* Commonwealth of Australia, Canberra, 2016.

Australian Antarctic Division, 2018, *Building Antarctica's First Paved Runway,* Australian Antarctic Division, Kingston, cited December 10 2019, http://www.antarctica.gov.au/news/2018/Building-Antarcticas-first-paved-runway.

[21] Department of External Affairs, *Antarctica—Air Communication 1956-67 [A1838 1495/1/3],* Department of External Affairs, Canberra, 1967.

Department of External Affairs, *Selection of an Airfield—Antarctica 1958-59 [A705 7/1/2477],* Department of External Affairs, Canberra, 1960.

Wilson, H.O., *Thala Dan 1958-1950 – Report – Proposed Airfield – Vestfold Hills, Antartica [Includes 12 B/W Photographs] [Pl557],* Antarctic Division, Department of External Affairs, Canberra, 1959.

[22] Mellor, M., *Notes on Antarctic Aviation,* U.S. Army Cold Regions Research and Engineering Laboratory, University of California, Berkeley, 1993.

Riffenburgh, B., *Encyclopedia of the Antarctic*, Taylor & Francis, London, 2007.

[23] Australian Antarctic Division, 2018, *Building Antarctica 's First Paved Runway*, Australian Antarctic Division, Kingston, cited December 10 2019, http://www.antarctica.gov.au/news/2018/Building-Antarcticas-first-paved-runway.

Australian Antarctic Division, 2018, *New Davis Runway*, Australian Antarctic Division, Kingston, cited December 10 2018, http://www.antarctica.gov.au/living-and-working/travel-and-logistics/aviation/New-Davis-Runway.

Gooley, C., 2018, *Site Chosen for Antarctic Year-Round Runway near Australia's Davis Research Station*, ABC News, cited October 5 2019, https://www.abc.net.au/news/2018-05-18/year-round-antarctic-runway-site-chosen/9774282.

Joint Standing Committee on the National Capital and External Territories, 2018, *Maintaining Australia 's National Interests in Antarctica: Inquiry into Australia's Antarctic Territory*, Commonwealth of Australia, Canberra, cited September 5 2019, https://parlinfo.aph.gov.au.

Layton, P., T. Hallen & L. Bishop, *Australia's Antarctic National Air Power Futures*,

Air Power Development Centre, Canberra, 2019.

Chapter 24:

[1] Edwards, P. & G. Pemberton, *Crises and Commitments – the Politics and Diplomacy of Australia's Involvement in Southeast Asian Conflicts 1948-1965*, Allen & Unwin, North Sydney, 1992.

US Department of State, 2019, *The Australia, New Zealand and United States Security Treaty (Anzus Treaty), 1951*, Office of the Historian, US State Department, Washington DC, cited October 1 2019, https://history.state.gov/milestones/1945-1952/anzus.

[2] Coulthard-Clark, C., *The RAAF in Vietnam: Australian Air Involvement in the Vietnam War 1962-1975*, Allen & Unwin, St Leonards, 1995.

[3] 'Big Outlay on New Planes for RAAF and RAN', *West Australian*, August 25 1951, p.1.

[4] Brown, W., A. Cork, C. Faggo, & A.e. Donselaar, *Swift to Destroy: An Illustrated History of 77 Squadron RAAF 1942-2012*, Norman Morris Pty Ltd, Newcastle, NSW, 2012.

[5] Brindle, W., 1958, *Defence – Air – Sabre Jet Pilot Given Special Training in a Simulator at RAAF Williamtown near Newcastle, New South Wales [B&WNegative I Cellulose Acetate I Preservation Material [L28561]]*, National Archives of Australia, Canberra, cited September 9 2019, www.naa.gov.au.

[6] Law published a paper in the *Medical Journal of Australia* in 1960 entitled 'Personality Problems in Antarctica, exploring difficulties of men surving for a year off the communications grid. He identified the compensations as the adventure, magnificent scenery, and lack of financial anxiety. Bowden, T., *The Silence Calling: Australians in Antarctica 1947-97*, Allen & Unwin, St Leonards, 1997.

[7] RAAF service record, *Kichenside James Charles: Service Number 033628: Date of Birth 28/7/1930. Place of Birth: Marrickville NSW. Conflict—Korea*, National Archives of Australia, Canberra, ACT, 1954-1998.

[8] O'Neill, R., *Australia in the Korean War 1950-53: Volume I: Strategy and Diplomacy*, The Australian War Memorial and the Australian Government Publishing Service, Canberra, 1985.

[9] Brown, W., A. Cork, C. Faggo, & A.e. Donselaar, *Swift to Destroy: An Illustrated History of 77 Squadron RAAF 1942-2012*, Norman Morris Pty Ltd, Newcastle, NSW, 2012.

[10] Ibid., Royal Australian Air Force, *RAAF Unit History Sheets (Form A50) [Operations Record Book – Forms A50 and A51] No 77 [Fighter] Squadron Jan 1968 – Feb 1979 [Covers Operations at Williamtown, NSW, and Butterworth. Aircraft Flown: Sabre]. [A9186, 105]*, National Archives of Australia, Canberra.

[11] Defence Committee, *Directive to Officer Commanding Royal Australian Airforce Continent, Ubon, Thailand [A2031, 67/1962]*, Department of Defence, Canberra, 1962.

[12] Stephens, A., *The Australian Centenary History of Defence: The Royal Australian Air Force (Volume 2)*, Oxford University Press, Melbourne, 2001.

[13] Royal Australian Air Force, *RAAF Unit History Sheets (Form A50) [Operations Record Book-Forms A50 and A51] RAAF Ubon Jun 62 – Sep 68 [A9186, 258]*, National Archives of Australia, Canberra.

[14] Defence Committee, *Directive to Officer Commanding Royal Australian Airforce Continent, Ubon, Thailand [A2031, 67/1962]*, Department of Defence, Canberra, 1962. Defence Committee, *Stationing of SEATO Forces in Thailand and Employment of No 79 Squadron [A7942, T82 Part 2]*, Department of Defence, Canberra, 1962.

[15] Royal Australian Air Force, *RAAF Unit History Sheets (Form A50) [Operations Record Book-Forms A50 and A51] RAAF Ubon Jun 62 – Sep 68 [A9186, 258]*, National Archives of Australia, Canberra.

[16] GpCapt Ross Huggins Glassop DFC & Bar. Division), R.A.N., 2019, *Vale Au Revoirs*, RAAF Association (NSW) Division Fighter Squadrons Branch, NSW, cited December 1 2019, https://fsb.raafansw.org.au/vale.php.

[17] Brown, W., A. Cork, C. Faggo, & A.e. Donselaar, *Swift to Destroy: An Illustrated History of 77 Squadron RAAF 1942-2012*, Norman Morris Pty Ltd, Newcastle, NSW, 2012.

[18] As at 2018. Hamilton, E., 'Double Prize for 36 Sqn', *Air Force*, April 23 2015, p.7.

[19] RAAF service record, *Kichenside James Charles: Service Number 033628: Date of Birth 28/7/1930. Place of Birth: Marrickville NSW. Conflict—Korea,* National Archives of Australia, Canberra, ACT, 1954-1998.

[20] Royal Australian Air Force, *RAAF Unit History Sheets (Form A50) [Operations Record Book-Forms A50 and A51] RAAF Ubon Jun 62 – Sep 68 [A9186, 258],* National Archives of Australia, Canberra.

[21] Coulthard-Clark, C., *The RAAF in Vietnam: Australian Air Involvement in the Vietnam War 1962-1975,* Allen & Unwin, St Leonards, 1995.

[22] HistorySG, 2019, *Konfrontasi (Confrontation) Ends 12th Aug 1966,* Singapore Government Agency, Singapore, cited October 20 2019, http://eresources.nlb.gov.sg/history/events/f950e04d-44d7-47ad-al0c-16dfb0cc9ce3.

[23] French fighter armed with 2x30mm DEFA cannon, 5 hard points, bombs, rockets, max speed of Mach 2.2 (863km/h at sea level), range of 2400km, 136701b thrust, powered by one SNECMA Atar 9C turbojet. Isby,

D.C., *Fighter Combat in the Jet Age*, HarperCollins, London, 1997.

[24] Royal Australian Air Force, 2019, *RMAF Base Butterworth,* cited October 20 2019, https://www.airforce.gov.au/about-us/bases/overseas/rmaf-base-butterworth.

Chapter 25:

[1] RAAF Radschool Association, 2019, *RAAF Staff College,* cited October 5 2019, https://www.radschool.org.au/Course%20Photos/Staff%20College//Staff%20College.htm.

[2] *Commonweath of Australia Gazette No.50 (Thursday August 13),* Australian Government Publishing Service, Canberra, 1959.

[3] Wilson, S., *Dakota, Hercules and Caribou in Australian Service,* Weston Creek, Aerospace Publications, 1990.

RAAF Radschool Association, 2014, *Richmond,* Radschool Association Magazine, Queensland, cited November 9 2019, https://www.radschool.org.au/magazines/Vol46/Page12.htm.

[4] Stephens, A., 1995, *RAAFPolicy, Plans and Doctrine 1946-1971,* Air Power

Development Centre, Canberra, cited September 26 2019, www.airpower.airforce.gov.au.

[5] RAAF service record, *Kichenside James Charles: Service Number 033628: Date of Birth 28/7/1930. Place of Birth: Marrickville NSW. Conflict – Korea,* National Archives of Australia, Canberra, ACT, 1954-1998.

[6] Ibid.

[7] Royal Australian Air Force, *RAAF Unit History Sheets (Form A50) [Operations Record Book-Forms A50 and A51] Number 38 Squadron Aug 66 – Aug 82 [A9186, 81],* National Archives of Australia, Canberra.

Royal Australian Air Force, *RAAF Unit History Sheets (Form A50) [Operations Record Book-Forms A50 and A51]Number38 Squadron Det A'Sep 69 – Dec 76[A9186, 81]*, National Archives of Australia, Canberra.

[8] De Havilland Aircraft of Canada Ltd, *The De Havilland DHC-4a Caribou,* Ontario, CA, 1969, p.

[9] Royal Australian Air Force, *Volume 12 – No 38 Squadron, RAAF, Richmond – Personnel Occurrence Report 1/1969 – 49/1969, 1/1969 – 8/1969 Caf, 1/1969-11/1969 [A10605 1012/4],*

National Archives of Australia, Canberra, 1969.

[10] Department of Defence, 2019, *Air Force News: Diamonds in the Rough,* Commonwealth of Australia, Canberra, cited December 5 2019, https://web.archive.org/web/20031214124321/http://www.defence.gov.au/news/raafnews/editions/4521/history/story01.htm.

[11] Flight Officer JW Rydstrom (co-pilot) 0221706, Flight Lt RP Ewing (navigator) 0216341, Sgt AJ Fraser (loadmaster) A18456. RAAF Operation Order 3/69, 21 November 1969.

Chapter 26:

[1] RAAF service record, *Kichenside James Charles: Service Number 033628: Date of Birth 28/7/1930. Place of Birth: Marrickville NSW. Conflict – Korea,* National Archives of Australia, Canberra, ACT, 1954-1998.

[2] Ballard, J.R., 2000, *Air Power and Joint Forces: The Evolution of the Joint Force since 1945,* Royal Australian Air Force, Canberra, cited November 30 2019, http://airpower.airforce.gov.au/.

[3] Scully, P.J., 2007, *Adams, John Irwin (Bay) (1922-1990),* Australian Dictionary of

Biography, Canberra, cited October 8 2019, http://adb.anu.edu.au/biography/adams-john-irwin-bay-12118.

[4] *Australian Government Gazette No. G9 (Tuesday March 4)*, Australian Government Publishing Service, Canberra, 1975.

[5] Jordan, J.C., 'On the Occasion of Your Retirement' [personal communication], to J.C. Kichenside, Royal Australian Air Force – Office of the Air Vice-Marshal, Canberra, March 19, 1975.

[6] RAAF service record, *Kichenside James Charles: Service Number 033628: Date of Birth 28/7/1930. Place of Birth: Marrickville NSW. Conflict—Korea,* National Archives of Australia, Canberra, ACT, 1954-1998.

[7] He was buried at Woronora Cemetery in Sutherland, where both his mother and father rested. Australian Cemeteries Index, 1976, *Inscription 9965237 – Charles William Kichenside,* Australian Cemeteries Index, cited August 31 2019, https://austcemindex.com/inscription.php?id=9965237.

[8] *Award of the Polar Medal [A3211 1966/1147Part 1],* Australian High Commission, London, 1953-1966.

[9] 'Police Kill Lone Jumbo Hijacker', *Age*, Thursday April 5 1979, p.1. Singh, I.P., 'Tale of Two Hijackers: One Is Congress Candidate, Other Most Wanted', *Times of India,* April 3 2014, p.16., Weber, B., 'Nikoa Kavaja, Anti-Tito Hijacker of Jet, Dies at 75', *New York Times,* November 12 2008, p.11.

[10] Beazley, K., *Media Release: Air Services to Southern Africa (March 22, 1983),* Office of Hon. Kim Beazley, Minister for Aviation, Canberra, 1983.

Beazley, K., *Media Release: Air Services to Southern Africa (March 24, 1984),* Office of Hon. Kim Beazley, Minister for Aviation, Canberra, 1984.

Hayden, B., *Media Release: South Africa – Policy Review (June 5, 1983),* Office of Hon. Bill Hayden, Minister for Foreign Affairs, Canberra, 1983.

[11] Beazley, K., *Media Release: Air Services to Southern Africa (March 24, 1984),* Office of Hon. Kim Beazley, Minister for Aviation, Canberra, 1984.

Chapter 27:

[1] Agencies, 2017, *Can They Be Friends? 'Lunatic' Donald Trump Tweets About 'Short*

and Fat' Kim after North Korea Hurls Insult, South China Morning Post, Hong Kong, cited October 7 2019, https://www.scmp.com/news/asia/diplomacy/article/2119492/donald-trumps-bizarre-sundaymorning-tweet-i-would-never-call.

[2] Goh, E. *The Prospects for a Great Power 'Grand Bargain' in East Asia,* in *New Directions in Strategic Thinking 2.0: ANU Strategic & Defence Studies Centre 's Golden Anniversary Conference Proceedings.* 2018. Canberra, Australia: ANU Press., Grant, S., 2019, *We Haven't Seen the End of History. We Are Witnessing Its Bloody Return (January 1, 2019),* ABC News, Sydney, cited October 1 2019, https://www.abc.net.au/news/2019-01-01/stan-grant-2019-the-end-of-history/10675572.

[3] Australian Insitute of Health and Welfare, 2003, *Cancer Incidence Study 2003: Australian Veterans of the Korean War [PHE 48],* Australian Institute of Health and Welfare, Canberra, cited October 18 2019, https://www.aihw.gov.au/reports/veterans/cancer-incidence-study-2003-korean-warveterans/contents/summary.

Commonwealth of Australia, 2005, *Report of the Post-Armistice Korean Service Review,* Department of Defence, Canberra, cited September 26 2019, www.aph.gov.au.

Harrex, W.K., K.W. Horsley, P. Jelfs, R. van der Hoek, & E.J. Wilson, 2003, *Mortality Study 2003: Australian Veterans of the Korean War,* Department of Veterans Affairs, Canberra, cited October 19 2019, https://www.dva.gov.au

[4] Sim, M., J. Ikin & D. McKenzie, 2005, *Health Study 2005: Australian Veterans of the Korean War (June 2005),* Department of Epidemiology and Preventive Medicine, Faculty of Medicine, Nursing and Health Sciences, Monash University, Melbourne, cited October 19 2019, https://www.dva.gov.au

[5] Evans, N., 2018, *Foreign Minister Julie Bishop Renews Bid to Repatriate Australian Diggers Lost in Korean War,* The West, cited June 14 2018, https://thewest.com.au/news/australia/foreign-minister-julie-bishop-renews-bid-torepatriate-australian-diggers-lost-in-korean-war-ng-b88864929z.

[6] Walker, J., 2018, *Closure Now Closer for Families of Australians Lost in Korean War,* The Australian, cited September 19 2018, https://www.theaustralian.com.au/n

ation/defence/closure-now-closer-for-families-of-australianslost-in-korean-war/news-story/31591b929166dl007d3538644aee6e01.

BACK COVER MATERIAL

KOREA – A DEADLY NEW BREED OF AIR WAR

1950: World War II was over, the world longed for peace. But when conflict in Korea sucked dozens of nations into a savage new war, Australia immediately answered the call.

The pilots of No.77 Squadron RAAF were among the first into Korean skies. The odds were overwhelming. MOST had no combat experience. Their planes were obsolete. And the enemy were equipped with the Latest in jet air power.

The Korean Kid is the story of Jim Kichenside and the Australian pilots of the 'forgotten war' in Korea. Of the 340 Australians who perished, 41 were from 77 Squadron. In 1952. Jam Kichenside was the youngest pilot in the squadron. He entered the Korean theatre with just 8 hours of training on his Gloster Meteor jet, and became 'The Korean Kid', flying for his life in the first war of the jet age.

Follow Jim Kichenside's journey from deadly Korean skies to the frozen snows of Antarctica and the jungles of South East Asia: a memoir of

Australia's baptism of fire into the modern jet era and beyond.

www.ingramcontent.com/pod-product-compliance
Lightning Source LLC
Chambersburg PA
CBHW012003120726
47902CB00015B/2117

* 9 7 8 0 3 6 9 3 9 1 1 0 0 *